"Judith Jordan and Jon Carlson's new b
application of the profound Relational-Cu
in this impressive collection move the the
cutting edge of a relational lens. Since the relational is foundational, and this
perspective is the future of therapy, we recommend this book as an essential
read for all therapists."
—**Harville Hendrix**, PhD, and **Helen Lakelly Hunt**, PhD, co-authors of
*Making Marriage Simple* and *Receiving Love*

"*Creating Connection* is a landmark volume in the field of therapy for committed
couples. Its skillful integration of feminist awareness of our multiple and
intersecting identities and their effects on intimacy with an emphasis on
connection and empathy in relationship offers a refreshing perspective on how
to think about intimate relationships caught in struggle. It's accessible, not only
for therapists who wish to think differently about how to work with couples, but
also for couples themselves looking for a new paradigm for deepening and
strengthening connection. This is a book I'll use in my practice, and also in my
life."
—**Laura S. Brown**, PhD, ABPP, Director, Fremont Community Therapy
Project, Seattle WA; author of *Your Turn for Care: Surviving the Aging and Death of
the Adults Who Harmed You*

"This exciting volume brings the vital perspective of Relational-Cultural
Therapy to a diverse range of couples, focusing on ways to intervene therapeutically to overcome disconnections and foster positive relationship. The
distinguished authors fill a major gap in knowledge: no previous volume has so
specifically and clearly addressed the experiences of marginalized couples,
examined how social inequality affects intimate couple interactions, and
detailed ways to repair and rebalance destructive inequities and interactions.
This book will serve as a touchstone for all future work with couples, and is
relevant not only for therapists but also for people interested in how to support
loving, positive relationships."
—**Dana C. Jack**, author of *Silencing the Self: Women and Depression*, *Behind the
Mask: Destruction and Creativity in Women's Aggression*, and *Silencing the Self Across
Cultures: Depression and Gender in the Social World*

"Relational-Cultural Theory is a complete natural for couples work, and Jordan
and Carlson have put together a gold mine of tips and mind-expanding
reframings. Seventeen clinicians cover the theory, the tie-in with couples, the
basic cultural tools, and spot-on, ready-to-use applications to class, race, gender,
sexual orientation, sex, parenting, stepparenting, health, and power differences
and impacts—an essential compilation all couples therapists will treasure."
—**Christina Robb**, MA, author of *This Changes Everything* and Pulitzer Prize-
winning journalist

# CREATING CONNECTION

Relational-Cultural Theory (RCT) posits that people grow through and toward relationship throughout the lifespan. Rather than emphasizing movement toward autonomy and self-sufficiency, it focuses on the power of connection in people's lives. Culture and power are seen as formative in individual and social development. As a model, RCT is ideal for work with couples: it encourages active participation in relationships, fosters the well-being of everyone involved, and provides guidelines for working with disconnections and building relational resilience. *Creating Connection* helps readers to understand the pain of disconnection and to use RCT to heal relationships in a variety of settings, including with heterosexual couples, stepparents, lesbian and gay couples, and mixed race couples. In addition to an emphasis on helping couples find authentic connection, RCT points to the need for changing the cultural conditions that contribute to the problems of disconnection. Polarities of "you vs. me" will be replaced with the healing concept of "us".

**Judith V. Jordan**, PhD, ABBP in Clinical Psychology, is the Director of the Jean Baker Miller Training Institute at the Wellesley Centers for Women, and Assistant Professor of Psychology at Harvard Medical School. She is a founding scholar of Relational-Cultural Theory.

**Jon Carlson**, PsyD, EdD, ABPP, is Distinguished Professor in the Division of Psychology and Counseling at Governors State University, and a psychologist at the Wellness Clinic in Lake Geneva, Wisconsin.

# THE FAMILY THERAPY AND COUNSELING SERIES

## SERIES EDITOR
### JON CARLSON, Psy.D., Ed.D.

Kit S. Ng
*Global Perspectives in Family Therapy:
Development, Practice, Trends*

Phyllis Erdman and Tom Caffery
*Attachment and Family Systems:
Conceptual, Empirical, and Therapeutic
Relatedness*

Wes Crenshaw
*Treating Families and Children in the
Child Protective System*

Len Sperry
*Assessment of Couples and Families:
Contemporary and Cutting-Edge Strategies*

Robert L. Smith and
R. Esteban Montilla
*Counseling and Family Therapy with
Latino Populations: Strategies that Work*

Catherine Ford Sori
*Engaging Children in Family Therapy:
Creative Approaches to Integrating Theory
and Research in Clinical Practice*

Paul R. Peluso
*Infidelity: A Practitioner's Guide to
Working with Couples in Crisis*

Jill D. Onedera
*The Role of Religion in Marriage and
Family Counseling*

Christine Kerr, Janice Hoshino,
Judith Sutherland, Sharyl Parashak,
and Linda McCarley
*Family Art Therapy*

Debra D. Castaldo
*Divorced Without Children: Solution
Focused Therapy with Women at Midlife*

Phyllis Erdman and Kok-Mun Ng
*Attachment: Expanding the Cultural
Connections*

Jon Carlson and Len Sperry
*Recovering Intimacy in Love Relationships:
A Clinician's Guide*

Adam Zagelbaum and Jon Carlson
*Working with Immigrant Families:
A Practical Guide for Counselors*

Shea M. Dunham,
Shannon B. Dermer, and
Jon Carlson
*Poisonous Parenting: Toxic Relationships
Between Parents and Their Adult Children*

# THE FAMILY THERAPY AND COUNSELING SERIES

## SERIES EDITOR
## JON CARLSON, Psy.D., Ed.D.

David K. Carson and
Montserrat Casado-Kehoe
*Case Studies in Couples Therapy:
Theory-Based Approaches*

Bret A. Moore
*Handbook of Counseling Military Couples*

Len Sperry
*Family Assessment: Contemporary and
Cutting-Edge Strategies, 2nd ed.*

Patricia A. Robey,
Robert E. Wubbolding, and
Jon Carlson
*Contemporary Issues in Couples
Counseling: A Choice Theory and
Reality Therapy Approach*

Paul R. Peluso, Richard E. Watts,
and Mindy Parsons
*Changing Aging, Changing Family
Therapy: Practicing With 21st Century
Realities*

Dennis A. Bagarozzi
*Couples in Collusion: Short-Term,
Assessment-Based Strategies for Helping
Couples Disarm Their Defenses*

Katherine M. Helm and Jon Carlson
*Love, Intimacy, and the African American
Couple*

Judith V. Jordan and Jon Carlson
*Creating Connection: A Relational-Cultural
Approach with Couples*

# CREATING CONNECTION

## A Relational-Cultural Approach with Couples

*Edited by Judith V. Jordan and Jon Carlson*

Routledge
Taylor & Francis Group

NEW YORK AND LONDON

First published 2013
by Routledge
711 Third Avenue, New York, NY 10017

Simultaneously published in the UK
by Routledge
27 Church Road, Hove, East Sussex BN3 2FA

*Routledge is an imprint of the Taylor & Francis Group, an informa business*

*Library of Congress Cataloging in Publication Data*
Creating connection : a relational-cultural approach with couples / edited by Judith V. Jordan & Jon Carlson.
pages cm
Includes bibliographical references.
1. Couples therapy. 2. Marital psychotherapy. 3. Cultural psychiatry. I. Jordan, Judith V., editor of compilation. II. Carlson, Jon, editor of compilation.
RC488.5.C74 2013
616.89'1562–dc23
2012040805

ISBN: 978–0–415–52991–4 (hbk)
ISBN: 978–0–415–81758–5 (pbk)
ISBN: 978–0–203–11734–7 (ebk)

Typeset in Baskerville
by Keystroke, Station Road, Codsall, Wolverhampton

# CONTENTS

CONTENTS

# EDITOR BIOGRAPHIES

**Judith V. Jordan** is the Director of the Jean Baker Miller Training Institute at the Wellesley Centers for Women, and Assistant Professor of Psychology at Harvard Medical School. She is a founding scholar of Relational-Cultural Theory and has written and lectured throughout the world about this relational model. Dr Jordan authored the book, *Relational-Cultural Therapy* in 2010 as part of the American Psychological Association's "Theories of Psychotherapy" series. She also co-authored the book, *Women's Growth in Connection* and edited *Women's Growth in Diversity: The Complexity of Connection and the Power of Connection.* She has published over forty original reports and twenty-five chapters.

Dr Jordan is the recipient of the 2010 Distinguished Psychologist Award from the American Psychological Association "in recognition of her outstanding accomplishments and significant lifetime contributions to the field of psycho-therapy." She is also the recipient of the Massachusetts Psychology Association's Career Achievement Award for Outstanding Contributions to the Advancement of Psychology as a Science and a Profession. She received the annual psychiatric residents' "Outstanding Teacher of the Year" Award at McLean Hospital and is included in *Who's Who in America*. Dr Jordan holds a diplomate in Clinical Psychology. She received a special award from the Feminist Therapy Institute "in recognition for outstanding contributions to the development of feminist psychology" (2002). She is on the editorial board of the *Journal of Clinical Psychology: In Session* and the *Journal of Creativity and Mental Health*. She has written, lectured, and conducted workshops nationally and internationally on the subjects of women's psychological development, gender differences, mothers and daughters, mothers and sons, empathy, mutuality, the power of connection, marginalization, and a relational model of self. She has sought to shift the primary models of psychology from an emphasis on the "separate self" to an appreciation of the centrality of relationship in people's lives. Dr Jordan believes that shifting the paradigm from separation to connection will transform not only the practice of psychotherapy, but also society.

## Recommended books

- *Relational-Cultural Therapy*, Judith V. Jordan
- *Women's Growth in Connection*, Jordan, Kaplan, Miller, Stiver, & Surrey
- *Womens Growth in Diversity*, (Ed.) Judith V. Jordan
- *The Complexity of Connection*, (Eds) Judith V. Jordan, Maureen Walker, Linda Hartling
- *The Power of Connection*, (Ed.) Judith V. Jordan
- *This Changes Everything*, Christina Robb

**Jon Carlson**, PsyD, EdD, ABPP, is Distinguished Professor, Psychology and Counseling, at Governors State University and a psychologist at the Wellness Clinic in Lake Geneva, Wisconsin. Jon has served as editor of several periodicals including the *Journal of Individual Psychology* and *The Family Journal*. He holds Diplomates in both Family Psychology and Adlerian Psychology. He has authored 170 journal articles and 60 books, including *Time for a Better Marriage*, *Adlerian Therapy*, *Inclusive Cultural Empathy*, *The Mummy at the Dining Room Table*, *Bad Therapy*, *The Client Who Changed Me*, *Their Finest Hour*, *Creative Breakthroughs in Therapy*, *Moved by the Spirit*, *Duped: Lies and Deception in Psychotherapy* and *Never Be Lonely Again*. He has created over 300 professional trade videos and DVDs with leading professional therapists and educators. In 2004 the American Counseling Association named him a "Living Legend." In 2009 the Division of Psychotherapy of the American Psychological Association (APA) named him "Distinguished Psychologist" for his life contribution to psychotherapy and in 2011 he received the APA Distinguished Career Contribution to Education and Training Award. He has received similar awards from four other professional organizations. Recently he syndicated an advice cartoon, *On The Edge*, with cartoonist Joe Martin. Jon and Laura have been married for forty-five years and are the parents of five children.

# CONTRIBUTOR BIOGRAPHIES

**Stephen Bergman**, MD, PhD, is a doctor, novelist, playwright and activist. A graduate of Harvard Phil Beta Kappa, a Rhodes Scholar at Balliol College Oxford, and a graduate of Harvard Medical School, he was on the faculty of Harvard for three decades.

Under the pen-name of "Samuel Shem," he has been described in the press as "Easily the finest and most important writer ever to focus on the lives of doctors and the world of medicine," and, "He brings mercy to the practice of medicine." *The Lancet* called *The House of God*: "One of the two most significant medical novels of the 20th century." Its sequel, *Mount Misery*, is about training to be a psychiatrist; and *Fine* is about a psychoanalyst.

His 2008 novel, *The Spirit of the Place*, about a primary care doctor in a small town, was reviewed as "The perfect bookend to *The House of God*." It won the "National Best Book Award 2008 in General Fiction and Literature" from *USA Book News*, and the Independent Publishers National Book Award in Literary Fiction 2009.

With his wife Janet Surrey he wrote the Off-Broadway hit play *Bill W. and Dr. Bob*, about the founding of Alcoholics Anonymous, which won the Performing Arts Award of the National Council on Alcoholism 2007. Website: www.billwanddrbob.com

Also with Surrey, he wrote the nonfiction book *We Have to Talk: Healing Dialogues between Women and Men*, winner of the Boston Interfaith Council's Paradigm Shift Award, 1999.

He has written an article on "Fiction as Resistance" (*Annals of Internal Medicine*), given over fifty commencement speeches on "How to Stay Human in Medicine," including Harvard Medical School in 2009, and lives in Boston and Costa Rica. Website: www.samuelshem.com

**Dana L. Comstock-Benzick**, PhD, is a Professor of Counseling and Chair of the Department of Counseling and Human Services at St Mary's University, San Antonio, TX. She has extensive training in Relational-Cultural Theory and integrates it into all aspects of her work. She is the editor of *Diversity in Development: Critical Contexts that Shape Our Lives and Relationships*, the first

RCT-based counseling text, published in 2005 by Wadsworth/Brooks-Cole. Among her many publications, she was featured in the first RCT casebook *How Connections Heal: Stories from Relational-Cultural Therapy*, published by Guilford Press and *The Complete Guide to Mental Health for Women*, published by Beacon Press.

**Mona DeKoven Fishbane**, PhD, is the Director of Couple Therapy Training at the Chicago Center for Family Health in Chicago, IL. She has contributed chapters to *Handbook of Clinical Family Therapy* (Wiley, 2005), *Neuroscience & Family Therapy: Integrations and Applications* (AFTA Monograph Series, 2008), *Spiritual Resources in Family Therapy, 2nd Edition* (Guilford, 2009), *Clinical Casebook of Couple Therapy* (Guilford, 2010), and *Normal Family Processes* (4th Ed.) (Guilford, 2012). She has also contributed articles to *Journal of Marital & Family Therapy* and *Family Process*. Dr Fishbane's book, *Loving with the Brain in Mind: Neurobiology and Couple Therapy* (New York: WW Norton, 2013), is part of the Norton Series on Interpersonal Neurobiology.

**Natalie S. Eldridge**, PhD, a psychologist and life transition coach, serves on the Faculty of the Jean Baker Miller Training Institute and on the Board of Directors for the Life Planning Network. She is chief editor and contributing author to the recent release, *Live Smart After 50! The Experts' Guide to Life Planning for Uncertain Times*. She is a contributing author to *The Complexity of Connection*, *Women's Growth in Diversity*, and to the Working Paper Series at the Stone Center at Wellesley College. She authors the *Action on Purpose* Newsletter at www. EldridgeWorks.com and has written and presented on relational mindfulness, lesbian and gay family psychology, feminist ethics, and women's career development.

**Pamela Geib**, EdD, is a Licensed Clinical Psychologist and Certified Internal Family Systems therapist. She is a lifetime member of APA, and a former Clinical Instructor in Psychology, Department of Psychiatry, Harvard Medical School. She has taught family therapy at the Cambridge Hospital, and now teaches IFS couples therapy. She also is the co-creator and co-teacher of the Internal Family Systems Mastery Seminar. She has presented widely on diverse methods of family and couples therapy. Her publications include co-authoring a chapter in *On Intimate Ground: A Gestalt Approach to Working with Couples* (Jossey-Bass, 1994), co-authoring a chapter in *Work in Progress* (Stone Center Working Papers Series, 1995), co-authoring a chapter in *The Voice of Shame: Silence and Connection in Psychotherapy* (Jossey-Bass, 1996), and authoring a chapter in *Touch in Psychotherapy* (Guilford, 1997).

**Constance A. Johannessen**, PsyD, is a clinical psychologist and managing partner at Woodland Professional Associates, a private practice in North Hampton, NH. For over 25 years she has provided individual, marital, and group therapy to adults struggling with depression, anxiety, trauma, self-esteem, and cancer. She has presented locally and in Canada on the Relational-Cultural Theory Cancer Groups for couples; the Emotional Aftermath when Surviving Cancer; Women and Competition; Marital Therapy; and Women's Self-Esteem. As an advanced clinician in the Jean Baker Miller Training Institute's Practitioners Program at Wellesley College, she expanded her practice from assisting caregivers and individuals with cancer to offering Relational-Cultural Theory-based groups for couples coping with cancer.

**Harriet Lerner**, PhD, is one of our nation's most respected voices on the psychology of women and family relationship. For over two decades, she was a staff psychologist at The Menninger Clinic and a faculty member and supervisor in the Karl Menninger School of Psychiatry. Currently in private practice in Lawrence, KS, she is the author of numerous scholarly articles and eleven books, including *The New York Times* bestseller, *The Dance of Anger, Women in Therapy*, and, most recently, *Marriage Rules: A Manual for the Married and the Coupled Up*. Lerner blogs for *Psychology Today* and *The Huffington Post*.

**Kumkum Pareek Malik**, PsyD, is a clinical psychologist with over 30 years of experience. She is the founder of Dr Malik & Associates, and maintains offices in Wellesley and Norfolk, MA. Dr Malik specializes in working on motherhood as real work that deserves respect. She is a member of the American Psychological Association and the Massachusetts Psychological Association, where she has also served as Board Member. Dr. Malik has been associated with the Jean Baker Miller Center and has used Relational-Cultural Theory in her work for over 20 years.

**Randy Markey**, MSW, LICSW, was educated at Brandeis University and received his Master of Social Work from the Simmons College Graduate School of Social Work. He completed special studies at the New England Conservatory. He is a professional actor, singer, and writer; a member of the Screen Actors Guild and the American Federation of Television and Radio Artists. His art greatly informs his psychotherapy. Randy has been published in the Washington Post, and other newspapers on the subject of physician–patient relationships. He has lectured at SUNY Stonybrook Medical School, Tufts Graduate School of Public Health, and delivered the keynote address for the American Pediatric Oncological Social Workers national convention. He was also privileged to testify to the United States Congress as an expert witness. Randy is currently finishing a film about men in relationships called *If Guys Are So Stupid, How Come You Want One?* He lives in Newton, MA and credits all of his practical knowledge about relationships to his lovely wife Marcia and their son Max.

**Marsha Mirkin**, PhD, is an Associate Professor of Psychology at Lasell College in Newton, MA. Her work explores culture, relationships, and societal power dynamics, particularly as they impact couples and families. She also writes and provides workshops on relational psychological interpretations of Biblical family stories. Her more recent books include *The Women who Danced by the Sea: Finding Ourselves in the Stories of our Biblical Foreparents* and the edited texts *Psychotherapy with Women: Exploring Diverse Contexts and Identities* (with Karen Suyemoto and Barbara Okun) and *Women in Context: Toward a Feminist Reconstruction of Psychotherapy*. Previously, Dr Mirkin was a Resident Scholar at the Brandeis Women's Studies Research Center and on the faculty of the Jean Baker Miller Institute, Wellesley College.

**David M. Shannon**, LICSW, is a psychotherapist in private practice in Boston, MA. He specializes in gay men's health and in working with individuals and groups healing from trauma and abuse, sexual addiction, and homo/bi/transphobia. For about 15 years, he has consulted with various health care and rape crisis centers and provided training and education to law enforcement, court personnel, and healthcare workers in how to provide sensitive and culturally competent care. David also provides clinical supervision and consultation to mental health trainees and clinicians.

**Karen Skerrett**, PhD, APRN is a Clinical Associate Professor at Northwestern University, Department of Psychology and senior staff at the Family Institute of Chicago/Center for Psychological Studies. She is a longtime faculty member of the Chicago Center for Family Health, teaching and supervising in the families and health program.

She formerly taught at the University of Illinois College of Nursing, Adler and Illinois Schools of Professional Psychology and most recently at the University of San Diego, where she was the Director of Advanced Practice Programs in Psychiatric Mental Health Nursing. She has maintained a private practice in marital and family therapy for over 30 years and consults widely in healthcare settings.

She has contributed articles to the journals *Families, Systems, & Health* and *Family Process* and is currently completing two books, one for Routledge with Jefferson Singer, PhD on couple therapy and another for Springer with Karen Fergus, PhD on the cultivation of relational resilience.

**Meg I. Striepe**, PhD, is a clinical psychologist. Her private practice in Concord, MA focuses on human sexuality and trauma. She completed a fellowship and was on the faculty at the Program in Human Sexuality, University of Minnesota Medical School. Her focus on the relational aspects of sexuality led her to study the overlap with trauma and sexual development. She was a therapist and supervisor with the JRI Trauma Center in Brookline, MA. She has published and taught in the areas of women's sexual health and how to include sexuality in trauma therapy.

**Janet Surrey**, PhD, is a Clinical Psychologist in Private Practice in Newton, MA. She is a Founding Scholar of the Jean Baker Miller Training Institute, Wellesley College and is on the Faculty and Board of the Institute for Meditation and Psychotherapy, Cambridge, MA. She was on the Faculty of Harvard Medical School for 20 years. She is co-author of *Women's Growth in Connection*, contributing author for *Women's Growth in Diversity*, and *Mindfulness and Psychotherapy*, and co-editor of *Mothering Against the Odds: Diverse Voices of Contemporary Mothers*. With her partner, Stephen Bergman, she has co-authored *We Have to Talk; Healing Dialogues Between Women and Men* and the play: *Bill W. and Dr. Bob*, the story of the founding of Alcoholics Anonymous.

**Maureen Walker**, PhD, is a licensed psychologist with an independent practice in psychotherapy and multicultural consultation in Cambridge, MA. She is Director of Program Development at the Jean Baker Miller Training Institute of the Stone Center at Wellesley College, as well as an Associate Director in MBA Program Administration at Harvard Business School.

The author of several papers in the Stone Center Works in Progress Series, Dr Walker has also written several articles and textbook chapters. She is co-editor of two books: *How Connections Heal* and *The Complexity of Connection*.

Dr Walker completed her graduate training in psychology at Georgia State University and the University of Texas at Austin.

# SERIES EDITOR'S FOREWORD

Right from the moment of our birth, we are under the care and
kindness of our parents, and then later on in our life when we
are oppressed by sickness and become old, we are again dependent on the kindness of others. Since at the beginning and the
end of our lives we are so dependent on others' kindness, how
can it be in the middle that we would neglect kindness toward
others?

The Dalai Lama (quoted in *The Sun*, January 2012)

Relational-Cultural Theory and Therapy (RCT) were developed by and for
women because the existing model of psychology was developed by and for
men. The model of what constituted a healthy psyche was not something a
healthy woman could relate to. But according to Randy Markey, "as men
became more committed to having emotional lives in their marriages and
relationships, and more aware of those holes in our lives; we also became aware
of our need for connection. And that is how and why this model is so deeply
important for men, even though we don't always 'get it' the way women do."

Because relationships are at the heart of RCT, this model seems perfectly
suited for working with couples. The RCT model seems to be a blending of
several different approaches. Readers will easily identify person-centered,
narrative, systems, and feminist underpinnings. I really resonate with this model
as it seeks to help people create healthy connections in their lives. I have long
held the belief that a mentally healthy person can be defined as one who gets
along with all the significant people in their life.

Relationships rather than the "self" are the foundation of the psychological
and physical states (Robb, 2006). According to Relational-Cultural Theory, the
goal of development is not forming a separated, independent self, but rather the
ability to participate actively in relationships that foster the wellbeing of everyone involved (i.e. growth-fostering relationships).

Because mutual empathy plays the central role in intimacy, love is the
product of mutual empathy. This process is a core component in Relational-
Cultural Therapy with couples and requires one to be able to engage as well as

to detach. You completely understand another but never leave your self. Jean Baker Miller and Irene Stiver (1997) define mutual empathy as "a joining together based on authentic thoughts and feelings of all participants in a relationship" (p. 29). It is through this process of expansion that relationships can grow and heal as our eyes are magically opened to the previously unseen.

This is not a new concept, for therapists such as Carl Rogers (1961) and others have preached it as a central component of the helping process, and Harville Hendrix (1991) and others have stressed its importance in creating and maintaining an intimate relationship. The difference seems to be in the depth and breadth in which the Relational-Cultural therapist works in connecting couples to each other and all aspects of their existence.

Dr Judy Jordan and the contributors to this book will help the reader to appreciate the pain and suffering of the chronically disconnected and what can be done to create a healing connection. The reader will have the opportunity to experience how to use this important approach in a variety of settings including with heterosexual couples, lesbian and gay couples, and mixed-race couples. The chapter authors also look at current relational challenges such as parenting, stepfamilies, sexuality, and illness from the lens of Relational-Cultural Theory. I hope you enjoy this collection of papers by the leading practitioners of Relational-Cultural Therapy.

Jon Carlson, PsyD, EdD
Series Editor

# References

Hendrix, H. (1991) *Getting the love you want: A guide for couples*. New York: Harper.

Miller, J.B. & Stiver, I.P. (1997) *The healing connection: How women form relationships in therapy and in life*. Boston: Beacon.

Robb, C. (2006) *This changes everything: The relational revolution in psychology*. New York: Farrar, Straus, & Giroux.

Rogers, C. (1961) *On becoming a person: A therapist's view of psychotherapy*. Boston: Houghton Mifflin.

# 1

# COUPLES THERAPY AND RELATIONAL-CULTURAL THERAPY (RCT)

*Judith V. Jordan and Jon Carlson*

The pioneers and original developers of the field of couple and family therapy were men. The thinking in therapy, including couples work, was also dominated by men. Their thinking permeated treatment until the late 1970s, when four women met in New York to create what has become known as Feminist Therapy. Marianne Walters, Betty Carter, Peggy Papp, and Olga Silverstein formed the Women's Project in 1977. They were frustrated because the therapies practiced did not meet the needs of women and persons of other devalued cultural groups. This gender-sensitive approach was quickly embraced and has become a mainstay of contemporary psychotherapy.

Around this same time, four women were meeting in the Boston suburb of Brookline to create another approach that encompassed strong feminist principles as well as aspects of multiculturalism and social justice. This new approach became known as Relational-Cultural Therapy (RCT), with a main focus on the primacy of relationships. That is, relationships are both the indicators for, and the healing mechanism in, psychotherapy that lead toward healthy living. The developers of RCT were psychiatrist Jean Baker Miller and psychologists Judith V. Jordan, Janet Surrey, and Irene Stiver. The Stone Center at Wellesley College became the physical center of the approach and of the development of "working papers." These papers became the heart and soul of RCT, known as works in progress.

The traditional models of human development and psychotherapy do not accurately address the relational experiences of women and persons in other devalued cultural groups. The main focus of RCT is the primacy of relationships. Relationships are the indicators and mechanism in psychotherapy for creating health and wellness. The goal of RCT is to create mutually growth-fostering relationships in which both parties feel that they matter. These are relationships where all parties experience the "five good things" (Miller & Stiver, 1997): (1) a sense of zest, or energy; (2) increased clarity and knowledge

1

of oneself and the other person in relationship; (3) a desire to take action both in the growth-fostering relationship and outside of it; (4) an overall increased sense of worth and (5) a desire for more connectedness, a reaching out to create a community of mutuality (Robb, 2006). These signs of relational health are what we work toward in RCT couples therapy.

Judith Jordan summarized the core RCT tenets (2010):

1. People grow through and toward relationship throughout the life span.
2. Movement toward mutuality rather than separation characterizes mature functioning.
3. The ability to participate in increasingly complex and diversified relational networks characterizes psychological growth.
4. Mutual empathy and mutual empowerment are at the core of growth-fostering relationships.
5. Authenticity is necessary for real engagement in growth-fostering relationships.
6. When people contribute to the development of growth-fostering relationships, they grow as a result of their participation in such relationships. All participants in growth-fostering relationships benefit.
7. The goal of development is the realization of increased relational competence and mutual empathy over the life span.

Relational-Cultural Theory posits that we grow through and toward relationship throughout the life span. The model examines the importance of what are called growth-fostering relationships in people's lives (Miller, 1976; Jordan et al., 1991). Other models have looked at the importance of the early mother–infant bond (Bowlby, 1982; Ainsworth et al., 1978; Schore, 1994), at the dynamics between people paired in couples or at the complicated interactions between members of a nuclear and even extended family. RCT posits a more central acknowledgement of relationships: we come into being in relationship. We are relational beings. Relationships, not selves, are the basic building blocks of human experience. Thus RCT addresses the ways in which all relationships become either growth-inducing or limiting forces in our lives. In expanding our understanding of the power of relationships in people's lives, it makes sense to attend to the special rewards and stresses that occur in what are thought to be our most intimate connections: our primary couples.

Models of development emphasizing independence and autonomy become prescriptions for separation and "standing on your own two feet". The broader culture as well as the field of psychology has supported the development of the Separate self. Further, there has been an emphasis on self-interest, self-actualization and the primacy of the individual. Alongside this valuation of the separate self, there has been an intense romanticization and privileging of dyadic couplings. Socialized in a context that lauds separateness and individual freedoms, at some point, adults are supposed to come together to form a nuclear family built around a primary pairing based on love, respect and shared interests. Relational-Cultural Theory points to the importance in creating these pairings of mutual empathy, characterized by a desire to contribute to the growth of others as we also flourish in the relationship.

Raised to be autonomous and separate, we are then expected to move easily into connection and couplehood. The expectations themselves for the development of separate selves may pose particular challenges for couples forging primary love relationships in this prevailing context of separation. If one spends one's whole life becoming "my own person", how then does one develop the skills necessary to come together with another person to form a couple, the nucleus of a family? What support is there in the culture for our mutual growth? Where can we turn for help in weathering the hard spots, raising the children, finding an equitable balance of labor? A separation context does not support relational skills.

Rather than building separateness, RCT encourages the establishment of growth-fostering relationships. These are relationships characterized by zest, clarity of experience, a sense of worth, productivity and the desire for more connection. Nowhere in RCT is there an expectation that the primary couple will meet all the needs of the individual; nor is there a denial of inevitable interdependence in our coupled relationships. The key to growth and empowerment is mutual empathy. In mutual empathy each person brings an openness to being affected by the other and cares about the impact he or she has on the other. This is the ultimate trust. *I invite you in to my life and I will be open to being changed by you, changed by my responsiveness to you. I will also take responsibility for the ways in which you are changed or affected by me. I will bring myself as fully as possible to this relationship with you (authenticity); at times that will include bringing in aspects of myself that may come into conflict with aspects of you. I will not react to those differences or conflict with aggression or dominance. I will work on co-representing difference and growing through these conflicts. I ask the same of you. I will allow you to see my vulnerability, the ways in which I am open to being changed by you. When necessary, to protect myself and preserve the relationship, I may have to move into strategies of disconnection . . . these are ways I have learned to keep important parts of myself alive and safe when those parts are not respected or welcomed by the other person. I do this to serve the relationship and to respect the vulnerability of each participant.* Empathy is cognitive-affective resonance, joining with the other person in a shared state of human connection. There is compassion, a lessening of the suffering of separation. Mutual empathy moves us toward one another, out of isolation (Jordan, 2000).

In heterosexual couples, the coming together in vulnerability and strength can be complicated by gender prescriptions. Boys and men in our culture are particularly pressured to stand alone, to be like a rock . . . strong, separate, invulnerable, rational. Girls and women are given far more latitude for dependence, emotional expression, staying in touch with their need for connection. Boys and girls are raised in very differing peer cultures, even when parents make every effort to downplay the gender stereotypes that shape both sexes. Boys are taught to act, to take risks, to be free of dependencies on others, not to show their vulnerability. They are actively shamed for any behaviors that appear "girl-like". The worst thing for a boy is to be called a girl. A soccer mom shared the following anecdote: She is a feminist and had raised her 10 year old boy to be extremely respectful of girls. There was in fact a girl on his otherwise all-male soccer team whom he admired; she was one of the best players on the team and she was fun. At their first soccer game of the season, however, a boy from the opposing team came up to her son after the first quarter and said, tauntingly "You have a girl on your team . . . you're all girls, you're all girls!" She reported watching a shadow cross her son's face and his lower lip quivered with held-in tears. He then drew himself up to his greatest height and said "We're not girls, we're not girls!!!!! We're . . . . . . WOMEN!" This was one boy, who coura-geously (and creatively) held on to the gift of respect for females his mother had encouraged in him. But the constant demeaning of girls by boys (and boys by girls at different times) contributes to the burdens of the heterosexual pairings that the majority of people engage in as adults. This is not to say that same-sex couplings are free of all stereotypes or conflicts around difference. They unfold differently.

Although the gender differences may appear complementary (he's strong, she's weak; he's hard, she's soft; he's silent, she's talkative; he's task-oriented, she's relational), to the extent that they apply or shape a person's presentation, they can become the sources of misunderstandings and disappointment. We are imprisoned in old images of who we should be; it is common for men and women to assume different roles based on old scripts although they may well state conscious determination to remain gender-stereotype-free. It is not uncommon for same-sex couples to mirror these gender stereotypes: the fem and butch, the top and bottom, the husband and wife, and therefore to be caught in some of the same limiting images.

To the extent that RCT values and believes in the power of connection, one might ask if males are disadvantaged in this approach to working with couples. There is the phenomenon of "relational dread" (Bergman, 1991) whereby men, feeling inadequate in relational arenas, begin to dread the moments when their incompetence in these areas is revealed. One might make an argument that with RCT it would be especially helpful to have a male and female therapist in the room with the heterosexual couple, capable of accurate empathy and supporting each of the individual's areas of vulnerability.

Tasks that face couples in therapy include the following:

1. Learning how to participate in mutually empathic exchanges with one another.
2. Practicing responsible authenticity. Each person represents his or her experience as fully as possible.
3. Engaging in "good conflict". This is not about winning, dominating or hurting.

4

4.  Finding a way to express radical respect. Appreciation and gratitude feed respect.
5.  Attending to the needs of the partner and the needs of the relationship.
6.  Developing an appreciation for the primacy of connection and learning ways to contribute to the wellbeing of the relationship, the "we".
7.  Supporting the growth of each person in the relationship.
8.  Healthy use of humor and lightness.

Mutual empathy is the cornerstone of relational health for couples. Empathy involves careful listening, being open to being "moved" by another person, tuning into our own resonance, moving beyond prevailing ego interests that might not allow the other's experience to impact us. Defensiveness, protecting an image that we have of ourselves (as loving, "right", strong, empathic, etc.), inevitably closes down empathic listening. The first step in working with couples is to make a safe space for each person to bring themselves ever more fully into the present moment, here with a therapist, to speak and listen. Each member of the couple needs to work on developing responsiveness and eliminating reactivity, the knee-jerk, amygdala-driven responses that diminish our ability to be open to the other's experience. In communicating our responses to one another, we are guided by our need to expand our own truths but also by anticipating the possible impact of our response on the other person. In RCT we talk about developing "anticipatory empathy". We anticipate, based on our increasingly integrated understanding of the other person, the impact we might have on the other person and we bring that portion of the truth to the exchange that will expand the relationship. We care about our impact on others. Mutual empathy also involves allowing our responsiveness to be seen. In order for empathy to promote growth, both people need to be able to see, know and feel that they are having an impact on one another, that they matter. Working with this paradoxically delicate and robust dance of mutuality is at the core of couples work. The heart of the work is in helping each member of the couple to see their impact on the other and helping them enhance each other's potential to love, care and empower each other and the relationship.

Authenticity is crucial to relational health. Being authentic does not involve "telling the whole truth" or "brutal honesty". When we find the truths that need to be spoken in relationship it is our responsibility to find the ways in which those truths can be spoken that will lead to growth, not damage. RCT does not encourage blurting out every thought that runs through our minds. We find what Irene Stiver (personal communication) called "the one true thing" that can be said, that needs to be spoken. Mutuality grows to the extent that we can represent our experience more and more fully. When we cease bringing ourselves fully to relationship, the relationship becomes less and less alive; there is less energy, less clarity, less investment in the relationship. In couples work we help individuals find ways to assist people in speaking their truths empathically. All responses need to be filtered through relational awareness. What impact will this have on our relationship? On US? On what we seek to build together?

Creating good conflict is a challenge for most couples. Most of us are conflict-avoidant. Either we suppress our responses, or we use aggression and dominance to silence others' realities. Jean Baker Miller once said "Authenticity and subordination are totally incompatible" (Miller, 1988). She meant that in power-imbalanced relationships those with power will not invite those with less power to represent their experience fully (authenticity) if their reality clashes with that of the dominant group. So the powerful silence and isolate those in subordinate positions (Miller, 1976). "Isolation is the glue that holds oppression in place" (Laing, 1998). Healthy conflict depends on being able to articulate and respect difference. And we work toward new understandings and resolutions rather than enforcing existing power structures and strategies. Helping couples address conflict is also about working with the power dynamics that exist in any dyad. How are differences resolved? How are divisions of labor negotiated? How are needs honored? How are individual feelings expressed and heard? What structures can be put in place to ensure safe representation of difference?

Respect encourages trust and growth. Respect involves an empathic appreciation of the other person's reality. We listen attentively; we allow the other person's experience to alter ours. Respect involves an open curiosity and responsiveness to the other person's needs. We have to let go of our images of what the other person "should" be for us and begin to notice and appreciate the gifts, the limitations that this person actually brings to the relationship. Respect helps to eliminate the invisible demands of entitlement and invites gratitude. When we are operating from entitlement, nothing the other person does or brings to the relationship is really seen or accepted. It is our due. It should happen without acknowledgement. We deserve this or that. We do not have to do anything to deserve special treatment. By our race, sex, class, etc. it is our "right". Entitlement is the enemy of gratitude and respect. It sucks the life out of empathy. It renders invisible the gifts that are offered. And it weakens relational mutuality.

A part of lessening the grip of entitlement is developing an appreciation of the primacy of connection. What do WE need? What can each of us contribute to the relationship, to make it stronger so that the relationship can become a source of nurturance for both people? In western dominant cultures we are so preoccupied with "self-development" that we forget when we enter a relationship that we must develop consciousness about "relational development" and relational health. This is the responsibility of both members of a couple. In many heterosexual couples, this work is handed off to the woman. It is seen to be woman's work: the nurturing and sustaining of relationship. Often therapists have to explicitly remind couples with the question: Is this good for the relationship? Will this grow the relationship? WE consciousness can be expanded in this way. Together therapists and couples can develop shorthand ways to remember to factor in the needs and health of the relationship. Our culture is saturated in Separate Self thinking and there will be a strong pull back to the dominant narrative.

This is not an either/or, black-white, selfless vs. selfish model. We do not pit the individual versus the relationship. We want to help people see the ways in which relationships need to be nourished so that the relationships can in turn support individual growth. We are not inviting people to surrender the need for personal wellbeing or sacrifice themselves to the relationship. In fact if the flow of mutuality is too out of balance, if intractable self-centered behavior prevails at the expense of the connection, often people must consider the possibility of leaving to find new relationship possibilities. RCT does not condemn people to unending efforts to make bad relationships better or to relinquish personal needs for the benefit of the other person or the couple. We seek to help people differentiate healthy mutuality, which will empower both people and sustain relationship, from patterns of disconnection that are hurtful and do not promise growth for either person. In helping people make these differentiations, we also suggest that in cases of entrenched, non-mutual and hurtful relationships the individual may choose to find a healthier relational context elsewhere. RCT does not encourage "going it alone" or getting increasingly independent in those conditions. The answer is found not in moving into "splendid isolation", it is in finding more positive relational possibility in other relationships.

Finally, we want to add, that in addition to respect, humor may be one of the more important sustainers of good connection. There is a refrigerator magnet that says "Laughter is the shortest distance between two people". Mutual laughter and humor (not aggressive humor which is aimed at undercutting or demeaning others) allows joining. In laughter together we often feel real, zestful, creative, worthy, and an increased desire for more connection . . . the five good things. Being able to laugh with ourselves, at ourselves depends on the capacity to step back just that little bit. Similar to what happens in meditation, we gain just enough perspective not to be swallowed up in the urgency of our own need to maintain a self-image, or convince someone else of how "right" we are. Humor allows relaxation into connection. It makes room for something new to emerge. It brings people into a better state of brain chemistry. Together we create the possibility for change.

Most people do not welcome change. We tend to get comfortable with what we know . . . even when what we know is painful. This is true for individuals and couples. The success of working with couples depends on each person being able to move into expanded possibility together . . . on getting present in this moment. Relational-Cultural Theory provides some guidelines to assist that movement: mutual empathy, engagement in authentic listening and speaking, dedication to respecting and honoring the We.

In this book we have invited both experts with established theories in couple therapy and therapists who are at the cutting edge of developing new approaches. While most of the authors are immersed in the field of Relational-Cultural Therapy, some are not affiliated with RCT in a formal way; they bring a more loosely defined relational approach to their work. And they bring new ideas to RCT. We have attempted to provide foundational work in the understanding of couple dynamics through an RCT lens and we have also sought to examine special applications of RCT thinking. We hope that our interest in the power of culture (and the culture of power) as well as our respect for the importance of neurobiology is evident to the reader. While this volume does not explicitly focus on the importance of social change and movement toward social justice, as clinicians (and outside our offices), this bias informs all our work with RCT. We acknowledge the power of context and the importance of naming the distorting impact of stratification and dynamics of power (power differentials) on individuals, couples, families and communities. Gendered power arrangements are also central to any understanding and intervention with couples.

We begin the book with an introduction of some of the core premises of RCT. Judith Jordan is one of the four founding scholars of RCT and Carlson, a world-recognized authority on couples, has been an appreciative supporter of this approach. We then turn to an interview with Janet Surrey and Stephen Bergman (written up by Jordan); Jan and Steve did much of the original work of applying RCT principles to the functioning of couples. Early on they named the importance of attending to the "we", and they created techniques for working with couples in groups. Their sensitivity to "male relational dread" (a dynamic named by Bergman) allowed them to effectively and sensitively intervene with both men and women in couples work.

Marsha Mirkin and Pamela Geib focus on the cultural and societal norms that impact people in relationships. Often work with couples involves making the context conscious. This allows individuals in couples to move out of a blaming stuckness. These authors examine the central relational paradox that RCT therapists work with both in individual and couples therapy.

Next Karen Skerrett develops her view that love stories are the essential building blocks of resilient relationships. She addresses the importance of sharing these stories in therapy, and illustrates these dynamics through an in-depth case presentation. Maureen Walker points out that mixed-race couples are becoming increasingly commonplace, accounting for approximately 15% of all new marriages in 2010. Walker provides an extensive treatment discussion through which to examine the complexities that arise for these couples. In particular she examines the role of shame. Natalie S. Eldridge's chapter on couples work with lesbian couples traces RCT themes in couples therapy (relational movement toward resilience, waging good conflict and uncovering the relational paradox). Eldridge notes the stresses of coming out in a heterosexual world and also marks the importance of the changing social context for same-sex partners, with the growing legal acceptance of same-sex marriage and civil unions. David M. Shannon brings RCT to bear on our understanding of couple dynamics for gay men. He examines the power of cultural shame, homophobia, biased messages about gay relationships and relational strengths of gay male couples.

Meg I. Striepe focuses on the integration of a relational and sexual health approach to concerns about sexuality in couples. She notes that most couples that present with sexual problems are actually struggling with finding ways to build a safer and more resilient connection with one another. Randy Markey addresses the challenges that men face in coming into couples therapy. He then brings these challenges to life with several detailed case vignettes. He examines what he calls the "gendered stress response" and points out ways to help couples see how each cares for the other, though often differently.

Kumkum Pareek Malik examines the ways in which the failure to fully appreciate the competencies, tasks, and stresses of motherhood can create barriers between partners. She points to the importance of validation at a very concrete level of the complexity and conflicting pressures that motherhood and being a member of a couple may create. Mona DeKoven Fishbane notes the ways that couples can enter therapy feeling stuck and polarized. She then looks at the underlying neurobiological processes (e.g. amygdala reactivity) that may precipitate movement out of a sense of safety within the couple. She also names the "empathy gap" that can exist for many heterosexual couples and demonstrates the way she uses "neuroeducation" to assist couples in becoming more aware of their own reactions, thus cutting down on reactivity. Constance A. Johannessen reports on her use of couples groups to assist couples in which one member has been diagnosed with cancer. She integrates RCT and relational neurobiology into her understanding of how healing occurs in couples work. Dana L. Comstock-Benzick, in a chapter both personal and historical, examines the history of the institution of marriage in order to better understand the often hidden biases that many people hold about divorce. She brings an RCT perspective to bear on the pain of chronic disconnection, the shame and sadness that ensue when a treasured relationship is no longer salvageable. In the final chapter by master couples therapist Harriet Lerner we are given wise insights into the extreme difficulties that often mark the stepparent–stepchild relationship. Lerner points out that stepfamilies are becoming the dominant family form. And helping couples challenge the myths that exist about stepparenting fosters health and resilience in the stepfamily. Lerner provides concrete suggestions to help reduce the potential toxicity of these relationships. The insights in this chapter should be a part of every couples therapist's toolbox in their efforts to support healthy relationships.

In the conclusion, the Editors bring us back to the "big picture": what are the greatest hopes of putting RCT into practice in our therapies and in our lives? Building on the insights gained through working with couples as well as individuals, families and groups, we return to our base of working for social change, bringing about justice and mutual respect in all our relationships in order to expand our sense of human possibility and contribute to a kinder, more compassionate world.

# References

Ainsworth, M., Blehar, M., Waters, E. & Wall, S. (1978) *Patterns of attachment: A psychological study of the Strange Situation*. Hillsdale, NJ: Lawrence Erlbaum Associates.

Bergman, S.J. (1991) *Men's psychological development: A relational perspective*. Work in Progress, No. 48. Wellesley, MA: Stone Center Working Paper Series.

Bowlby, J. (1982) *Attachment and loss, Vol. 1: Attachment*, 2nd edition. New York: Basic Books.

Jordan, J.V. (2000) The role of mutual empathy in relational-cultural therapy. *In Session: Psychotherapy in Practice*, 55, 1005–1016.

Jordan, J., Kaplan, A., Miller, J.B., Stiver, I. & Surrey, J. (1991) *Women's growth in connection*. New York: Guilford Press.

Jordan, J. (2010) *Relational-Cultural Therapy*. Washington, DC: American Psychological Association.

Laing, K. (1998) Katalyst leadership presented at In Pursuit of Parity: Teachers as Liberators, Boston.

Miller, J.B. (1976) *Toward a new psychology of women*. Boston: Beacon Press.

Miller, J.B. (1988) *Connections, disconnections and violations*. Work in Progress, No. 33. Wellesley, MA: Stone Center Working Paper Series.

Miller, J.B. & Stiver, I. (1997) *The healing connection: How women form relationships in therapy and in life*. Boston: Beacon Press.

Robb, C. (2006) *This changes everything: The relational revolution in psychology*. New York: Penguin.

Schore, A. (1994) *Affect regulation and the origin of the self: The neurobiology of emotional development*. Hillsdale, NJ: Lawrence Erlbaum Associates.

Stiver, I. (1995) Personal communication. Finding the "one true thing".

# 2

# RELATIONAL-CULTURAL COUPLE THERAPY

## From Impasse to Movement

*An Interview with*
*Stephen Bergman and Janet Surrey*


Relational-Cultural Therapy (RCT) focuses attention on the movement of relationships rather than on internal intrapsychic change. It explores cultural constructions of gender, race, class, and sexual orientation. Therapists assist couples in coming into the present moment of relational being. The movement from I or you to WE is essential to increased mutuality and relational health (Bergman and Surrey,1994; Shem and Surrey, 1998).

### Gender Dialogues

Janet Surrey and Steve Bergman began their work with couples by bringing together men and women in couples' gatherings. Prior to gathering couples in intensive workshops, they had spent ten years studying male–female relationships in corporations, schools, and other organizations. There they developed an interest in encouraging something they called gender dialogues. They were both involved at a core level in the development of Relational-Cultural Theory, had an abiding interest in meditation, and had studied and written about the development of AA (Shem and Surrey, 1990). In their gender/couple workshops they immediately saw that they had to shift the emphasis from the I to the WE, from Self to Relationship. One of the first innovations they provided was to ask couples to introduce "the relationship" to the group rather than presenting each self in the relationship. When asked, people came up with metaphors for the relationship that were quite striking and became the kernel for understanding many of the characteristics of the relationship. Often they mentioned animals or natural elements: a deer, a scared cat, a porcupine, a deep river.

The couples workshops that Surrey and Bergman conducted typically met for a beginning intensive three-day session; thereafter they often reconvened once a month. But each group determined the specific form the meetings took;

they were a work in progress. In these groups one of the first steps was to break into gender groups where men would be supported by men and women by women.

Before dividing the larger group into same gender subgroups, Janet and Steve framed questions for the gender groups to explore: (1) name three strengths the other gender group brings to relationship; (2) what do you most want to understand about the other gender group? and (3) what do you most want the other gender group to understand about you? In separate groups of men and women, these questions were explored and answered. The leaders hoped that this would stimulate respect, curiosity, interest and empathy for the other group. Interestingly the men found it easier to answer the question about women's strengths (i.e. nurturance, capacity for feeling, sensitivity, realness, interest in working on relationship). The women often had difficulty with this; some groups even said "none". But they also saw men as caretakers, with deep loyalties, lifting heavy objects, using rational thinking, having the ability to focus on one thing at a time. The women saw each strength as the other side of a liability, depending on "how it is used" in relationship to support or to shut down the other and the relationship. For example, the ability to focus on one thing could mean shutting out the other or could work to support the other or the relationship.

Having already written about male relational dread (Bergman, 1991) which he defined as a man's sense that he will not be enough and therefore has to withdraw or attack, Steve knew that special attention had to be paid to the discomfort of the man in a relational context such as therapy. Steve and Janet also recognized that women often feel lonely and angry being the sole caretaker of the emotional part of relationship. The naming of man's experience (relational dread) seemed to provide relief to many of the men and their partners. It helped move people out of self-centered loops, to see themselves as inevitably tied to one another and mutually responsible for the relationship.

## Building the WE

The emphasis is on cultivating the strength of the "WE", remembering what drew them together and nourishing and cultivating the good problem-solving they are capable of. The work acknowledges the inevitable gender impasses, based in acculturation in a society that privileges male strengths and perceptions. It is not a "problem-centered" approach. The emphasis is on naming and cultivating the relational strengths that exist, sometimes in spite of the context in which each partner has been situated.

Together they asked "What is a healthy WE?" It is characterized by shared purpose, mutual responsibility, finding ways to hold the relationship and appreciate the cultural impact on men and women coming into relationship together. Part of working on building a strong WE involved examining the culturally expectable and idiosyncratic impasses that arise for any couple (Shem and Surrey, 1998; Bergman and Surrey, 1994)

## Working with Impasses

Impasses inevitably are illuminated in the therapy. These impasses are treated as relational: they reside not in one person or the other but in the process between them. A typical impasse is the dread/anger impasse; the man, feeling relationally incompetent, dreads engagement with his partner while she finds herself getting more angry and critical of his avoidance and withdrawal and withdraws herself.

A relational impasse occurs when a relationship is stuck, static, or unmoving. Typical impasses arise around gender-stereotyped roles. The inevitable impasses that couples come to are dealt with by helping them to see "we got into this together and we can only get out of it together. It's our work." We help people value this struggle and investigation of how can WE move forward together. The therapist clearly allies with the relationship. Having both a man and a woman therapist facilitating these groups was essential. In particular Steve was able to assist men in getting to know and name their vulnerability.

Given the high expectations held for dyads in this culture where the nuclear family is anchored in the couple (especially committed marriage relationships), it is striking how isolated most couples feel in terms of sharing their real experience with others. The gender dialogue is at the core of the work on impasses in couples therapy. In this work the therapists help hold the "arc of relationship".

Humor is a constant in both the workshops and couple therapy. The absurdity as well as the pain of many of the conflicts is gently explored. There is a steady movement away from blame and judgment to looking at ways to empower the couple. The experience of "difference" is altered when "WE consciousness" and mutuality are emphasized rather than when the individual Self is at the center. Contrary to popular wisdom at the time to "keep it in the I voice", Bergman and Surrey found that persistently emphasizing the WE made a difference. People "got" it and it led to significant shifts in their dynamics. Often Steve and Janet would ask "Where's the WE right now?". If there was no basis for the WE, this would show up in the sessions as a drop in energy, lack of clarity, and often it was predictive of the ultimate break-up of the relationship.

## The Complexity of Couples

Janet and Steve were weaving together gender, cultural issues, relational theory and their work with substance abuse to form an appreciation of the complexity of couple dynamics. Their witnessing and reminding people to move to the WE is at the core of the work. The couples therapist allies with the relationship again and again. A part of strengthening the relationships is about learning to fight or work with conflict and differences. Both people always have the right to say, "Stop" as an argument unfolds. But they must agree to come back to the disputed issues or feelings within 24 hours.

## Shared Vulnerability

The message is "We are in this together". The suffering is shared. What are WE going to do? All of this flies in the face of American culture: no self, no fixed structure of relationship. In a highly individualistic culture with a gender construction that privileges male dominance, the anger of women is inevitable. As the man feels safer in bringing his vulnerability into the room, the woman's anger often softens and conversely, both man and woman come to a place of mutual vulnerability. The group leaders often bring their vulnerability to the meeting as well: "We don't know how to do it either". It's hard stuff. With a man both modeling and witnessing male vulnerability, there is an opportunity to shift some of the engrained cultural gender patterns. The femininization of relationality starts to ease. The context that serves to keep gender prescriptions in place is examined in the sessions and becomes part of the expanding consciousness of each couple. We are not alone. This is not just about our failures or our individual histories. There is a huge contextual piece to these impasses and this suffering.

This work has grown in a cultural relational perspective. The emphasis is on moving toward more mutuality, where both people feel seen, valued, understood, where both can serve as partners in the growth of connection, of the WE. By cultivating a stronger, clearer WE, the fabrication of self is deconstructed in important ways.

Miller has written that relationships are always in movement . . . toward either better connection or increasing disconnection (Miller, 1986). Disconnections occur in all relationships and are inevitable. In growth-fostering relationship they become a stimulus for relational growth. When disconnection cannot move into reconnection, there is an experience of impasse. When impasses in couples endure, both people and the relationship suffer. As Miller and Stiver write, "When yearnings for connection are stimulated, so are all the protective strategies each person has developed to stay out of connection based on a relational experience and cultural learning" (Miller and Stiver, 1997). In heterosexual couples these are often based on past relational images.

## Core Relational Principles for Couples Therapy

While the couple and therapist emphasize the connection to self and other, RCT places the relationship at the center. Holding relational awareness is something that the therapist brings to the meetings; eventually both people in the couple will develop the skill to do this. New positive imaginable ways of describing and naming the "we" strengthen the awareness of resources for the relationship. The language of connection and disconnection itself helps couples describe their experiences. The therapist works toward empathic connection; each person moves into greater authenticity. Holding an empathic under-standing of each person's experience and vulnerabilities provides a template for mutual empathy. The therapist holds the ongoing possibility of connection through difference and vulnerability.

## Mutual Responsibility for the Relationship

The therapist works to facilitate mutual responsibility for the relationship. Initially women feel burdened, as they already feel "too" responsible for the relationship. Appreciating the importance of mutual impact also helps move the couple out of power or control struggles. When both people feel they have an impact on the relationship, they are moving from a "power over" model to a model of "power with": mutuality. Gendered experiences of power are explored. And the awareness of the other's experience and the needs of the relationship grow. This is what is meant by growth in connection. Couples, with a heightened awareness of the WE, can create satisfying, mutual growth and provide anchors for growth-fostering experiences in families and communities.

---

### From Impasse to Relational Movement: A Vignette of Session One

Tom and Ann (a composite couple) come into the office so angry at each other and so discouraged about their marriage that they cannot even look at each other, so they face me, the therapist (Steve). Tom is a tall, athletic-looking middle-aged WASP with graying blond hair and horn-rimmed glasses. He owns a small computer software company. Ann is a youthful-looking, dark-haired, Jewish woman with intense dark eyes. She is headmistress of a private school. Both wear business suits. They have two teenage sons. Immediately they start talking about the faults of the other person, referring to each other in the third-person pronoun:

*Tom:*  Nothing I do is enough for her.
*Ann:*  I'm tired of taking care of this relationship.
*Tom:*  She's so demanding! And oversensitive. I try and try, and nothing seems to work
*Ann:*  He's so closed; he never talks. If we start to have a discussion that involves feelings, he changes the subject or gets angry and walks out. I feel shut out and alone. I told him that unless he came to therapy, the marriage is over.
*Tom:*  Nothing I do is enough. I even went into individual therapy for her—to try to work on myself.

They fall silent. The relationship is stuck. I get a sense that this is the endpoint of an impasse, the result of many painful attempts to connect. I feel for them. A traditional couples therapy approach is to try to have each person stay in the "I" (first person) rather than to be in the "you" (second person). This couple however, wasn't even in the second person, but the third—"he" and "she". My initial attempts to get them to stay in the "I", making statements such as "I feel" or "I think", failed miserably.

Tom:     I feel that she always makes me feel like a failure.
Ann:     I feel that he's treating me like his mother!

I could follow up on "mother", which might lead to significant family history. Using the relational model, however, the first priority is the quality of their connection, which is always in the present moment. And so I actively try to shift the paradigm away from self and/or other, to their relationship. There are three reasons for this: to see what the relationship, in fact is, its potential, and its history as seen by each of them; to shift away from the idea of "psychopathology" residing in one or the other; and to see if this paradigm shift might help move things in the present movement.

   With a sense of concern, I say that they are stuck in an impasse, not moving and that this stuckness is not because of a "sickness" in him or her, not the fault of either, but rather a difficulty in how they are meeting. I introduce the idea that in addition to "self" and "other", maybe we can also look "the relationship" almost as a thing with qualities, a past and quite possibly a future. I ask what they can say about the relationship.

Tom:     What relationship? There is no relationship here.
Ann:     (starts to cry) It feels dead. Boring and dead. So different from where we began.

This may not seem like much, but in fact it is a relational statement, the first time that either has used the "we" and referred to "it", the relationship. I say, "I know it seems pretty hopeless right now, but maybe you can describe what the relationship was like when you met".

Ann:     He was different . . . so open and trustable.
Steve:   (interrupts) Sorry, I didn't mean to ask about him. I meant the relationship.

16

This surprises them. For the first time they look at each other. They begin to talk, more and more animatedly, about how the relationship in the past was—in Ann's words, "safe and love, a lot of trust, and we used to be really free, do the wildest things—go to concerts, go dancing". Tom talks about how he was attracted to Ann's depth of feeling and how, wanting to impress her on their first date, he got tickets to Symphony Hall—only to find that it was "Barbershop Quartet Night". Now there is a palpable shift in the room—they are making eye contact. They laugh. They are talking about the past history of the relationship, but they are not in the past—they are in the present, making contact, in connection. There is a real sense of things coming unstuck, things moving. What is moving is the relationship. I begin to sense their potential.

After a while, now that they are connected, I try to build on this relationship exercise. Each tries to get an image of the color of the relationship, the texture, the sound, the climate, the animal.

*Color?*

*Ann:*    Red, cool blue.
*Tom:*    Black, purple.

*Textures?*

*Ann:*    Lumpy, mud.
*Tom:*    It started out smooth, now it's sandpapery.

*Sound?*

*Ann:*    Ocean.
*Tom:*    Distant rain.

*Animal?*

*Ann:*    Cat.
*Tom:*    Tiger.

I point out how there are real similarities in their images, as well as clear differences, and say that the shift back—sandpapery to smooth—will happen. I tell them that the problem isn't the shift or the conflict; it's how to be in creative movement rather than in deadness, impasse.

*Ann:*      I guess we really don't know each other.

*Steve:*    I have a sense that you really do know each other pretty well. What you don't know right now is how to move in relationship.

The session ends with my affirming that there is in fact a relationship here, a "we" with a history. Ann says that she knows it, but that Tom often seems to forget. Coming back from a business trip recently, he hung up his coat on the rack at the door and walked past her to his answering machine without even saying hello. I suggest that they can try to be creative, even playful, about working together on the relationship. For, instance they might put up a sign over the coat rack inside the door "Danger: There is a relationship here." They laugh. Now we are, to a certain extent, all on the same side; all three of us working together for the sake of the relationship. I feel empathy with the pain in each of them and with the way they are connecting and disconnecting.

*Steve:*    You're both very vulnerable right now and the relationship is vulnerable too. It is important that each of you take care right now not to do more harm, not to hurt each other or the relationship any further.

They sense my concern, agree, and ask how they can do that. I suggest two tools they can use: the check-out and the check-in. The check-out can be used when the couples are in a fight and one person wants to stop. He or she says so but then has to say when they will bring up the subject again. Either person can call for a check-in, which consists of each person in turn telling what he or she is feeling in them and in the relationship. The other listens, without asking for elaboration, and just says "I hear you". The check-in is a simple but powerful way to make a connection in the moment. I ask if they'd like to try a check-in right now, suggesting they look at each other as they do it.

*Tom:*      *(looking at Ann directly)* I'm afraid to say anything because we might start up again. I feel shell-shocked.

*Ann:*      I feel you're really trying, Tom but . . .

*Steve:*    Can you just stay with your own experience for now?

*Ann:*      *(pause)* I feel kind of lost and scared to trust you again. But I hear you, Tom.

*Tom:*      And I hear you.

There is a palpable shift at this authentic statement from each of them to the other.

Finally, I suggest that before the next session they try to write a "relational purpose statement". Together, on one sheet of paper, write down the purpose of the relationship and purpose of their "WE". This is a way of seeing whether or not a couple share the same basic world view and values on which much can be built. We've found that how far a couple gets on this shared project is a fairly reliable predictor of how the therapy will go.

As they are leaving:

Tom:     Thanks. You brought back the idea that there is a relation-ship here and that it does have some good to it.
Ann:     Yes, it helps to keep the focus on the relationships, not just on him.
Tom:     (joking, with poignant truthfulness) So, if I take care of it, it'll take care of me!
Steve:   Yes, and right now each of you have to take care of it, the relationship. This is possible.

They leave with a sense that together we three have broken through an impasse, a first step has been taken; a feeling that they are moving again in however tenuous a connection—which guides greater faith that this is possible. They have a sense of great relational resilience (Jordan, 1992), of relational presence and that someone is really with them and with their relationship, which helps them to have a sense of the reality of the relationship too, and its potential. A seed has been planted that they can act together to move to greater connection. This we call "relational empowerment" (Surrey, 1987); that is, locating the power of capacity to act in the relationship.

The core relational principles guiding couples therapy are: (1) holding relational awareness; (2) working toward mutually empathic connection; (3) mutual responsibility and mutual impact; and (4) the gendered "WE".

## Vignette: Session Two

In the second session of the therapy with Ann and Tom, they reported that things were better, but still difficult. Both felt that getting in touch with their history of the relationship had been useful. But as they had started to work on a relational purpose statement, they had gotten into an impasse.

*Tom:*    We started out well enough and decided that one purpose was to "provide a loving environment for the growth and protection of our children and ourselves"—that was easy. But then she wanted more and got in her "we're not close enough" issue . . .

*Ann:*    Wait a sec . . . I didn't say "not enough". I just want it better.

*Tom:*    You're insatiable—as you said . . . the sky's the limit.

*Ann:*    What's wrong with that?

*Tom:*    There's no limit to the sky. Nothing's ever good enough.

*Ann:*    You just want to stay stuck in the mud . . . as if mud's good enough.

Steve stops the process. This may seem like bad news, but in fact I was delighted. In the first session they were totally stuck in an impasse, not even looking at each other. Now they are in an impasse, but engaged on a growing edge—trying to move. There's more to work with. They are actively struggling with each other. And they actually started to work on their relational purpose statement. I have a sense of liking them.

Now that they are connecting, there is room for me to start to use all the various ways to work empathically with each of them and with their relationship. I acknowledge to them that this could be really hard work and that both of them are trying their best. I say that it's not unusual for impasses to come up around trying to do the purpose statement. I ask them to tell me more of what happened.

It turns out that their relational styles in doing this were much different: she wanted to toss things around in dialogue and then write something down at the end; he wanted them each to make a list and then put them together. He had felt lost in her "looseness" and she had felt shut out by his "structure". This is a product/process impasse (Shem and Surrey, 1998), common between men and women. He wants to fix it. Women often want to think in dialogue to get clearer.

20

And men have a difficult time believing that such a process can actually get anywhere. Steve can reframe their impasse in terms of how what each of them is doing is influenced by the different ways each gender has learned to move in relationship. The problem isn't difference itself; it's not being able to see difference clearly and without judgment. to work with and move with difference in relationship.

Steve ends the second session by sharing: "Our priority together has to be, first and foremost, connecting. If we're not in connection, there's room for all kinds of trouble to creep in: the past, accusation about family ('you're like your father'; 'you're like your mother'); gender stereotypes ('you're like all men'; 'you're like all women'); and ethnic issues ('you're like all WASPs or all Jews'). In connection we can talk respectfully about any of these differences, such as religious, ethnic and class differences, without stereotyping. "Today by hanging out through the disconnections, you've managed to make an even better connection." I mention the idea of the continuity of connection (an awareness that the relationship continues to exist even when they are apart or feeling disconnected). Often just saying "I was thinking about what we were talking about yesterday" conveys the sense of continuity of connection and reminds us that we are held in someone's heart.

In summary, there are several core principles in working with couples from a Relational-Cultural perspective: (1) Hold the relationship, with awareness, faith and "in process"; (2) connections comes first; (3) reframe therapy in terms of relational movement, gender movement and movement through and toward connection; (4) work with the concepts of impasse and breakthrough; (5) make use of strategies to create mutuality: check-in, check-out, purpose statement, creativity; (6) work in the present moment; (7) create mutual empathy and engage around difference; (8) reframe depression, autonomy and dependency in terms of the movement or stasis of the relationship, not in terms of intrapsychic forces operating on either individual; (9) work with continuity and transition. The inquiry isn't so much "what do you do?" as "what do you do NEXT?" What follows the disconnect? While "hanging out in the disconnection" we make room for movement toward mutual authenticity; (10) Open to spirituality. RCT and relational work suggests something greater than self and other. This movement in connection, toward mutual relationship, greater than self and other, brings people to an awareness of being a part of something larger. This is at the heart of helping people—couples—to heal both their cultural and their personal wounds.

# References

Bergman, S. (1991) Men's psychological development: A relational perspective. *Work in Progress*, No. 48. Wellesley, MA: Stone Center Working Paper Series.

Bergman, S. and Surrey, J. (1994) Couple therapy: A relational approach. *Work in Progress*, No 66. Wellesley, MA: Stone Center Working Paper Series.

Jordan, J. (1992) Relational resilience. *Work in Progress*, No 57. Wellesley, MA: Stone Center Working Paper Series.

Jordan, J. (2010) *Relational-Cultural Therapy*. Washington, DC: American Psychological Association.

Miller, J. (1976) *Toward a new psychology of women*. Boston, MA: Beacon Press.

Miller, J. (1986) *Toward a new psychology of women* (2nd ed.). Boston, MA: Beacon Press.

Miller, J. and Stiver, I. (1997). *The healing connection: How women form relationships in therapy and in life*. Boston, MA: Beacon Press.

Shem, S. and Surrey, J. (1990) *Bill W. and Dr. Bob: The story of the founding of AA. A play*. www.billwanddrbob.com

Shem, S. and Surrey, J. ( 1998) *We have to talk: Healing dialogues between women and men*. New York: Basic Books.

Surrey, J. (1987) Relationship and empowerment. *Work in Progress*, No 30. Wellesley, MA: Stone Center Working Paper Series.

# 3

# WHEN 1 + 1 DOES NOT EQUAL 2

## The Impact of Context on Couples Therapy

*Marsha Mirkin and Pamela Geib[1]*

We want to begin by discussing the goals and values that inform our work. We share the values of the Relational-Cultural Theory developed at the Jean Baker Miller Training Institute at Wellesley College (Jordan, 2009). This model focuses on a connection-centered rather than autonomy-centered way of thinking. It emphasizes the importance of sustaining and improving connection, the need to identify and repair ruptures in relationship, the importance of cultural humility, and the centrality of mutual empathy. The values of Relational-Cultural Theory help us approach the therapeutic relationship more collaboratively and with greater curiosity, inviting the couple to expand their formerly narrow story.

As Relational-Cultural family therapists, we focus on the influence of family, cultural, and societal norms and values on individuals and their relationships. As we will see in this chapter, differences in culturally prescribed power, privilege and marginalization in the lives of a couple and between the couple and the therapist can contribute to blame and ruptures in relationships. Most importantly, identification of these contexts can lead to stronger connections. This is what we call "context made conscious."

## Consciousness of Context in Clinical Practice

To illustrate what consciousness of context means in clinical practice, we would like to introduce Ann and Peter,[2] a white, middle-class couple who came into my office in matching states of blame. Peter said Ann was unsupportive and critical. Ann said Peter was uncommunicative and showed no understanding of how hard she was working.

Their lives had been impacted by the economic downturn when Peter lost a job he valued. Up until then, they had both worked and shared household tasks. Peter's job was higher paying and had required longer hours than Ann's, so they had agreed that she would do somewhat more of the home chores. All in all, they felt that they had shared equally in the overall earning and housekeeping domains.

Now that Peter was without work, he had become withdrawn and uncommunicative. Ann expected him to do more of the house chores, as he was at home all day looking for work online. She was angry that he was not accomplishing the chores, that he had no leads on possible employment, and most of all, that he had withdrawn from their once vibrant relationship.

Peter said that Ann did not understand what he was going through, although he had trouble elaborating on what that was. Ann was frustrated by what she perceived as his neediness. She was busier than usual. Her work place had laid off staff, and was asking current employees to do more work than before the recession. She felt she had no choice but to comply since jobs everywhere were becoming scarce.

This is an example of a couple blaming each other in a narrow, problem-saturated story, without awareness of the cultural assumption that was influencing them. In this case, the assumption was the belief that individual effort reaps success, and that failure must be a result of individual fault. It is remarkable that this cultural story still held sway for them in an era in which the media was full of stories about how financial institutions had caused the crisis. But the cultural narrative of individual responsibility has great power. Thus, Ann and Peter were attributing personal failings to each other (he could do better; she could do better), and failing to see how the larger context was impacting them.

In addition, gender roles are often entrenched even with couples who advocate for and seem to live in more gender-aware and equitable ways. I wondered if it was psychologically harder for women with unemployed or underemployed husbands than for men with unemployed or underemployed wives, since the dominant cultural mandate is for husbands to support their wives and masculinity is often defined by work status. I wondered if this was part of their experience and kept my ears open to that possibility.

Their lack of contextual perspective was obvious to me but my therapeutic approach is to encourage inquiry in the client rather than to give "expert advice." So rather than telling the couple to look outside themselves, I asked them to explore what was going on inside as they complained about each other.

When Peter accused Ann of being unempathic, I asked him what was going on for him as he said that. He identified the anger first. As I collaborated with him with curiosity and without judgment, he was able to get in touch with the wounded part of him that the anger was protecting. He was able to realize fully just how bad he felt about himself for losing the job. His self-esteem had plummeted, as he had identified himself as a successful man through his climb up the corporate ladder. Going even deeper, he connected with feelings of hopelessness about regaining his footing in his field of employment. Hopelessness slowed him down in his efforts to search for jobs. Ann had seen his depressed behavior as a lack of initiative rather than the underlying hopelessness and shame he was experiencing. Her impatience stemmed from her need for him to recover quickly and resume the path of success he had been on.

As Peter explored his own inner world with interest and compassion for himself, Ann was able to listen more compassionately. In connecting with Peter, she began to be aware of the larger frame that was impacting him. She began to feel indignant, not at Peter, but at the larger system that had let him down, even as he had worked well and hard at his job. Because curiosity and compassion had entered the conversation, Ann's story was beginning to include the impact of the larger context (in this case, the economic context).

I also helped Ann explore her own inner experiences. She discovered that the sharp criticisms of Peter were protecting a part of her that was scared about their financial problems. We also explored what was going on inside when she took such a dismissive stance toward his unhappiness. She came to see that she had unacknowledged resentment towards the extra unpaid work she was doing at her company. She had been aiming that resentment at Peter rather than at the company. As she looked deeper, she also found that she was afraid that her own job security was at risk, so it had been safer for her to resent her husband than show anger at her workplace.

Hearing this, Peter was able to react with compassion to his new understanding of her fear and resentment. He began to feel indignant that her company was burdening and scaring its employees.

As they became more aware of their own and each other's internal systems (Schwartz, 2001) they were able to talk about how they both were experiencing the loss of their former vibrant relationship. They turned toward each other rather than against each other. Their energy was no longer drained by mutual blaming and defense but the fear and anger had not gone away; it still needed expression.

Because they now had a broader picture of the context of their difficulties, they were able to mobilize their anger by turning toward the system that had caused the problems with which they were struggling. They began to focus anger on the financial system that had so changed their lives. Because Peter felt safer with Ann, he told her in more detail about how his company had fired many middle managers and kept reaping profits for senior management. Ann's compassion for Peter increased, as did her anger at how he had been treated. Peter felt the unfairness of Ann doing more work for the same pay and joined her in resenting the fear the company engendered to keep workers compliant. Mutual empathy had been restored to the relationship.

With a common understanding of the bigger picture, they looked for ways to counter their helpless feelings with action. They joined in reading articles about how the financial crisis had arisen, and engaged with online groups that were trying to pass new regulations. This led to several meetings in their own neighborhood, where they met people who were invested in political action to change the financial systems. With their new awareness, they were able to face the external "enemy" and took arms against a sea of cultural inequities.

This new intimacy allowed Peter and Ann to express gender expectations that had remained hidden. They both experienced their marriage as modern and free from outdated gender stereotypes. Ann was able to share that, in the difficult times, a part of her had felt let down, as this part had always expected that her husband would earn more money that she did. Peter talked about how one factor in his depression was that he had felt less "manly" because he wasn't living up to the masculine role of breadwinner. Neither had felt comfortable with these feelings, having prided themselves on a modern sense of role equality, and freedom from old gender stereotypes. In retrospect, they could share with each other their surprise and embarrassment at not being free of societal gender roles. Now they could laugh about this. It is important to note that they were learning to discover what contextual norms were affecting them. They terminated their therapy with a new skill: contextual awareness.

*This is a case of context made conscious.* Peter and Ann's new awareness allowed them to question their former interpretation of their situation by broadening their vision to include a larger economic and societal context. They became empowered to make new choices, which unblocked the flow of connection, agency and pleasure in the relationship.

It is satisfying to know that Ann and Peter were helped to reconnect in this way. Yet their inability to see the obvious, to see the problem that was hiding in plain sight, may seem surprising. Since Ann and Peter had the privilege of being white, upper middle-class, heterosexual, educated white-collar workers, why was this broader perspective not immediately obvious to them? From a cultural context, this inability to see is not surprising. After all, it is a privilege of the privileged to be blind to privilege (Hardy, 2008). Ann and Peter experienced racial, sexual, class and educational privilege, and were not confronted by the daily micro- and macro-aggressions of those who are subjugated (Sue, Capodilupo, Nadal & Torino, 2008). When Ann and Peter's economic situation changed, they became personally confronted by injustices that they never before had to see.

A primary factor contributing to this not seeing is that our culture emphasizes individual effort and individual failure. So pervasive is this assumption that it can blind individuals to the contexts that impact them and therefore impact their relationships. There is a profound belief in "rugged individualism" in our society—exemplified in the iconic stories of Horatio Alger, the early twentieth-century author whose novels featured white, heterosexual young men who, in spite of impossible circumstances, always managed to prevail and become financially successful.

The Horatio Alger narrative, in some form or another, tells us that context doesn't matter. That no matter what your circumstances, turns of fate, or limitations, physical or fiscal, you can do anything you want if you work hard and are of good moral fiber. If you don't succeed it's your own fault. Notice also that Horatio Alger is a male, and the sense of personal responsibility for economic success still weighs heavily on the shoulders of many men.

This Horatio Alger narrative prevented Ann and Peter from being aware of the broader context that was impacting them both. In this chapter, our intention is to look at this issue of context in many of its manifestations. The inability to be aware of context is problematic in many ways—whether the context is race, class, gender, sexual orientation, religion, ethnicity, immigration status, or any other identity that is privileged or marginalized in our culture. In the life of a couple, we often explain difficulties we're having by attributing them to personality weaknesses and character flaws (preferably our partner's, not our own). What is often lacking is a consciousness of the power that context exerts in creating our limitations and misunderstandings.

This may seem strange in a society in which racism, gender inequality, homophobia and other issues are much discussed in the media. Yet however much diversity is discussed, "micro blame for macro problems"—that is, individual attribution—is often what dominates our private lives, and the power of those in the dominant culture dictates whose story is heard and valued and who is unheard and blamed.

This dynamic certainly affected Ann and Peter. We will deepen and expand the understanding of how context affects intimate systems by describing other clinical vignettes in which facilitating an awareness of context has been essential in our work with couples.

## Blocks to Connection as Stuck, Blaming Narratives

The story of Ann and Peter's work illustrates that no matter how much we value connection and empathy, we often don't see these qualities when couples enter our offices. Why not? Everyone has a theory about the difficulty couples have with connection. We believe, along with Michael White (2007) and many other narrative therapists, that we all create stories about our lives and relationships, and that by creating new narratives and forming new and richer understandings of existing narratives, we can transform ourselves and our relationships.

By the time that couples enter our waiting rooms, they have developed a story about their relationship that is so problematic that it no longer allows them to be empathic toward each other. A hallmark of these problematic stories is how small and still they have become. Complexity and ambiguity have narrowed into tiny, redundant, blaming or defending statements. Movement and narrative possibility have been frozen. In the midst of this confining, stationary story sits the couple, feeling incompetent and disempowered, unable to tell a more satisfying new tale.

By this point, chances are these stories of blame are so entrenched that the couple is looking more for a judge than a therapist. Have you ever had a couple come in and say they want help expanding their constricted narrative? Not often. Often couples are looking for someone who will say that one is right, the other is wrong, and then go about changing the other so that the relationship will work. We don't want to accept that invitation. So, what do we do?

## Reconnecting through Expanding the Context

What tools can we utilize to expand the narrow story? The method we're describing today we call "expanding the context" (revised from Mirkin & Geib's (1999) "pushing out the context"). This is an exploration of the larger contexts that impinge on relationship. Some of these contexts are personal, such as the influence of family of origin messages or the impact of abuse history, which in turn are often embedded in cultural messages. Some of the effects of context are embedded in the social fabric itself, such as attitudes and messages regarding race, class, gender, ethnicity, and sexual orientation. We try to help couples notice and name the personal and cultural messages that are causing trouble in the relationship.

This naming is important. Because many of society's messages are part of the dominant cultural story, they are often so pervasive as to be invisible. They are implicit, and do their work in private. Naming them makes them less powerful and gives the couple more space for creative movement. It brings these assumptions into a level of awareness where they can be questioned, challenged, and re-understood. By expanding the context in this way, we can help the couple externalize some of the problems they have been blaming on each other, thus restoring their relationship.

## Case Commentaries

We want to illustrate these ideas by speaking further of clinical work in which we've helped couples expand the context in order to have more satisfying connection. In addition to describing these clinical vignettes, we'll be commenting on some of the methods we use, the "how to" of this particular work.

Let's begin with a few words about this "how to." Our goal is to work collaboratively with clients, avoiding the extremes of passively following or omniscient leadership. We do assume that because we do not have to live inside the narrow, problematic stories of our clients, and because as therapists we have been thinking about just these issues, we may glimpse more of the impinging contexts than do our clients. We do not, however, wish to impose our meaning on them; this is bombastic and unhelpful. It would ignore the facts that our clients are the experts on their lives and about their experiences of privilege and marginalization. Further, we may have blind spots related to our own areas of privilege, as will be discussed later in this chapter. Living with the paradox of being with and standing apart from our clients' stories is a piece of what we will be describing. We'll be seeing this in action in the following case.

## *Sarah and Jean: The Context of Sexual Orientation*

Sarah and Jean, a white, lesbian couple, are in their thirties and have been in a committed relationship for six years. They arrived at therapy at an impasse with Jean feeling disconnected and lonely, and Sarah unsuccessfully trying to make things better while feeling misunderstood and unappreciated.

Jean has been out as a lesbian with her family and friends since early in the relationship, and her family is accepting of Sarah. Sarah has not told her family or her colleagues about her relationship with Jean, and she has not publicly identified them as a couple. Jean feels rejected by Sarah, and believes that if Sarah truly valued her, she would be out and possibly even get married.[3] No matter how often Sarah tells Jean that she loves her, Jean still feels degraded by Sarah's lack of public acknowledgment. Once again we see an impasse. We try to break the impasse by contextualizing the difficulties. We ask Sarah and Jean to share their experiences as lesbians in this society.[4] This move involves them letting go of blaming the other and instead exploring their own experience while expanding the context beyond the individual relationship to include societal impingement.

It turns out that their experiences have been very different. Jean is a social worker in a group practice where several of her colleagues are lesbians and all the women feel safe being out about their sexual orientation. Sarah, on the other hand, works at a politically sensitive job at the State House, and feels that acknowledgment of her homosexuality could jeopardize her job. This makes Sarah anxious because Jean earns so little money, and the couple depends on Sarah's salary. Sarah sees her caution as in the service of their relationship and coming from a concern for the financial wellbeing of both of them. Jean is stunned by Sarah's explanation. Jean had always assumed that if Sarah lost her job, she'd easily find another because of Sarah's enormous talent and expertise. Sarah never had that much confidence in her own ability, or in the job market, and was touched that Jean had such faith in her, although her anxiety over potential job loss was not alleviated.

With these issues on the table, we could ask whether they were angry at each other, or at a society in which there were often real life consequences for lesbian partnership. The issue was redefined not as whether Jean loved Sarah more than the reverse, but how they could manage to live a loving life in the context of a homophobic society. They developed a number of playful and crafty ways to do this. For example, Jean wrote a love letter to Sarah, signed with the letter "V" that hid her identity but implied victory, which Sarah brought with her to work in her attaché case. They also discussed whom it was safe to tell, and why Sarah felt uncomfortable coming out even among her few supportive friends and family. They brainstormed ways of dealing with the difficult financial realities they could face should Sarah lose her job.

Once the context was expanded, Sarah and Jean were freed up to grasp the empathic bond that connects them and empowers them to deal with their unempathic surroundings. They moved away from the mutual blaming stance with which they entered therapy, and their mutual support enabled them to start exploring some deeply disturbing aspects of their lives and relationship.

### The Story Unfolds: The Importance of Timing

This further exploration was able to take place because the stuck story of blaming around the context of sexual lifestyle had been loosened, and its meanings expanded. In this section, we describe the subsequent unfolding of other important issues in order to illustrate the importance of timing. The sequence in which new issues emerged in treatment points up the importance of the therapist's willingness to let the client set the agenda, even if certain problems are obvious to the therapist by virtue of her awareness and training. We want to emphasize the importance of trusting that the clients will address issues when the setting has become sufficiently trustworthy. Thus the therapist who is well trained in recognizing the importance of social contexts needs to feel out which level of context is currently most available for conversation.

After having explored the ways that homophobia had impacted the relationship, Jean and Sarah were able to open up the topic of difficulties they were having with Sarah's two sons from a previous marriage. The problem focus was on the boys' inability to accept that their mother is a lesbian and their subsequent resentment of Jean. They seemed to feel that Jean had "made" their mother homosexual, and framed the solution to the family problem as getting rid of Jean. This was not an easy way for Jean to enter the already difficult arena of step-parenting. Because of her status as step-parent, she was an easy target for such scapegoating. Complicating matters was the fact that the father, who had joint custody, seemed to share the boys' feelings and judgments.

As we met with various subgroups of the family and alone with just the couple, we used awareness of the pervasive impact of homophobia to empathically connect with each member of the system. This expanded the story from one in which either (1) the boys and father were to blame for being intolerant and cruel or (2) the mother Sarah was to blame for causing her family pain, into a story in which homophobia, named and externalized, was affecting every member of the family, causing disconnection.[5]

After having named the culprit, homophobia, we asked the boys to talk about how homophobia (not their mother or Jean) was causing them misery. They talked very movingly about how awful they felt in the middle of the intense homophobic jokes and mean stories about gays that were current at their school. They told of how embarrassed they felt, even though they made sure that no one knew about their mom.

Several meetings were held with friends of theirs who went to another, more progressive school that had workshops on tolerance and diversity. We talked about how that school was putting up a fight against homophobia. The father was helped, by the therapist, to talk with the boys about the cultural messages about sexual identity he had received growing up, about how he had been called a sissy for liking to read and do school work. He began to attend meetings of PFLAG, a support and advice group for friends and families of lesbians and gays. Blame was lifted all round, and new, if tentative, conversations emerged.

But the treatment wasn't over. In the course of more work, other problems surfaced, each in its own time. It took the safety of an ongoing relationship, and the confidence that came with mastery of the preceding work, to allow the most difficult, shame-laden, issues to surface.

With an expanded, less adversarial family story around homophobia, Jean became more able to share her very real difficulties with being a step-parent. This spoken vulnerability helped Sarah become more aware that the process of step-parenting was not an easy one. At this point in the therapy, Jean trusted that admitting "I'm having trouble with your children" would not trigger blame. Thus we were able to help Jean release the shame she was feeling, and assist Sarah in getting some distance from blame that came up by addressing the difficulties inherent in step-parenting.

It was essential that the issues of homophobia and step-parenting were able to emerge at the couple's own pace, as they came to the foreground of awareness and could be dealt with productively. Expanding the context and externalizing helped create a safe environment in which some of the more raw parts of the story could be told and reworked.

It is distressing that this layered approach is often not easily accessible to clients of limited economic means, and that class privilege rather than equal access to services enabled Jean and Sarah to have the time to work on issues at the pace they set. As therapists, we can begin to address the disparity in services by offering reduced fees and extended hours (for low-income clients with no work hour flexibility) and by advocating for single payer systems and mental health parity (which has been achieved to some degree in Massachusetts but is decontextualized and available only for "biologically based illnesses").

## John and Judy: The Contexts of Race, Gender, and Ethnicity

We've been talking about the importance of recognizing specific aspects of context. These include, but are not limited to, race, class, gender roles, gender identity, religion, ethnicity, able-bodiedness, sexual identity, age, and immigration status. In our clinical work, it is crucial to recognize that context is not unidimensional, and we generally see a number of social contexts woven together in one couple system. After all, we all have many different identities, some of which are privileged in this society and others that are oppressed. In Jean and Sarah's case, they experienced class, race and educational privilege as well as gender and sexual orientation oppression. When we work on our own self-awareness and when we help clients see how cultural mandates impact their lives, we examine intersectionality, or the interactions among our privileged and oppressed identities (Crenshaw, 1989). In the following case, these intersections that make up the multi-contextual nature of our work are exemplified.

As in the past two cases, John and Judy have been in a committed relationship for six years. John is an African-American man who was brought up in the South. Judy is a white woman whose low-income grandparents immigrated to the Northeast United States from England when they were children. Judy arrived at our session feeling disconnected and lonely, while John felt hurt and angry.

33

As they described their marital problems, they did not mention race. When I asked what it was like for them to work with a white, female therapist, they responded that it wasn't a problem. When I inquired about the experience of being a biracial couple, John said they lived in a tolerant community. Yet, in their arguments, issues of race and gender were both visible and unacknowledged. Judy shared that she was lonely because John didn't care for her as a person, only as a "possession," who was expected to do what he wanted and not have her own ideas or needs. John responded angrily that Judy was the controlling one who had to have her own way, and who treated him like a "n____."

John and Judy were locked in a struggle, each feeling controlled by the other, astounded that the other could perceive him or her as the controlling one, and furious at the other's perception. To defuse the struggle, and make way for empathy and authenticity, I helped them look beyond their relationship to the context in which their relationship is embedded (Imber-Black, 1990). Since they used the language of control, I wondered with them about their past experiences of feeling controlled. Initially, John could not remember any such experiences. Judy felt that in her family, her ideas were often ignored in favor of her brothers, who were seen as more credible simply because they were male. She went on to explore her experience that this dynamic was recreated at her job when her expertise was taken seriously only when presented by her male counterpart. She recalled incidents of harassment that went unreported but were seared on her consciousness.

As Judy explored both the inner and outer experiences of gender oppression, John became animated. He told me that he had believed that since I am a therapist (he did not at this point specify "white therapist"), I am only interested in his experience in his own family-of-origin and not in the larger society. However, when Judy spoke about gender oppression at work, and I was interested in her experience, John felt that he could share his experiences of racial oppression in the larger society. John recounted stories in which white colleagues and neighbors made false and hurtful assumptions about him because he is African-American. He felt that in spite of his class privilege, decisions are made about him over which he has little influence because of his race. John reported feeling guarded at his job because success and failure were viewed not simply as his own, but as a reflection on his entire race. He angrily shared an example of a white applicant who came to his office, saw him, and respectfully

34

inquired when the director was returning. John is the director. Examples such as these reminded John daily that no matter how much he worked, how high he reached in his profession, he would always have to be vigilant because racism just doesn't go away. Racism looms large even if the subject of race is ignored in therapy. Even a white spouse who loves John dearly can have a blind spot, born of racial privilege, about race. As Hardy (2008) wrote, "The denial or lack of awareness and sensitivity to race does not negate or diminish its pervasive significance in our lives" (p. 77).

I wondered aloud whether they were playing out these highly charged racial and gender experiences within their marriage, and I reminded them that when they shared their stories, they used the words "possession" and "n____." As they explored the meanings of race and gender in their marriage, they brought up cultural differences as well. This was a critical moment in the therapy, since when race, gender, and other cultural differences weren't seen or acknowledged, serious misunderstandings followed.

John's Southern grandmother emphasized collectivity and sharing, values that were transmitted to John and that he respected. John was appalled at Judy's individuality and aloofness. Judy's British family taught her that respect required space and distance, so she saw John as intrusive and disrespectful. John was sensitive to others fearing him for no reason other than his being a black man, and he was hurt by the times when Judy seemed afraid of him. Judy, who had a sister who was raped and a friend who was battered, was aware of how often women are violated. She was brought up in a family that insisted on quiet, discreet discussions, and was frightened by John's loud expressions of anger. Without understanding these differences in culture, Judy and John interpreted each other's behavior in a way that led them to assume the worst about each other.

Their conflict escalated when John's aunt and uncle came to stay without first calling or receiving an explicit invitation. While this is acceptable behavior in collectivist cultures, it is unacceptable in individualistic cultures (Kliman, 1994). After the family spent the afternoon and early evening together, Judy left to make an extended phone call. John was angry at what he perceived was Judy's rudeness toward his relatives, and he felt shamed in front of his aunt and uncle. Judy thought John's relatives were rude for arriving without an invitation, and was angry that John wasn't setting more limits around his aunt and uncle's visit. Judy also felt resentful because the arrival of two extra people meant that someone had to perform more household tasks, and she felt she was expected to take on the extra work.

John and Judy were at war, hurt and angry. Their perceptions of each other's behavior and motivation were dictated by their own life experiences with culture and context, and their lack of familiarity with the culture and context of their spouse. The impasse was broken as Judy and John expanded the context to include the experience of the other. They contextualized their problems based on Southern black heritage and British white heritage. What Judy saw as invasive was defined by John and the culture in which he grew up as hospitality; what John saw as rude was Judy's culturally sanctioned need for privacy. They were beginning to develop mutual empathy.

As John and Judy processed these incidents, John was surprised at how disadvantaged Judy felt based on being female, given her race privilege. Judy was equally surprised at how disadvantaged John felt in their relationship given his gender and class privilege. Their mutual blaming was replaced by curiosity about self, other, and the relationship they were creating. The challenge they took on was to work out ways to name and appreciate cultural differences as they create their relationship. As John and Judy included gender, race, and ethnicity in their discussions, they could begin to develop a marriage that is inclusive of not just the two of them, but of the relationship and commitment they have to their cultural and ethnic backgrounds.

Toward the end of therapy, John impishly reported that he initially said that it didn't matter that the therapist was white and female because he didn't trust me enough to choose to be honest and share his discomfort with a privileged white woman. This caution around trusting institutions and their representatives (such as the mental health system and therapists) is a necessary adaptation for people who have been victimized based on racial or other oppressed identities. Boyd-Franklin (1989) names this idea "healthy cultural paranoia."

## Tracking and Concretizing Context

The previous two cases demonstrate the multiplicity of contexts we often encounter in a single couple system. We find it helpful to explicitly keep track of these contextual issues as they emerge.

Sometimes we do this visually with what we call a "star diagram" on which these contexts can be tracked.

This diagram keeps the contextual material available for discussion and reinforces the idea of context. The following is a verbal description of the visual chart that we created as therapy with John and Judy unfolded.

First, Judy raised the issue of gender. We drew a gender axis on our flip chart. The conversation about gender oppression helped John bring up his experience of racial oppression. A line bisecting the gender line was drawn and named as the racial parameter. We put each contextual variable on the diagram with a mention of how it was impacting the relationship. For example, along the dimension of gender we put Judy's meaning of being a "possession" and "ignored." Along the dimension of race we put John's experience of being seen as a " n___" and "controlled" by a white society. With these meanings and experiences so visible, we could refer to them when they were stirring up trouble in the relationship.

The couple then discussed the cultural differences that were woven into the other impingements in the relationship. We drew the dimension of "British values" and on it Judy's meaning of "respect" and John's experience of this as "distance." Another line was drawn for the variable of Southern black values, with John's meaning of "sharing" and Judy's experience of "intrusion."

We kept this diagram available at all our meetings. By having it there, the couple became attuned to the possibility that whatever they were struggling with had many contextual components. The diagram was a reminder that the story can always be expanded to include context when it threatens to become too narrow.

Kliman (2010) suggests that a more expansive visual graphic be utilized so that clients and therapists can diagram the degree of proximity to and distance from the dominant culture that is experienced for each of one's identities. She presents a wheel with spokes, each spoke related to another identity. For example, if one is white, poor, Jewish, transgendered, and able-bodied, one would map oneself as in the center of the diagram for race and physical ability, further away from the center for religion, and at the far end of the spoke for gender identity and income. The resulting diagram maps out privilege and marginalization in multiple arenas and makes visible what may otherwise remain invisible and unnoticed in the therapeutic conversation.

## Relational-Cultural Paradox

Essential to RCT is the central relational paradox, the concept that we yearn to be in relationships but that our fear of being rejected leads us to hide parts of ourselves, the parts we find most shameful or unlovable, from the relationship (Miller et al., 2004). This leads to a lack of authenticity that keeps us from participating in the very relationships for which we yearn.

A number of years ago at a faculty meeting of the Jean Baker Miller Institute, I (MM) wondered whether we could extend that idea to cultural identity, thus developing the term "relational-cultural para-dox" (RCP). After all, connections and disconnections occur at the sociocultural level (Walker, 1999), and Jordan and Hartling (2002) suggest that silence, shame, and isolation are hallmarks of these socioculturally based disconnections. A person from an oppressed group may be required to or want to work with, supervise or be supervised by, become friends with, or simply feel comfortable with a person from a privileged group. In order to do so, the person who is oppressed may feel a need to hide part of his/her culture and the meaning that culture has to him/her in order to "fit in." This is an understandable adjustment to a society that accepts or rejects people based on their cultural (racial, ethnic, class, religious, etc.) backgrounds but in the effort, parts of oneself go into hiding.

So, for example, in the film *Mi Familia* (1995), a child of Mexican immigrants grows up to become a lawyer and takes his wealthy, white fiancée and her parents to meet his large, low-income family in the barrios. In this tragic-comic scene, it becomes clear that the young lawyer feels shamed by his family when his parents call him by his childhood name, "Memo." He explains to his puzzled fiancé and future in-laws that Memo is the diminutive for Guillermo, the name he was born with, just like they call him Bill instead of William. In this film, Memo hid parts of himself (his birth name as well as his nickname) in order to be accepted in the dominant culture. Would Guillermo have gotten the job in the law firm? Would Memo have been introduced to his fiancé? Would her parents accept him as Memo or Guillermo? But what price did he pay for becoming Bill? Could the part of him that is Memo find a place in his life as a husband to a privileged, US-born woman? Could the part of him that is Bill be comfortable and authentic in his family of origin? What did he need to hide in service of relationships and how did that impact him and his relationships?

Because of cultural dynamics of privilege and oppression, many of our clients from oppressed groups struggle with this relational-cultural paradox.

The RCP was played out in the relationship between a young, low-income, Mexican-American female law student and her white, Catholic, upper middle-class husband. Both Maria and Jake were concerned that Maria was depressed and that their marriage felt distant. Disconnect loomed large. Jake described their life before Maria became depressed in glowing terms—they were both doing well in law school, had friends, attended church together regularly, had occasional Sunday dinners with his family who lived in driving distance, and that Maria kept in close phone contact with her family and sent them money that they had saved from internships and clerkships. Maria thought that she should be happy with her life—it was everything that she and her parents had wanted for her (although her parents would have preferred for her to marry a Mexican-American law student). Yet, as therapy progressed, Maria became willing to share the part that was hidden. She felt angry at Jake—she accused him of trying to make her fit into his life and ignoring hers. She yearned to go to a church that resembled the Mexican Catholicism that mattered so much to her; she yearned to speak Spanish; she yearned to have someone who would truly welcome her family for extended visits. There were so many yearnings. But Maria kept them hidden out of fear of losing Jake; and Jake, who came from a place of privilege, thought that Maria would be thrilled to leave her life in the barrios. It had not crossed his mind that there was something in that life that she could be missing. The hiding was exhausting for Maria and it provided fertile ground for shame and depression to grow.

Because Maria was able to search underneath her anger to discover her longing for being accepted as her authentic self, the therapy was able to go forward. Her ability to do this demonstrates that therapy can bring into the couple's awareness longings and assumptions based on cultural identities—identities that, because they are not privileged, have been underground. Thus we enable the couple to find a way to authentically include the marginalized, and not just the privileged, aspects of identity.

There are many times when a person consciously chooses to hide aspects of an identity that is oppressed in the larger culture as a way to subvert the biased behavior of those in the dominant culture. For example, Jean did not tell her employer or colleagues that she is a lesbian. Those are choices one makes to avoid harassment and to maintain some degree of power in a situation, and these choices can be healthy. RCP discussed above is problematic because at least one partner is hiding parts of herself from the very same relationship in which she wants authentic closeness. In our example, Maria needed a home that felt like a safe haven from the storm of prejudice and bias. She longed for true intimacy with Jake, hid part of herself that she feared he would reject, and then felt exhausted and depressed from wanting Jake to love her for who she is, all of who she is, while also feeling shamed by the internalization of societal messages about her immigrant identity and the class of her family of origin.

There is no guarantee that the more privileged spouse will commit to this more authentic relationship, or that the less privileged spouse will want to continue in a relationship that literally and figuratively is so foreign. We always respect the possibility that the authenticity we facilitate will lead to disconnection. Yet we often find that the couple's desire for relationship with each other will hold the relationship, as we help them honor their own and their partner's stories in this cultural terrain. It wasn't until Jake visited a Mexican Catholic church with Maria that he understood the loss she experienced when she attended the church that was familiar to him. Jake became much more aware of his Western-European identity when he attended the Mexican Catholic church, and reported that he had not experienced being a minority at a gathering in any other situation in his life. At the same time, he also reported that he had never experienced the commitment and mutuality of a community in the way that he did after he became a regular participant in the church introduced to him by Maria. He came to appreciate that this sense of community was important to him.[6]

Jake never agreed with Maria's cultural belief that it was her job to care for a brother with alcohol problems because her parents did not have the resources to do so, but they negotiated the different terrain and developed a bicultural marriage that took into account both of their needs. This work does not erase power and privilege differentials. We don't think Jake ever recognized the full extent of his privilege, but we do know that he supported Maria's decision to work as a legal aid attorney for a Latino clientele. They became members of Maria's church where their first child was baptized, and Maria described herself as once more feeling vibrant.

## Blind Spots in Clinical Practice

Although in this chapter we have discussed successful cases, we also encounter blocks and difficulties in our work. At times, because of our training, life experiences, privilege, and oppression, we keep certain aspects of context out of our awareness. These are our blind spots.

Often, blind spots are connected to our privilege since one of the privileges is that we do not need to be aware of the experiences of those who are marginalized. So when a couple comes to our office arguing about their child-rearing differences and the husband says that his 16-year-old daughter may not date, while the wife argues that the current young man interested in her is a good influence on her, we may make assumptions that the father is inappropriately overprotective and having difficulty with his daughter's sexuality. That assumption matches the dominant cultural beliefs about dating. However, if we move beyond our privileged blind spots and approach the couple with respect and curiosity about their experience, we may instead find immigrant parents who are trying to hold the values of the culture from which they came (in this case the father's position), while also adopting elements of the culture in which they are now immersed (in this case the mother's position). What is seen as differences in child-rearing ideas can be reframed as negotiating the yet-to-be determined borders and points of entry between the cultures of their original and adopted countries (Llerena Quinn & Mirkin, 2005).

Similarly, when couples do not seem trusting of us, we may attribute this lack of trust to some intrapersonal trait that we need to "work on" together. Doing so without looking at the larger cultural context is another privilege-based blind spot. For example, we are both white women. Perhaps a client of color does not trust us because we are members of a group responsible for the micro- and macro-aggressions that they have experienced (Sue et al., 2008). Why should we be deemed trustworthy just because we might think we are worthy of that trust? How arrogant of me to think that John would have let me in on his feelings about race during our first session. We earn that trust as we develop a relationship with the couple, provided that we do our own work. That work involves developing cultural awareness, a cognitive process; cultural sensitivity, an affective process; and cultural humility or the recognition both of how little we know about our clients' cultural identities and how much we need to learn (Falicov 2005; Hardy and Lazloffy, 1995). The work we do on our own cultural identities, privilege, and oppression and our accountability for this awareness can lead us to be more curious, less judgmental, less prone to fall into blind spots, and aware that we will at times hit up against those blind spots because this awareness of self and cultural is a journey. However, if we ignore our own race (or any other identity) and how our whiteness plays a role in therapy, then we have a huge blind spot that will impact our work with couples of all races.

There are other ways in which the therapist can be blind to, or out of contact with, the context and experience of the client. For example, blind spots can exist in areas we just don't know enough about to recognize. This is called ignorance and we all are ignorant of certain realities. We believe the remedy for this is humility, that is, the ability to imagine that there are realities we're not familiar with, and the willingness to be taught by our clients.

We can also develop blind spots about something that is invisible because it is so close in, so part of our identity or our meaning system that it becomes unseen. We have both experienced this particular state[7]. For example, when either one of us works with a heterosexual couple, we can lose all awareness that there are two women and only one man in the room, and that this configuration can make a difference. Fortunately, some male clients are brave enough to point this out, and express what this is like for them. We continue to remind ourselves to "see" this place in which our awareness tends to disappear.

## Conclusion

This chapter is our attempt to describe ways in which the narrow, limiting and blaming stories of couples can be enlarged to include a consciousness of context. By helping clients explore the vulnerability beneath their anger and blaming and externalize the contextual impingements, we can empower them as a team to expose negative societal assumptions that are affecting them. We help couples externalize their conflict, and in doing so strengthen mutual empathy. Our challenge as therapists is to maintain an inquiring stance rather than making ethnic, gender, class or racial assumptions. Through inquiry, we avoid stereotyping people, and we also avoid ignoring differences. By creating a partnership with our clients we learn from them about their experience of context. Through active efforts at educating ourselves in this area, we can become more culturally aware, sensitive and humble therapists.

## Notes

1   This chapter is a revision and elaboration of an article by the same authors in *Journal of Feminist Family Therapy*, 1999, 11(1). That article was based on the Stone Center Work in Progress # 73, 1995. Marsha Mirkin, PhD, is an Associate Professor of Psychology at Lasell College and at the time of this writing was also a Resident Scholar at the Brandeis Women's Studies Research Center. Pamela Geib, EdD, taught for many years at the Cambridge Hospital Couples and Family Training Program. She is now in full-time private practice, which includes individual and group consultation. She is a Certified Internal Family Systems therapist and is on the staff of the Intimacy from the Inside Out Couples Training Program, and is a co-creator and co-teacher of the Internal Family Systems Mastery Seminar. The two authors contributed equally to the chapter.
2   All cases in this chapter are composites combining many families and changing all identifying characteristics.
3   Gay and lesbian marriage is legal in Massachusetts.
4   The authors did not actually see this case together. Since both of us had several similar cases, we created a composite of the case and of how we would combine our work in co-therapy treatment.

5   See White (2007) for an expanded description of externalization.
6   We want to thank Dr Roxana Llerena-Quinn for her discussion with MM about the benefits to the person in the dominant culture when engaging in a relationship with someone whose culture is not dominant. Dr Llerena-Quinn also discussed hiding of aspects of oneself, due to shame, whether one identifies with a dominant or a subjugated culture. This hiding of self has implications for the relationship. We hope to examine in the future RCP in relation to the person from a dominant culture: One of the unearned privileges of being a member of the dominant culture is that our culture is assumed to be the norm and therefore does not have to be hidden for us to gain acceptance. However, in an interview by Randall C. Wyatt (2008), Dr Kenneth Hardy suggests that white people will often censor what is said in a group with people of color because of fear of saying something that can be interpreted as racist. Fear of being challenged or rejected for one's racism, whether the racism is intentional or unintentional, may result in self-silencing and lack of authenticity within a relationship rather than to further self-exploration about racism. The lack of authenticity can further undermine the relationship.
7   The term "countertransference of context" was developed by Pamela Geib.

# References

Boyd-Franklin, N. (1989). *Black families in therapy: A multisystems approach.* New York: Guilford Press.

Crenshaw, K. W. (1989). Mapping the margins: Intersectionality, identity, politics, and violence against women of color. *Stanford Law Review,* 43(6), 1241–1299.

Falicov, C. J. (2005). Training to think culturally. *Family Process,* 34(4), 373–388.

Hardy (2008). Race, reality and relationships: Implications for the revisioning of family therapy. In M. McGoldrick & K. Hardy (Eds), *Re-visioning family therapy,* 2nd edition. New York: Guilford Press.

Hardy, K., & Lazloffy, T. (1995). The cultural genogram: Key to training culturally competent family therapists. *Journal of Marital and Family Therapy,* 21, 227–238.

Imber-Black, E. (1990). Multiple embedded systems. In M. P. Mirkin (Ed.), *The social and political contexts of family therapy.* Needham, MA: Allyn & Bacon.

Jordan, J. (2009). *Relational-Cultural Theory.* Washington, DC: American Psychological Association.

Jordan, J. V. & Hartling, L. M. (2002). New developments in relational-cultural theory. In M. Ballou & L. Brown (Eds), *Rethinking mental health and disorder.* New York: Guilford Press.

Kliman, J. (1994). The interweaving of gender, class, and race in family therapy. In M.P. Mirkin (Ed.), *Women in context: Toward a feminist reconstruction of psychotherapy.* New York: Guilford Press.

Kliman, J. (2010). Intersections of social privilege and marginalization: A visual teaching tool. *AFTA Monograph,* 6, 39–48.

Llerena-Quinn, R. & Mirkin, M. (2005). Immigrant mothers: Mothering in the borderlands. In M. P. Mirkin, K. Suyemoto, & B. Okun (Eds), *Psychotherapy with women: Exploring diverse contexts and identities* (pp. 87–110). New York: Guilford Press.

Miller, J. B., Jordan, J., Stiver, I., Walker, M., Surrey, J., & Eldrige, N. (2004). Therapist's authenticity. In J. Jordan, M. Walker, & L. Hartling (Eds), *The complexity of connection* (pp. 64–89). New York: Guilford Press.

Mirkin, M. & Geib, P. (1999). Consciousness of context in relational couples therapy. *Journal of Feminist Family Therapy*, 11, 31–51 (reprinted from Stone Center Working Paper #75, 1995).

Nava, G. (Director) (1995). *Mi Familia* [Film]. Agoura Hills, CA: New Line Cinema.

Schwartz, R. (2001). *Introduction to the internal family systems model*. Oak Park, IL: Center for Self Leadership.

Sue, D. W., Capodilupo, C. M., Nadal, K. L., & Torino, G. C. (2008). Racial microaggressions and the power to define reality. *American Psychologist*, 63, 277–279.

Walker, M. (1999). Race, self, and society: Relational challenges in a culture of disconnection. Wellesley, MA: Wellesley Centers for Women.

White, M. (2007). *Maps of narrative practice*. New York: WW Norton & Co.

Wyatt, R. C. (2008). *Kenneth V. Hardy on multiculturalism and psychotherapy*. Retrieved from www.psychotherapy.net/interview/kenneth-hardy

# 4

# RESILIENT RELATIONSHIPS

## Cultivating the Healing
## Potential of Couple Stories

*Karen Skerrett*

> Love consists in this, that two solitudes protect and touch and
> salute each other.
>
> (Rainer Maria Rilke)

"I was complaining to Jen just the other day . . . it used to be we got more years out of our appliances. Now you pay all this money and they run down faster. Think it's the same for marriage??"

Don Dore slaps his knee as punctuation, looks first to Jen, then to me, and smiling somewhat sheepishly says: "So here we are again."

As they begin to chronicle their latest "challenges", I find my mind wandering over the years we've known each other. I think of the blessing/curse aspects of working with couples over the long haul. The blessing of being witness to the miracles of human resilience, the triumph of growth out of pain, the mysteries of repair and reconciliation; the curse in that I find I could recite their issues before they even verbalize them. Fortunately, these days, I ponder less that the redundancy of their issues is exclusively my therapeutic failure and appreciate the wisdom of pioneering researchers and couple therapists (Gottman & Gottman, 2006) who remind us that 65% of the issues between partners are enduring. I pull myself back into the room, re-engaging with two pairs of eyes that reflect myriad emotions. I choose to focus on the glimmer of hope.

Jen replies to Don's comment by asking if he remembered a few years back when he would call during the middle of the day to ask how she was, if she wanted him to bring dinner home or go out. Don nodded that he remembered and Jen's eyes locked his. "Then why is it that now I dread getting your calls and sometimes don't even pick up?"

At the center of this exchange, Jen has told a "love story"—a moment of connection between a couple that defines and directs their relationship. Jen shares this anecdote to remind both of us what she feels she has lost, of what they're here to regain if their relationship is to recover its meaning and vitality. Don's silent head nod and look of recognition is his responding story, signaling a moment of mutuality that I understand to be the heart of relational resilience.

In this chapter, I share the view that love stories—created, recovered and made anew—are the essential building blocks of resilient relationships. Couples that can find their stories, that can share them first with each other, then with family, friends and a larger community, are more likely to preserve a vision of partnership that sustains and nurtures over a lifetime of togetherness (Skerrett & Singer, 2013). The fact that Relational-Cultural Theory and Therapy (Jordan, 2010) has as its goal mutual growth-fostering relationships and views relationships as both the indicator for and the healing mechanism toward mental health and wellness makes it an ideal framework for our consideration. Further informed by a developmental/neurobiological and narrative perspective of experience, particularly the works of Walsh (2006), Sharpe (2000), Singer (2011) and Siegel (2012), I will share highlights of the couple treatment of the Dores in order to demonstrate how an understanding of resilient processes can be applied in the service of individual and couple healing and growth.

## The Early Work: Individual Stories

I first met the Dores 12 years ago. Jen was 45 years old and had contacted me for therapy because she had heard that I worked with many families struggling with chronic illness. Despite her sunny "we try harder" disposition and carefully appointed make-up, Jen's puffy face, bloated extremities and bright eyes were characteristic of steroid use. Indeed, she reported a long history of physical problems, primarily autoimmune and most notably Crohn's disease. Having had numerous "bad doctor" experiences, she had become expert at advocating for her own health and worked with a team of specialists and complementary and alternative medical (CAM) practitioners. As a physical therapist, she knew her way around medical jargon and generally wasn't intimidated by the demands of living with chronic illness. Lately, however, she felt something more was going on because she was experiencing a recurrence of nightmares, headaches and generalized tension that she was unable to relieve with her usual routines. In describing the details of the nightmares, she admitted to a history of physical, sexual and emotional abuse while growing up and panic episodes as a young adult, but believed she had "dealt with all that" during her individual therapy 10 years earlier. She thought her current stressors centered around her frustration with her "workaholic husband" and her wider family's generalized unwillingness to believe or accept the ongoing challenges of her condition. Tearfully, she described feeling "totally alone", as if she carried the heaviest load in the family despite feeling like the "weakest link". Her twin 20-year-old daughters and her 18-year-old daughter treated her like the "hired help" and she knew she wasn't consistent in setting limits with them. We discussed sleep hygiene, possible medication side-effects, techniques she was using to manage stress, and reviewed deep breathing and relaxation techniques. She agreed to invite her husband to join us for our next session.

My initial impression of Don was that of an overweight, boyish, very affable man intent on impressing me with his willingness to "lend a hand to help Jen get better". As a partner in a mid-sized accounting firm, Don worked long hours and often brought work home on weekends. He seemed blissfully unaware that Jen was feeling so disconnected from him or that she saw his lifestyle choices to be partly responsible for her recent illness flares.

## Struggling to Connect

In many ways, Jen and Don are similar to other couples in my practice. They were longing to connect with one another in meaningful ways while struggling to make decisions in lives filled with overwhelming choices and competing priorities. Like other couples, they were two well-meaning people who believed they wanted the best for each other and their family. But with no guidelines to navigate relationships, they kept moving, losing a sense of what they had accomplished together and the ways in which they had blessed each other's lives. Eventually, they found that habit and inattention had filled the gaps in their lives with negative stories—repetitive complaints, tales of shortcomings, and narratives of disappointment and disconnection.

McAdams's lifestory model of identity (2001) has been pivotal in developing the notion that individuals in modern society provide their lives with meaning and purpose by regularly constructing internalized and evolving narratives of their experience. Meaning-making by making stories is one of the crowning achievements of human development and is the way we transform despair into hope, problem into possibility, make peace from conflict and learn how to navigate life (Skerrett, 2010). Postmodern and social constructivist approaches (Gergen, 1991) have been applied by narrative therapists (Freedman & Combs, 1996; Lieblich, McAdams & Josselson, 2004; Madsen, 2009; White, 1993), who claim that therapy is fundamentally a process of story reformulation and repair. Gottman and Silver (1999) write that a critical component to couple functioning is the capacity to share their stories, find meaning and dream out their lives together.

Jen's individual story reflected competing but equally defining themes. Her earliest relational images (Jordan, 2010) were those of someone who deserved to be judged, criticized, and evaluated. She always felt she came up short in the eyes of her parents, particularly her mother. Other images were that of the perpetual caretaker who was expected to suppress her own needs in order to hold her mother together emotionally and protect younger sibs from paternal wrath. Her father, a lifelong alcoholic, would subject the family to his drunken rages, then offer the olive branch to Jen to manipulate and cajole her to maintain the role of "second mother". Many nights, his drinking would culminate in his fondling both Jen and her younger sister. Attempts to tell their mother resulted in vicious attacks or being blamed for an "overactive imagination". Jen believed that because her prior therapist was a male and didn't really "get" her feelings, she hadn't fully relinquished such negative relational images and was very vulnerable to reactivation with Don. Given such a difficult history, Jen was proud of her educational and professional achievements and particularly pleased with the myriad ways she'd positively rewritten her history as an adult.

Don's individual story was also peppered with ongoing family of origin problems. As the oldest in a sibship of four, he was the "overfunctioner"— caretaking an anxious, highly phobic mother and an alcoholic father. He described being called to pull his father out of bars from the age of seven until leaving for college. His winsome smile and roll-up-your-sleeves attitude hid a furious, fearful man who never had a childhood.

Jen and Don grew up in the same blue-collar, working class neighborhood filled with Irish and Polish immigrants. Many were city workers—fire, police, construction, and low-level government employees. The local Catholic Church not only symbolized sacred space but defined the mores and behavior of the community. This included looking the other way at drunken parents, child abuse, domestic violence, truancy, and petty thievery. As long as you opened your door to the good priest on a Friday evening, you were a member in good standing in the neighborhood.

Jen and Don met at a parish bingo night when they were 16 and immediately became inseparable. As one another's only confidants and protectors, they forged first tenuous, then instrumental relationships with each other's families— aligning with, troubleshooting for, and generally serving to take some of the pressure off for one another.

As I sat with them in that first joint session, I recall puzzling along with them how they had gotten to such a place of disconnection when each clearly referenced the other as their "best friend and soul-mate". Don appeared more perplexed than Jen as to how, with so many resources and solid financial security, Jen could be so miserable. Both agreed that they wanted to regain the sense of connection and feelings of closeness that had characterized their early years together. They also agreed that they wanted to be more honest and relaxed with one another and "didn't have a clue how to get there".

## The Relational "Dance"

Jen and Don behaved as long-habituated allies with a connection that seemed superficial; they were agreeable to the extent that no differences were exposed or expressed. The Dores' attachment was fragile and dependent on the maintenance of high levels of security and safety, and this required the utmost respect and care in response. Jen was tentative in expressing disappointment or dissatisfaction at Don's behavior; both seemed to tacitly agree that it was her job to reinforce his self-image as the "good guy". She even had difficulty naming a problem a problem.

One of the first examples she tentatively offered was recently telling Don about her fatigue and need for more sleep, to which he responded by scheduling a barbecue with extended family for that weekend. As she tried in our session to describe how undercut she felt and frustrated by his "unwillingness to hear" her, she began to tear up and turn her body away from Don. He became defensive and offered first one rationale, then another. Such early and infrequent requests for change were typically met with defensiveness, anger and elaborate rationalizations about how hard he tried. Jen needed considerable support and encouragement to speak her truths, and Don needed support and encouragement to listen and respond in new ways. I regularly needed to challenge gender-based assumptions: Don's socialization for dominance and control and Jen's for selfless service and care-taking. Because both Jen and Don held negative relational images and misattributed blame to themselves during disconnections, I knew to carefully attend to my capacity to maintain connection to each. Don tended to tightly guard his feelings of shame and uncertainty and Jen went silent, concluding she was unworthy of getting her needs met. Staying attuned to my own levels of reactivity helped me be aware of their experience of disconnection and expand my empathic responsiveness, which, in turn, expanded their levels of self/other compassion.

One of the key advantages our early collaboration benefited from was their interest in and responsiveness to my perspective that their disconnections and communication challenges were just another reflection of their biological make-up. Originally trained as a nurse, I have always utilized a holistic and strengths-based perspective as a therapist and find that most couples respond well to a normalizing and integrated approach to their problems. Also, I find that many individuals, with some initial education, can make the link from physically expressed symptoms (sleeplessness, stomach or headaches, heart palpitations, etc.) to behavioral dynamics. This was particularly the case for Jen and Don, given that her chronic health problems had taken such a center stage in their relationship. It had unfortunately become their currency to express all manner of interpersonal injuries. We needed to create a space between Jen's illness and their relationship. The challenge was to find ways to capitalize on Don's need to be needed while attending to Jen's symptom reduction—so crucial to alliance building.

They were particularly receptive to understanding the neuroscience of both Jen's condition and connection/disconnection. While Don knew of Jen's trauma history, neither had considered the long-term behavioral implications and Don had never considered himself as having a trauma history. This understanding not only had the effect of leveling the field between them but provided another way to identify and empathize with one another. We went over basic explanations regarding our evolutionary hard-wired tendency to protect ourselves when threatened, the effects of chronic stress and the ways in which dissociation in response to trauma represents a breakdown of neural integration and plasticity (Cozolino, 2010). Teaching such essential brain basics and the neurobiology of "We" (Siegel, 2012) oriented them away from blame and shame and toward their shared biological nature. They expressed relief and gratitude to understand that the pathophysiology of trauma involves abnormal fear circuits and that resilience would involve learning to avoid overgeneralization of fear cues. Jen, in particular, remarked that now she could give up one more thing she blamed herself for. I shared my definition of health as a state of integration—the linkage of differentiated parts that occurs in the body and in relationships. We discussed neuroplasticity—the brain's capacity to change patterns of energy and information or neural connectivity in response to new experiences (Siegel, 2012). What we pay most attention to defines us. I explained that when partners work through a stressful set of circumstances in their lives and arrive at a state of greater well-being, they have moved toward a condition of greater neural integration within a system of mutual regulation (Atkinson, 2005; Cozolino, 2006). They could see how biologically we are wired to see into the other's internal state before recognizing our own. Such an amazing regulatory system highlights the interactive, mutual nature of couple resilience (Solomon & Tatkin, 2011). Don really "got" that when Jen exposed a vulnerability, it triggered vulnerabilities for him to which he responded by shutting down. Scheduling a family barbecue after Jen described feeling fatigued did not serve to restore her to her over-functioning role but rather increased the cascade of negativity and disconnection. Jen could understand that she was misreading Don's anger as lack of caring for her rather than as anger at himself for not being able to help. These conversations also established a context for our therapeutic work such as the primacy of safety, gradual exploration of fears, recrafting meanings, and supporting shifts from helplessness to personal agency (Feder, Nestler, Westphal & Charney, 2010). Several sessions focused on helping each learn to read their own emotions—particularly when aroused, so critical to both self and relational empowerment. I taught them several self-soothing techniques to practice at home as reinforcement of our in-session work. They began to have first-hand experience of the ways in which self-attunement contributes to an increase in genuine empathy with the other. In fact, self-attunement and empathy with others appear to utilize the same resonance circuits in the brain (Siegel, 2010).

## Growth toward Connection through Stories

I regularly work to make the linkages between presenting concerns and opportunities for growth very explicit, particularly for couples like Jen and Don who had such a fragile, undifferentiated connection. A critical dimension of healthy integration is narrative coherence. When we tell our stories, we are forging neural pathways and grounding change in relational experiences. Ongoing research with couples (Skerrett, 2013) supports the idea that by expanding partner perspectives as to the meaning, continuity, and importance of each other's life concerns through understanding their abiding life themes, partners are better able to understand and invest in the other's change processes. Assisting Jen and Don to isolate the old themes that had outlived their usefulness and were contributing to current impasses focused change efforts. We did this by way of a structured storytelling exercise.

I asked each of them to independently write a brief version of their life story and select a dominant theme to highlight. I also asked them to list several current goals, and their hopes and dreams for the future, and bring these to our next session. I explained that when we shared this, I expected the experience would be helpful to understand the linkages between the current impasse and their personal development goals. My experience with other couples had been that this process also helps to interrupt the negative and stuck storylines and embed current problems within thematically patterned life struggles in self and other.

Both Don and Jen reported that the life story writing was harder than they had expected but gave them a lot to think about. Excerpts from each are described below.

*Jen:* "I realize I had a hard life. I don't like to think about it—I prefer to think about how far I've come and how successful I am. I understand my parents had a hard life too and probably did the best they could, but they still placed too many burdens on me. Maybe that is why I've achieved so much, but I also wonder if the trauma resulted in all these illnesses. I hate the flares because they remind me of being helpless and out of control and I hate not being able to help myself. I know I need to focus more on myself—that that is what will help me get well—but I am such a helping person that it feels easier to do for my family than for myself. I know I don't always show Don and the kids that I'm having a bad day or a hard time and that that is an old, bad habit. I know that I'm wearing out. But I like thinking of myself as someone who can just push past the obstacles and not let anything get me down. So I guess I'd say that's my theme . . . 'Make the best of what you have'."

*Don:* "It's always felt important to me to help my family and well, anybody that needed something. When I was growing up, our family seemed like such a mess that I wanted to make a difference and also not give them any more to worry about. I never thought about not helping—it's just always been who I am. I like to think I make Jen and the girls proud of me 'cause of what we have and what I can provide. I know I never thought I'd be the most successful person in my family. Makes me feel good. I don't like to focus on problems—just solutions. I'm known around the office as the go-to guy and I really like that. My theme is 'make lemonade'."

The shared experience of witnessing the reading of their stories in their entirety was quite moving. Being "just a listener" and freed of the expectation of reacting and/or responding elicited more affect, particularly from Don. He remarked: "There was something about reading this aloud all at once and having her just listen that got to me. A lot of the stuff I wrote about I never think about anymore, and then to write it out and share it with Jen . . . kinda overwhelming." Jen commented: "I can forget how awful it was for Don most of his life, I really understand that in the face of all that criticism he felt like he never dared make a mistake—just like now."

They both commented that they were struck by their similarities and could re-appreciate why they got together in the first place. They said that the sharing helped crystallize for them the degree to which they were both "fixers", and that it was difficult to expose what they perceived as a weakness in front of the other. They could at least intellectually grasp that without a capacity to expose vulnerability, they were limited in response-ability as well as capacity to empathize.

I was reminded of McAdams's (2006) depiction of the uniquely cultural brand of American storytelling he calls "redemptive". Both Jen and Don's stories had this overarching theme: one meets up with an obstacle, works to overcome it, and becomes a "better" person in the process. Because this theme is so embedded in the collective consciousness of Americans and is so tied to our notion of "rugged individualism", it is often very challenging to help partners accept the limitations of such a view and the ways in which this can preserve the status quo and block opportunities for growth. Don and Jen did, in fact, have difficulty relating their themes to their goals for change. We had a number of fruitful conversations in which they identified the interactions between the storylines created and the ways they each tended to engage with life. For example, Jen recognized the ways in which she would either disappear emotionally or take on too much just when she was feeling the most needy. This resulted in Jen's identifying that she wanted to learn to make herself a higher priority and to learn to express her needs and ask for what she wanted. After initial attempts at goal setting ("I want Jen to be well", "I want to make Jen happy"), Don eventually could recognize how ruthless his "Mr Fixit" could be and identified his goal as learning to recognize a personal limit and listen to it. They were enthused when they could see that both individual goals represented a rescripting of their longtime themes and, while challenging, had great potential to bring them closer to their overall desire for deeper connection.

## "Good Enough Stories"

I shared with them my impression that they had each crafted what I've come to call a "good enough" life story (Skerrett, 2010). Simply put, this is the life-script that has the potential to help us grow throughout our lives, and has the following characteristics:

(a)  an active, conscious interpretation of life experiences that clarifies how one got from point A to point B
(b)  an internal consistency or overall coherence

(c) motifs of resilience and the recasting of negative events into positive meaning.

Ideally, good enough stories evolve across time into a greater balance of thoughts/feelings/actions, a greater flexibility of adaptive style, and greater interdependence with others.

## Individual to Couple Story

Just as one's sense of self is crafted in story, so too is the couple narrative a mutual, ongoing creation. Couple stories, the stories shared by both partners about their relationship, also lend a sense of meaningful coherence and guide for engagement. A couple story reflects a mutual identity that couples spontaneously describe as the experience of "We-ness". Initially identified by Surrey, Shem and Bergman (1998), it refers to the couple's sense of the lived experience of their relationship. It is evidenced by a kind of thinking that reflects reciprocity and integration of the other's perspective into their own and has been found to have adaptive qualities throughout a couple's relationship (Fergus, 2011; Skerrett, 2003, 2004). Couples who focus on themselves as a team and put concerns for individual fulfillment in the background are more likely to build a strong base for mutual satisfaction, empathy for one another's needs, and a recognition of the importance of balancing personal goals with the mutual goals they establish together (Mills, Clark, Ford & Johnson, 2004; Reid, Doell, Dalton & Ahmad, 2008). Of particular relevance to the Dores is the evidence that couples who adopted a "we" orientation in relation to one partner's serious illness have been found to demonstrate greater resiliency and capacity to cope with the demands related to the illness (Fergus, 2011; Skerrett, 1998, 2013). Connor, Robinson, & Wieling (2008) emphasized the value of developing a common story for managing a painful medical condition. Just such a level of self/other and relationship awareness is what creates the "we". Congruence between the partners' perceptions is a critical aspect in gauging the success of mutuality within the relationship since couple interactions and concurrent perceptions are intertwined in a continuous mutual feedback system. The capacity to shift from a self-centered perspective to a more systemic, altruistic perspective goes hand in hand with tolerating, supporting, and enhancing one's partner in doing the same. These capacities lay the foundation for connection, and for individual as well as relational growth.

However, I have learned over years of working with couples that very few present for treatment with any degree of "we-consciousness". The Dores never thought that part of their problems lay in the way they went about doing what they thought was best for their marriage. Each came at it from the position of "I"—what "I" am doing or need to do to help my partner or the family. While well intentioned, the heart of a resilient marriage resides in the question: "What do WE need to do that will best serve our relationship?" And of course this question can never be asked or answered alone but only in dialogue. "How will this benefit me?" is a very different question than "How will this [behavior] strengthen the bond we have forged together?"

Of course, most couples come for treatment with eroded or nonexistent levels of trust in one another. They have a hard time accepting that distrust or refusal to become vulnerable will sabotage most efforts to bring about great intimacy, satisfaction and understanding. Before being able to accept the idea of "We-ness" or couple first, a strong sense of safety and goodwill must be established.

Not long after I led the Dores through the individual life story exercise, I recommended they do the "couple story exercise". I instructed them to return to the individual life themes they had each identified and work together to develop a couple theme that they felt reflected the story of their relationship and the developmental issues identified as relevant. Utilizing the 3R process (see Appendix A, page 57), I suggested they shape their couple story so as to support both individual and relational growth. At this point, they had each grown in their reflective abilities and were well on the way to developing a couple consciousness. I was curious to see how they would respond. They reported really enjoying the process and liked trying to think about their relationship and how "each part fit into a whole". Don commented: "We've been together for so long, I hardly ever think about an Us anymore." They had immediately agreed that their story should reflect their mutual attraction as "people pleasers", focused on the expectations and caretaking of others. They first titled their couple story: "Give 'um what they want." In a conversation several days later, they spontaneously recognized that the most enduring conflict in their marriage was "never having much left over for ourselves or each other". Below is an abbreviated version of their story.

"We are two hard-working people who have overcome a lot of obstacles in our lives. We've always done the best we can for other people and have been very successful. You could call us resilient. We still like to look out for each other and do everything together. We're like two old horses who have been tethered together and keep plowing on. We do so much for everyone else, we don't have much left over."

This led quite nicely into our conversation about an alternative couple story that reflected where they would like to head, or what I call their "growing edge". It was moving to witness how much progress they had made in honest self-expression as each playfully offered first one title, then another. It was quite evident that they had taken more ownership of this aspect of their dynamics as well as the way it had backfired over the years. They finally agreed on the title "Pleasing ourselves and each other" and we began to talk about what that might look like in their day-to-day lives. I coached them to regularly notice the state of their relationship by asking questions of one another such as: "Is it working right now? What am I doing that is contributing to where we are at?" They were reminded that they were responsible to bring only their self-awareness to the other and were not responsible for the thoughts, feelings or behavior of their partner. This promoted the mutual ability to approach challenges from the question of "What do I need to learn to help us better function as a team?"

## Cultivation of "We-ness"

In recent years I have come to place the assessment of "WE" consciousness— a couple's awareness that they belong to a larger entity that transcends each of them as individuals—at the heart of my work. I have utilized a variety of methods for assessing the "WE" (Labunko Messier et al., 2008) as well as developed exercises to cultivate "We-ness" in the relationship, such as the couple story exercise above. Essential to all domains of possible intervention is the ongoing education of couples regarding the primacy of their relationship—that it is the cultivation of "We-ness" that operates as the safety and security system for both. They are in the care of one another. Without that understanding, neither can thrive. Helping couples to jointly focus on that third entity, their relationship, builds secure functioning and promotes the capacity to mutually amplify positive moments between them. Gradually shifting a couple's sights to their assets and strengths infuses the climate with positivity, hope and potential. Utilizing the Couple Resilience Boosters (see Appendix B, page 58) is useful in coaching for strengths. This is vital across all opportunities for couple contacts, but particularly so when illness injects fear, saps vitality and diminishes hope.

The work of Jordan (2010) and Walsh (2006) has been most instructive in these efforts. Both hold the development of empathy as crucial to relational resilience. The primary components I focus on clinically to build mutual empathy and WE consciousness are: (1) self/other and relationship awareness; (2) mutual engagement in supported vulnerability; (3) joint creation of meaning and (4) the cultivation of relational priority and the requisite skill sets to support it.

I knew that we were making progress on those dimensions when Don proudly told the following story. He had awakened one morning with a sense that Jen had had a sleepless night, and decided to ask how it had gone. Hearing her recount another nightmare, he made the decision to postpone going in to the office, instead holding her and encouraging her to talk about the nightmare. He admitted that previously he would have felt angry and helpless in the face of her pain and hastily left for work—the "perfect escape". Now he could recognize that his short-term avoidance contributed to Jen's long-term resentment, and reported relishing both her responsiveness and the feeling of renewed empowerment in their marriage.

Opening up the conversation to Don's alcohol use and its effect on Jen proved more challenging. Don had a considerable investment in being the problem solver as opposed to what he saw as the problem causer, and felt entitled to "a few relaxing drinks" given how hard he worked for the family. While willing to acknowledge the triggering effect of his drinking on Jen, he was unwilling to modify his behavior, which reinforced Jen's tendency to "put up and shut up". Adding insult to injury was Don's propensity to encourage Jen to drink with him and "party", overeat and join him in what Jen saw as his "self-destructive, excessive behaviors". Sharing her frustration that he was going down the path of his father or her fears that she'd lose him to illness and death did not appear to result in sustained change on Don's part. Gradually, as Jen became stronger, developed clearer boundaries and could self-soothe, she grew less reactive to Don's drinking. When invited to join him on a Friday night to bar-hop with his colleagues, Jen said, in a good-natured way, that she'd already made plans. She neutrally refused his attempts to have her join him on a weight-loss program and put limits on how much alcohol they would serve at family events. Jen's differentiating behaviors initially made Don very anxious and provided numerous opportunities to practice self-regulation and self-soothing. Our alliance now allowed me to playfully remind them of *both* aspects of their couple goal: "Pleasing self and other." Skills that supported this work of self-regulation were journal writing (Niederhoffer & Pennebaker, 2009), mindfulness-based stress reduction (MBSR) classes (Davidson, 2012), every-day acts of caring (Lyubomirsky, 2007) and gifts of gratitude (Emmons & McCullough, 2003).

Clearly, this was a partnership with many strengths. When we concluded our initial work, each was feeling more genuinely connected, a bit more willing to ride the waves of the relational paradox and fortified by the refocus on their individual and collective resilience. It was clearer to me the ways in which curiosity, generosity, healthy boundary setting, self/other compassion and interpersonal sensitivity contribute to the "bounce-ahead" quality of resilience and are critically essential to relational repair work during couple distress (Skerrett, 2004).

## The Evolving Story: "Back to the Future"

In the intervening years, I saw the Dores for two more episodes of work; once four years after our initial sessions and again two years after that. Both episodes were relatively brief, of a tune-up nature and triggered by concerns they were stuck in disconnection and passivity.

So as I faced them again, I wondered how much embarrassment and shame they might feel regarding their return to therapy; as if they had again failed to figure things out on their own. In response to their "love story", I reflected on the progress they had maintained. By sharing the story of her reluctance to take Don's phone calls, not only did Jen risk revealing her anger and disappointment in him but she was opening herself to the uncertainty of his reaction. Don refrained from defensive rationalizations, listened quietly and nodded as if to validate and encourage Jen's continued expression of feelings. Reminding them of their strengths and the clear evidence of their ability to sustain several of the skills we had worked on during our previous work reestablished our engage-ment as collaborators. Together we would reexamine the places the relationship was both moving and stuck and understand them as reflections of their wishes for and fears of intimacy and self-development. Together we would focus on "we" consciousness to activate relational strengths and recraft relational stories that would help restore optimal developmental processes and a balance between relationship and personal growth. Together we would mine the depths of their bond for deeper love stories—ones with ever more complexities and positive potentials.

We were off!

## Appendix A: Re-storying Exercises

### *Suggested sequence*

Request that each partner write a brief version of their life story to bring to session and read aloud to one another. Include current goals, hopes and dreams for future.

Help each identify the relationship of the presenting problem, as they see it, to a key issue each is working on in terms of their personal development.

Teach 3R process: *Reflect, Reorganize, Recreate.*

- *Reflect:* Spend time in quiet meditation in which each reflects on their life theme and how it is manifesting in their current life.
- *Reorganize:* Rebalance the components of their theme in light of their presenting problem.
- *Recreate:* Rewrite the problem in the direction of positive outcome(s).

Share with their partner.

### *Couple Story Sequence*

In session, help them blend their individual stories into a couple story, utilizing the life themes of each and the developmental issues identified as relevant.

Help them identify the challenges for the relationship posed in the couple story.

Recommend utilizing the 3R process again to identify ways to revise their couple story so as to support both individual and relational growth.

Identify a plan of action to support the above and reinforce with regular practice. Can be repeated/recycled as new issues emerge.

# Appendix B: Resilience Boosters for Couples

## *Gratitude Lists*

- Make a list of all the things you are grateful for and add to it weekly.
- Exchange lists with your spouse and talk about it on a regular basis.

## *Pleasure Breaks*

- Find one thing that brings you pleasure and do it daily.
- Identify a pleasure you and your spouse share; plan a way to do it weekly.

## *Signature Strengths*

- Visit the website www.authentichappiness.org
- Identify your signature strength and have your partner do the same.
- Plan a night together in which each of you uses your highest strengths.

## *Increase Optimism and Hope*

- Practice finding the universal causes of good events as well as the temporary and specific causes of misfortune.
- Practice disputing your pessimistic thoughts.
- Recognize them.
- Treat them as if they were uttered by an external person (a rival whose mission in life was to make you miserable).
- Stand back and check the evidence for your pessimistic belief.
- Examine the alternatives.
- Ask how useful it is to hold onto the pessimistic belief.

## *Thankfulness*

Thank one person a week for something they said or did that added to the quality of your life.

## *Compassion: Self/Other*

See resources and exercises at www.wisebrain.org

# References

Atkinson, B. (2005). *Emotional intelligence in couples therapy: Advances from neurobiology and the science of intimate relationships.* New York, NY: Norton.

Connor, J., Robinson, B., & Wieling, E. (2008). Vulvar pain: A phenomenological study of couples in search of effective diagnosis and treatment. *Family Process,* 47(2): 139–156.

Cozolino, L. (2006). *The neuroscience of human relationships: Attachment and the developing social brain.* New York, NY: Norton.

Cozolino, L. (2010). *The neuroscience of psychotherapy: Healing the social brain* (2nd edition). New York, NY: Norton.

Davidson, R. (2012). *The emotional life of your brain: How its unique patterns affect the way you think, feel and live and how you can change.* New York, NY: Hudson Press.

Emmons, R. & McCullough, M. (2003). Counting blessings versus burdens: An experimental investigation of gratitude and subjective well-being in daily life. *Journal of Personality and Social Psychology,* 84(2): 377–389.

Feder, A., Nestler, E., Westphal, M., & Charney, D. (2010). Psychobiological mechanisms of resilience to stress. In J. Reich, A. Zautra, & J. Hall (Eds.), *Handbook of adult resilience* (pp. 35–55). New York, NY: Guilford Press.

Fergus, K. (2011) The rupture and repair of the couple's communal body with prostate cancer. *Families, Systems & Health,* 29(2): 95–113.

Freedman, J. & Combs, J. (1996). *Narrative therapy: The social construction of preferred realities.* New York, NY: Norton.

Gergen, K. (1991). *The saturated self: Dilemmas of identity in contemporary life.* New York, NY: Basic Books.

Gottman, J. & Gottman, J. (2006). *Ten lessons to transform your marriage.* New York, NY: Crown.

Gottman, J. & Silver, N. (1999). *The seven principles for making marriage work.* New York, NY: Three Rivers Press.

Jordan, J. (2010). *Relational-Cultural Therapy.* Washington, DC: American Psychological Association.

Labunko Messier, B., Singer, J., Alea, N. Baddeley, J., Vick, S., & Sanders, R. (2008, July). *Measuring relationship mutuality: Development of marital engagement-type of union scale and partners apperception test.* Poster presented at the biennial conference of the International Association for Relationship Research, Providence, RI.

Lieblich, A., McAdams, D., & Josselson, R. (2004). *Healing plots: The narrative basis of psychotherapy.* Washington, DC: American Psychological Association.

Lyubomirsky, S. (2007). *The how of happiness.* New York, NY: Penguin Press.

Madsen, W. (2009). Collaborative helping: A practice framework for family centered services. *Family Process,* 48: 103–116.

McAdams, D. (2001). The psychology of life stories. *Review of General Psychology,* 5: 100–122.

McAdams, D. (2006). *The redemptive self.* Oxford, UK: Oxford University Press.

Mills, J., Clark, M., Ford, T., & Johnson, M. (2004). Measurement of communal strength. *Personal Relationships,* 11: 213–230.

Niederhoffer, K. & Pennebaker, J. (2009). Sharing one's story: On the benefits of writing or talking about emotional experience. In C.R. Snyder & S. Lopez (Eds.), *Oxford handbook of positive psychology* (pp. 621–633). Oxford, UK: Oxford University Press.

59

Reid, D., Doell, F., Dalton, E., & Ahmad, S. (2008). Systemic-constructivist couple therapy (SCCT): Description of approach, theoretical advances and published longitudinal evidence. *Psychotherapy Theory, Research, Practice, Training*, 45: 477–490.

Sharpe, S. (2000). *The ways we love: A developmental approach to treating couples.* New York, NY: Guilford Press.

Siegel, D. (2010). *Mindsite: The new science of personal transformation.* New York, NY: Random House.

Siegel, D. (2012). *Pocket guide to interpersonal neurobiology: An integrative handbook of the mind.* New York, NY: Norton.

Singer, J. (2011). Using self-defining memories in couples therapy. In G. Kenyon, E. Bohlmeijer, & W. Randall (Eds.), *Storying later life* (pp. 213–234). Oxford, UK: Oxford University Press.

Skerrett, K. (1998). The couple experience of breast cancer. *Families, Systems & Health*, 16: 281–298.

Skerrett, K. (2003). Couple dialogues with illness: Expanding the "We". *Families, Systems & Health*, 21: 69–80.

Skerrett, K. (2004). Moving toward We: Promise and peril. In W. Rosen & M. Walker (Eds.), *How connections heal* (pp. 128–149). New York, NY: Guilford Press.

Skerrett, K. (2010). "Good enough stories": Helping couples invest in one another's growth. *Family Process*, 49: 503–516.

Skerrett, K. (2013). *Couple adjustment to breast cancer: A ten year follow-up.* Manuscript under revision.

Skerrett, K. & Singer, J. (2013). *Cultivating "We-ness" in couple stories: A positive approach to couple therapy.* Manuscript in preparation.

Solomon, M. & Tatkin, S. (2011). *Love and war in intimate relationships: Connection, disconnection, and mutual regulation in couple therapy.* New York, NY: Norton.

Surrey, J., Shem, S., & Bergman, S. (1998). *We have to talk: Healing dialogues between women and men.* Rydalmere, Australia: Hodder Press.

Walsh, F. (2006). *Strengthening family resilience* (2nd edition). New York, NY: Guilford Press.

White, M. (1993). Deconstruction and therapy. In S. Gilligan & R. Price (Eds.), *Therapeutic conversations* (pp. 22–61). New York, NY: Norton.

# 5

# LIBERATING VOICE
# AND VULNERABILITY

## Relational-Cultural Perspectives on Conflict in Mixed Race Couples

*Maureen Walker*

Mixed race couples, once considered culturally anomalous, are becoming increasingly commonplace. According to data published by the Pew Research Center (Wang, 2012), the percentage of exogamous partnerships more than doubled in the past decade, with mixed race couples accounting for approximately 15% of all new marriages in 2010. Given the existence of anti-miscegenation laws well into the 21st century, this increase in exogamy represents a significant cultural shift.

There are, however, differing interpretations of the meaning of this shift. While some interpret inter-racial marriage as evidence of increased cross-racial tolerance, if not amity, others suggest that such an interpretation represents over-investment in the notion of racial transcendence. That is, the mere incidence of cross-racial coupling is taken as evidence of the lessening of racial tensions and the dilution of the power-over narrative of race that spawns personal and cultural disconnection. Advocates of this perspective tend to bolster the notion of racial transcendence with statistics indicating the number of younger Americans who self-identify as mixed race, repudiating traditional categories as at best non-descriptive and at worst diminishing (Kerwin, Ponterotto, Jackson, & Harris, 1993).

While the idea of racial transcendence has gained currency in popular discourse, it tends to over-rely on phenotypic markers, while ignoring or minimizing the meaning systems and multi-layered relational images that encode an individual's racial identifications. Further, while the increase in mixed race coupling represents dramatic change in terms of both legal precedent and cultural norms, it does not mean that race ceases to function as a potent strategy of disconnection in even the most intimate of relationships. In fact, the foundational tenets of Relational-Cultural Theory (RCT) suggest otherwise. According to RCT, we come to awareness of personhood through acting in culturally embedded relationship (Miller, 1976; Jordan, 1992; Walker, 1999). Specifically, self is emergent process: it is through the dynamic interaction of culture, biology, and particular relational histories that we experience the simultaneity (Holvino, 2010) that we come to call self. Therefore, the act of mixed race coupling itself cannot be interpreted as the transcendence of cultural divisions. Because each person enters the relationship embodying multiple biographies – familial, biological, as well as relational and cultural histories – inevitable and necessary conflict may in fact be engaged as multi-layered re-enactments of personal and political pain. In such cases, either or both partners may over-rely on cultural-racial interpretation to deflect opportunities for relational growth. Similarly, either or both may over-personalize the acute disconnections that are rooted in chronic cultural violation. Either strategy results in terror of vulnerability and disempowered voice in relationship.

In the case analysis that follows, a couple whom I will call Sam and Didi will represent a composite of issues that often surface in mixed race or interracial couples. By explicating critical junctures in the therapy of Sam and Didi, this chapter will illustrate the specific relational processes that allow mixed race couples to begin healing the wounds of cultural violation, engage the simul-taneity of their experience with greater consciousness, and enlarge their capacity for intimacy with each other.

## Meeting Sam and Didi

My first encounter with Sam and Didi happened by way of a phone call from their couples counselor, a woman whom I did not know but had met briefly during a workshop presentation. For the preceding four months, Sam and Didi had been in marital therapy with her (I will call her Dr K). Dr K described Sam and Didi as an attractive and articulate mixed race couple in their mid-thirties. Two issues prompted Dr K's request for a consult. First, over the course of the four month period, Didi had occasionally threatened to leave the counseling sessions because she felt "unsupported" by Dr K. Specifically, she suspected that as a white woman, Dr K could not "understand a black woman's experience". Second, Dr K explained that a few weeks earlier, Didi had "resorted to suicidal gesturing" during a heated argument with Sam. After thoroughly assessing the incident, Didi, Dr K, and Sam agreed that there was no imminent danger: that her purchase of a "stockpile" of over-the-counter sleeping pills and placing them by the bedside was an attempt to "scare Sam" into paying attention to his impact on her. They further agreed that the incident indicated a level of distress that might best be addressed in individual therapy. Both partners and Dr K happily concluded that Didi would benefit from "working through her own issues" with a black female therapist.

While their conclusion was thoroughly understandable, this first critical juncture in the conjoint therapy raised two concerns that I discussed with Dr K. The first involved my skepticism about the efficacy of demographic pairing. While conventional wisdom might suggest that similar or same race membership would facilitate the therapeutic alliance, seminal research by racial identity theorists suggests identity development or meaning-making is a more consequential factor (Helms, 1991; Jenkins, 1999; Sue & Sue, 2008.) Second, singling Didi out as the partner most in need of repair could exacerbate any problematic power dynamics operating in the couple's counseling process and in their marriage. Such a signal had the potential to disempower not only Didi, but also the conjoint counseling process itself. On one hand, being identified as the "damaged" partner could lessen her credibility both within the therapy hour and in the rest/most of their relationship. On the other, individual therapy – especially when approached from a Separate Self perspective – could function to discount the conjoint work. As I discussed my Relational-Cultural approach to therapy with Dr K, we agreed that both partners might benefit from individual psychotherapy. Specifically, Sam and Didi needed support to develop the intentions and skills that would allow them to engage their differences with mutual respect and courage. After the initial conversation, we decided on what we termed "an experiment". Dr K would convey both my interests and my concerns to Sam and Didi, who would then decide whether or not they wanted to invite me into their couples session. Three weeks later, I attended a session with Sam, Didi and Dr K.

The purpose of this initial joint session was to provide an opportunity for the four of us to (a) get to know more about each other and (b) make informed choices about the feasibility of combining individual therapy with the couple's counseling. Although both partners described themselves as mixed race, Didi insisted that she was only "technically" mixed race because of her darker skin. Didi was the youngest of three daughters of a Bahamian mother and a Dutch father. For the first three years of her life, Didi and her family lived in the Bahamas. Months after immigrating to the United States, her father left the family, returned to Europe, and as Didi reports, remarried and started a new family "weeks" later. Although the father continued to provide financial support for Didi and her sisters, her physical contact with him was limited to sporadic and typically unannounced visits. Sam, on the other hand was the only child of an African American father and white American mother. Although his parents remained married until Sam reached adulthood, the relationship was anything but harmonious. His father, whom he described as "professionally successful but emotionally decrepit" was given to serial infidelity. Sam described his mother as being "as beautiful as she is creative, but emotionally overwrought and high strung". Because both parents were absent from the home, sometimes for protracted periods, Sam was often left in the care of his mother's parents: grandparents who were as unrestrained in their affection for Sam as they were in their hostility toward his father. At the outset of the conjoint therapy with Dr K, Didi had one clear goal: to make Sam a better husband. His goal, on the other hand, was to quiet what he experienced as Didi's unbridled emotionality. Each partner felt that the success of the marriage required the other person to change. Each partner carried relational images that left them predisposed to flagrant re-enactments of familial distress, largely because they felt fundamentally unsafe and disempowered in connection. Each attempted to use power-over strategies of disconnection to quell their felt vulnerability. In the process, each lost some measure of voice.

In our first co-facilitated meeting, it was immediately clear that each partner felt blamed and victimized by the other. However, they both seemed somewhat intrigued when I described my role as a participant in a process that might help them become better conflict partners. Specifically, I expressed a desire to help them to heal some of the wounds that marred their experience of marriage and to help them become more effective in responding to the inevitable conflicts that arise in an intimate relationship. Further, I expressed my view that the primary goal of the individual sessions would be to foster a capacity for mutual empowerment, not to support the deeply entrenched patterns in which each partner attempted to gain power over the other. Because their typical conflict patterns left both partners feeling alienated and disempowered, Sam and Didi acknowledged that it was time to try something new. At the close of the session, we agreed that whatever ultimate decision Sam and Didi made about the future of their marriage, the focus of our individual psychotherapy would be to help each partner learn and grow through relationship. Didi and I agreed on a six month schedule, while Sam continued to meet individually with Dr K. It was further agreed that the therapist would share information "as needed" with the consent of both partners. In addition, we discussed the possibility of occasional sessions facilitated by both therapists. The couple left this initial joint session with the stated goal of addressing the issues that would enable them to make better use of marital therapy or relationship coaching at a future date.

## Getting to Know Didi

Didi was a striking presence. Tall and elegantly dressed, she strode into my office, flung her over-sized purse aside and said: "Had I known five years ago what I was in for, I would have chosen what was behind Door #3!" It was very clear during our first session that banter came easily to her. Charming, witty, and intellectually engaging, it was not surprising that she was on a fast track for tenure in the philosophy department at her university. Although Didi was given to flagrant displays of emotionality, there seemed to be only the most tenuous connection between her expressiveness and her actual experience. While I had no doubt that she carried deep pain, I was left with the impression that she "performed" her emotions. While her superior verbal facility and dramatic flair served her well in her career as a popular assistant professor, these talents were less adaptive in the rest of life as they functioned to distance and distract: strategies that left her disconnected from her partner, her therapists, and her own experience.

All prior agreements notwithstanding, from the start Didi was persistent in efforts to use her individual therapy to make the case that Sam needed to change.

On more than one occasion, she described herself as the Perfect Wife, attributing much of her husband's professional success to her ability to facilitate social contacts. Her numerous examples of his marital failings seemed to cluster around two themes: emotional unresponsiveness and insufficient appreciation of her value in the relationship. From Didi's perspective, to be married to Sam was to live with the constant threat of abandonment. In her mind, his apparent lack of devotion was evidence of not only a marital failing but also a spiritual weakness. For example, if Sam disagreed with her viewpoint in an argument with a third party, Didi would remind him of his Biblical duty to "forsake all others and cleave to his wife". When I asked Didi if she had had a chance to continue reflecting on goals for our time together, her answer came quickly and only half-jokingly. "Yes, do you think you can turn that frog I married into a prince?"

## You and Me against the World

Much of the work of Relational-Cultural Therapy involves engaging the relational images through which people construct meaning and gauge possibilities. These images are the cognitive-affective ideas and physiological processes that inform experiences of self, expectations of others, as well as decisions about the nature of relationship. In addition to early familial and interpersonal experiences, these images are shaped by the controlling images of the dominant culture (Collins, 2000). A fundamental proposition of RCT is that culture provides more than scenic backdrop or context for interpersonal encounters, but is actively implicated in shaping and defining the parameters of connection and disconnection. Relational-Cultural Therapy then necessarily involves recognizing and reworking the commingled sequelae of familial–interpersonal disconnections and cultural violation.

At no point were the commingled effects of Relational-Cultural ruptures more apparent than during my first few sessions with Didi. In contrast to more conventional models that might have focused on confronting her resistance to change, in Relational-Cultural Therapy strategies of disconnection (e.g. Didi's relentless pursuit of the "Change Sam" agenda) provide an opportunity to examine the relational images underlying constricted response capacity and distress in relationship. Didi's early comments about her husband's "failure to cleave" proved portentous for our relationship. From the outset, she attempted to forge an alliance with me by establishing Sam and Dr K as "Other"; in effect, she attempted to secure our relationship by creating an "Us vs. Them" dynamic. Rather than experiencing relationship as a generative process that offered the possibility for mutual growth and shared power, the images constituting Didi's relationship template mandated competition (*in order for Didi to feel in, someone had to be out)* and control (*in order for Didi to "win", someone had to "lose"*). Accordingly, uncertainty triggered intolerable levels of vulnerability and disagreement raised the ever-present specter of abandonment. To counteract that sense of powerlessness, Didi resorted to enactments of power-over. In our case, she began by remarking on how good it felt to be in therapy with me and not those "two white people" (Sam and Dr K). The implicit negotiation in this remark contained both an offer and a request/demand. The offer was an expression of allegiance or presumptive camaraderie based on phenotypic similarities. The remark also conveyed the implicit demand to cleave to her: that is, to agree with her assessment of Sam and of Dr K. My response to Didi did little to appease her. I told her that I was confident that we would find a way to connect with each other, and that we could do it without disparaging either Sam or Dr K. Furthermore, I assured her that our time was a safe place for her to explore all of her hurts, misgivings, and doubts about both Sam and Dr K. I then suggested a small experiment: that we both try to be as honest as possible in that sharing and to do so as if they are in the room with us. To paraphrase marital therapist Peter Pearson (2012), if conjoint therapy is to lead to movement and positive growth, individual therapy can't be a place to practice one's argument that the other person bears all the responsibility for changing. Didi let it be known quickly and forcefully that she was not amused.

Relational-Cultural Theory posits that all acts of power-over are based in fear and are in fact efforts to forestall powerlessness (Jordan, 2010). Rather than framing Didi's remarks as manipulative, her attempts to enact power-over in the therapy are more usefully seen as strategies of disconnection aimed at securing safety. For that reason the Relational-Cultural therapist "honors" the strategies of disconnection as an attempt by the client to be in relationship by the only means she perceives as available to her (Miller & Stiver, 1994). When I invited Didi to talk about what our racial differences and similarities meant to her, she elaborated on previous comments about being only "technically" mixed race. As she put it: "I don't look like my sisters: no one ever looked at me and thought I was anything but black." She went on to say: "And if you look at Sam, he's a straight-up white boy." As it turned out, Didi's joking manner belied deep-felt body shame. Much as in the larger culture, stratification based on racial phenotype was a source of disconnection within Didi's family of origin (Walker, 1998, 2011). She recalled that on more than one occasion, her mother had admonished her to do well in school because she would "never be able to get by on good looks". Her sisters, "the pretty ones", looked more like their European ancestors, while Didi's skin was in her words "even darker" than her mother's. For all of her posturing and protestations about being a Perfect Wife, Didi felt deeply unworthy of Sam, and this contradiction was a source of terrifying vulnerability. The shame that Didi carried was multi-layered: not only was she ashamed of her black body, she was ashamed of being ashamed of her black body. Her public persona – and indeed her persona within her marriage

– made no allowances for contradiction or ambivalence. Didi acknowledged that her "loud and proud" style was her way to silence all doubters, wherever they were: on tenure committees, in social circles, or in her own family. The problem, however, was that in quieting the voices of others, she had disconnected from her own voice. Her insistence on commanding the respect of others led her to forfeit any claim on respecting the complexity of her own experience. For this reason, notions of self-empathy seemed not only counterintuitive but downright wrong to Didi. In a poignant moment, she reflected that she only felt safe when she was able to take up as much space as possible in a room so that people would have to acknowledge her presence. The irony was that it was during those moments that she felt most fraudulent and alone. It was also during those moments that she felt most unworthy of compassion.

Jordan (2010) defines self-empathy as the ability to bring an empathic attitude to bear on one's own experience. While my goal was to help Didi become a more compassionate witness of her life, I also needed to respect her skepticism about this notion of self-empathy. The risk, it seemed to her, was that she would be weak and lose credibility; her ambivalence would be "out there" for everyone to see. We agreed that perpetual ambivalence was not a fitting career strategy; however, unremitting entrapment inside a one-dimensional persona was not a likely life strategy. Because she could not trust that she was worthy of love, Didi had learned to garner admiration – from all comers. Moreover, by focusing her energies on becoming the Chosen One, she had forfeited any personal claim on voice and choice. Over time, we came to call these strategies of disconnection "playing to the audience". A pivotal moment in our therapy occurred when Didi was able to acknowledge that playing to this unnamed and omnipresent audience left her feeling exhausted, angry, and ultimately disempowered. This acknowledgement notwithstanding, the path toward self-empathy was somewhat circuitous. In fact, in a light-hearted moment, I took a vow that I would never *force* empathy on her. Instead, I explained to her that in my experience, empathy is grounded in respect and curiosity about our shared humanity; that it is the intention that opens both people up to greater clarity and understanding.

Sensing that Didi was curious about curiosity as a facet of empathic experience (and frankly counting on her lively imagination), I suggested that we create something together. I said to Didi: "Suppose we were to design a curriculum for little black girls, and the only measure of success would be their discomfort with their bodies. Suppose that curriculum conveyed to all girls what matters most is how you look: and to black girls in particular, how you look is irredeemably wrong [Walker, 1999]. What would the curriculum have to include? And who would need to deliver it? What kinds of incentives or reinforcements would need to be in place to ensure life-long learning?" This was an approach to empathy that Didi could embrace with gusto. It was no surprise that the content of the curriculum she reported, rather than designed, was pervasive, penetrating every major developmental activity and function.

Likewise, the delivery systems were ubiquitous. From off-handed remarks of "color-struck" (indicating a preference for lighter skin) relatives to the acclaimed beauty of flaxen-haired princesses in fairy tales; from the Catholic school teachers who were less generous with their praise of her than of her lighter skinned counterparts to the "soft pastel colors of the Blessed Virgin"; from the conventions of language and thought that associate darkness with evil and undesirability to the near absence of any positive images of Africans in textbooks or television: Didi's journal was replete with examples from popular culture to lived intimate experience: all delivering the message that she would be an undesirable – that she had to work double hard just to be seen and heard. *"And this just gets us up to the third grade!"* she exclaimed.

She joked that upon discovering that "woolly-headed" meant stupid, she finally understood why math was so difficult for her. We laughed; we wept. Didi had never told anyone her greatest secret misery: that her father had left the family to join a white family because she – his youngest daughter – was too black. She had also never said out loud that Sam, with his white skin and wavy red hair, was her personal trophy: that it was a triumphal moment when she paraded him down the aisle, as evidence of her beauty and her worth. This recognition led to an even more painful question: did she ever clearly and open-heartedly choose Sam, or was she simply bound and determined to have him choose her?

In the following sessions, Didi's tears began to flow freely and unashamedly. This part of our work involved helping Didi to cultivate a measure of mindfulness and curiosity, thus enabling her to reconnect with her own feelings and thoughts. At one point, she smiled through her tears and said: "I told you this empathy wasn't all it's cracked up to be." I responded: "Yes, it can deepen your awareness of the hurt, and it takes away the isolation surrounding the hurt. You can be seen and heard and safe at the same time." One part of lessening the isolation involved "re-apportioning the shame" as we called it. Didi came to see herself as a carrier of an intergenerational legacy of cultural shame. She came to see that the commingling of cultural shame and personal grief resulted in painfully racialized re-enactments in her family home: from her sisters "flipping their long red pigtails in my face" to her mother's insistent reminders that she *failed* to embody the aesthetic values of the dominant culture. In a moment of speculation she surmised that perhaps the racialized shame and personal pain were too much for her mother to bear: that perhaps as the daughter who most resembled her mother she was forced to carry it with her. While this interpretation did not erase the pain of those childhood memories, it did widen the lens through which she viewed their relationship both past and current. She remembered those comforting private moments when she sat in the kitchen between her mother's legs on a Saturday night, while she brushed and oiled her hair readying her for Sunday services, how her mother would laugh and tell stories, sing songs, and if she wasn't too tired, show her the dances she danced as a teenager. It was in those moments that she felt precious in her mother's sight. And in the recall, she felt much more real.

## When Thumbs Wrestle

I had not yet heard about Didi's most recent threat to "leave" the marriage when I received the call from Dr K. In his individual session the night before, a clearly perturbed Sam had reported finding airline and real estate information for a city on the West coast. When asked about it, Didi nonchalantly explained that she planned to take a sabbatical year in California. According to Sam, one of the worst fights of their lives ensued when he wished her well and attempted to leave for the gym.

To say that Didi was "fired up" when she came to our next session would be an understatement. Once again, she recounted Sam's failings as a husband and bemoaned the fact that she hadn't married a "real black man". As we talked more about this latest marital crisis, it became clear that there were no plans for a sabbatical – on the west coast or otherwise. The threat to leave for a year was prompted by an incident that Didi experienced as a humiliating betrayal. In retaliation, she wanted to show Sam that he mattered as little to her she did to him. The downward spiral was accelerated by Sam's apparent non-response: in effect indicating that his "not mattering to her" didn't matter to him.

Over the previous weekend, Didi had hosted a dinner to welcome a new employee, a young white woman, to the firm in which Sam was a junior partner. Although Didi did not particularly like the young woman, her offer to host the dinner was a strategic effort to support Sam's bid for promotion into the senior ranks. During the course of the dinner, the young woman voiced her strong support of upcoming marriage equality legislation. Mindful of her role as host, Didi offered what she described as a "tempered" version of her strong opposition to the legislation – a view that was more in line with the church that she and Sam attended as well as with the opinions of the senior partners. Much to her consternation, Sam revealed that he strongly supported the legislation. Didi reported that she "played her part perfectly" during the dinner; afterwards; however, she confronted Sam about embarrassing her "in front of that white girl" *and* abandoning their faith. Sam, in response, suggested that she stop over-reacting and went to sleep.

Not surprisingly, Didi's account of this incident was punctuated by attempts to entice me to agree with the righteousness of her positions: both on the issue of marriage equality and on Sam's "obvious" transgressions. Like Sam, my response to her insistent demand for validation was admittedly feeble. I responded that she was obviously shaken and saddened and that I was sad to see her in such distress. As her interpretation of the conflict was becoming increasingly inflamed, my initial reasoning was that it would be more pro-ductive to help Didi connect with the pain and fear she was experiencing rather than delve into the content of the incident.

Fortunately for our relationship, my attempts to stay in neutral territory did not work. She asked directly: "What do you think. Aren't you a Catholic? Surely as a black woman you can't believe that this demand for same sex marriage is the same as the civil rights struggle." In that moment, I decided that Didi's challenge offered an opportunity for us to *do* conflict rather than talk about how to do conflict. In more words than would be appropriate for this chapter, I explained that (a) I indeed stood for the sanctity of covenantal love – irrespective of the genders of the people who make the commitment; (b) the black freedom struggle was a source of courage, helping me to name and stand against oppression however it manifests; and (c) freedom and dignity are human capacities that need not be apportioned as scarce commodities: that the dignity of my heterosexual marriage is not compromised by the inclusion of homosexual couples. I also said to Didi that I had no interest in convincing her to change her mind, but that I was deeply interested in knowing how she was feeling in the moment about us.

What followed was multiple iterations of power-over maneuvering. For example, Didi responded that she was disappointed but not surprised: she had never really gotten on well with African American women. In her view they tended to lack the intellectual heft and moral sturdiness of Afro-Caribbean women. She went on say that they had often wondered if I had grown up with "pretty girl privilege" – thus leaving me inured to the struggles of real black women. I responded with curiosity; Didi's repeated use of the word "real" provided an opening into a conversation about the complexity of authentic experience. For example, we talked about "oppression within oppression": how marginalized people within an oppressive dominant culture may jockey for rank by bartering with whatever privilege they may hold. In her case, claiming higher rank than African American women served two functions. First, as an immigrant family it was important *not* to be associated with the legacy of chattel slavery and its continuing degrading impact on American blacks. Second, Didi had learned that claiming a superior history was an effective counter to her young classmates' sneers at her occasionally accented English. Adding insult to racial injury was the fact that the "pretty girls" – the black girls (like her sisters) with lighter colored skin and longer hair – seemed to be more readily accepted by peers and rewarded by adults. Didi's apparent grandiosity was her effort to resist the ravages of everyday devaluation in the only way she knew. As a survival strategy, its usefulness was limited in that it required her to internalize the very values that deconstructed self-empathy, thus hobbling her efforts to move toward more real or authentic relationships.

I asked Didi how she wanted me to feel when she commented about the inferiority of African American women and "pretty girl privilege". She responded tearfully that she wanted to punish me for betraying her; that she hoped to feel stronger by making me feel bad – and that my feeling bad would help her feel less vulnerable.

Everyday devaluation is endemic to power-over cultures, and growing up in such a culture can be a soul-scarring experience. To resist its demeaning effects, Robinson and Ward (1991) speak of the necessity of cultivating a belief stronger than anyone's disbelief. For her part, Didi attempted to resist by creating stories or interpretations of reality and forcing herself and those with whom she wished to be intimate to live according to the dictates of her scripts. To paraphrase Wexler (2008), to force another person to inhabit one's story of reality is the ultimate act of power-over. Didi acknowledged that her stories made her feel powerful, but they ultimately kept her from confronting truths about herself, Sam, and their relationship. Two sessions later, we agreed that it was time to try another co-facilitated session with Sam and Dr K.

Their most recent crisis quelled, Sam and Didi seemed ready to try a new conversation with the hope of becoming more known to each other. Both partners seemed ready to embrace the risks of an authentic conversation: that is, of being seen, of being heard, and being changed. In a power-over culture in which romantic relationship itself becomes a measure of one's value – an object "to have and to hold", the risks of mutual influence are indeed daunting. In Relational-Cultural Therapy, mutual empathy is the process that enables growth and healing (Jordan, 1997, 2002, 2010). In other words, participants in the relationship must be willing to be transparent about the impact that others have on them. Sam and Didi had to risk sharing out of their authentic experience, and in so doing, share the power that each attempted to withhold from the other in order to feel safe. To facilitate movement toward mutual empathy, I proposed that the partners hold these questions:

1. What do you genuinely want to know about your partner?
2. What do you need in order to feel safe telling what is true for you?

As an exercise in anticipatory empathy, I suggested that each partner ask the question: "How do I want her/him to feel when I say _____?"

With these guidelines in mind, Sam volunteered to begin. As it turned out, he had long been puzzled by Didi's distinctions about being "technically" mixed race and had grown to resent her imputing racial motives to each conflict. "Why can't a fight just be a fight?" The couple talked openly about their different developmental experiences of race – experiences mediated by class differences and different familial race loyalty demands. Though Sam admired and longed for relationship with his philandering African American father, loyalty to his mother and grandparents had created a seemingly unnavigable distance in their relationship. Their different developmental experiences manifest in conflicting expressions of racial consciousness.

According to a model proposed by Helms (1991), Sam appeared to be anchored in pre-encounter consciousness. That is, he often did not apprehend the racial import of an incident. At other times, he deliberately ignored the possibility of racialized meaning, in part to quiet Didi. He acknowledged that this response style had often left Didi "in the lurch", holding whatever racial tension that did exist for both of them. Didi in turn acknowledged that her vehement remonstrances in light of those incidents was an attempt to feel "less crazy" by making him feel some of the pain. Didi seemed to hold tenaciously to encounter consciousness, ferreting out evidence of racial insult in the most benign incident. She, in turn, acknowledged her attempts to force Sam into a model of black manhood that would help her feel less alone and afraid. Sam explained that he equated Didi's emotionality with his mother's excessive need for reassurance and validation. Since he was afraid to anger her by disagreeing or expressing his own views, he simply kept quiet. Didi tearfully explained that she equated his silence with her father's abandonment – a loss too great to bear again. The couple began to reinterpret stories of past fights, this time with more tears and laughter than recrimination. Further, they were able to perceive the perfect complementarity between their strategies of disconnection. In their effort to manage their vulnerabilities by silencing the other, each partner had lost a measure of their own authentic voice.

As the session came to a close, Dr K shared an image from neuroscientist Dan Siegel and wondered if it might be helpful to Sam and Didi. Closing her hand into a fist, she described the executive functions of the cortical regions of the brain and the functions of the limbic system represented by the thumb. As she explained it, the limbic region was focused on surviving threats and personal survival. When it was doing its job and the amygdala was firing full tilt, there wasn't much room for mutual empathy or any of the skills that would allow them to grow closer and become more real with each other. In that sense, it was absolutely "normal" that each would either shut down or attempt to shut down the other. At one point Didi exclaimed: "Sam, I can't believe we've spent the past five years in a thumb wrestling contest!" To which Sam replied: I don't think we'll have a winner until we unlock thumbs and join hands."

## Embracing the Possibility of Something New

According to Gottman and Silver (1999), the eradication of conflict is not the hallmark of a successful marriage. Instead, successful marriages are marked by the couple's willingness to repair inevitable conflict. Likewise, Jean Baker Miller (1976) theorized that authenticity grows in relationship only to the extent that the participants are willing to wage good conflict. An earnest effort to repair requires each partner to embrace the vulnerability of shared power. Contempt and power-over breed stagnation and violations of trust and dignity. In other words, each partner must listen for and encourage the shared humanity in the other's voice. Sam and Didi came to see that to the extent that they engaged in "thumb wrestling", they would remain mired in suffering and chronic disconnection.

Didi remained in individual therapy with me for another six months and Sam with Dr K for a similar period. During that time, they did not pursue conjoint counseling *per se*, but each indicated that he or she felt prepared to do so whenever the time came. Didi and I continued to work on what she laughingly (and genuinely) came to call "her empathy thing". What was most important for her was coming to feel and to know that empathy did not require abdication:

that, in fact, the process allowed her to feel more fully seen and heard when she approached others with the intention to respect and understand. As she put it, she no longer had to build a wall of words around herself; nor did she need to hide behind the mystifications of cultural "rules" and labels or hyper-religiosity. From time to time, she reported that she and Sam hit a communication snag, owing to different cultural or expressive styles and other times because of their different temperaments or needs. What was absent in these conflicts was either partner's need to disempower the other through blame or shame. This new relational awareness allowed Didi to use her words caringly and courageously. As she became more compassionate toward her own experience, she was less fearful of being known. As they became more accepting of their personal contradictions and their shared vulnerability, each became more capable of responding to truths and possibilities that evolve in mutually empowering relationship.

# References

Collins, P.H. (2000). *Black feminist thought: Knowledge, consciousness, and the politics of empowerment.* Boston: Unwin Hyman.

Gottman, J.M. & Silver, N. (1999). *The seven principles for making marriage work.* New York: Three Rivers Press.

Helms, J.E. (1991). The measurement of black racial identity attitudes. In J.E. Helms (Ed.) *Black and white racial identity: Theory, research, and practice* (pp. 33–47). Westport, CT: Praeger.

Holvino, E. (2010). Intersections: The simultaneity of race, gender, and class in organization studies. *Gender, Work, and Organizations,* 17(3), 248–277.

Jenkins, Y.M. (1999). Salient themes and directives for college helping professionals. In Y.M. Jenkins (Ed.) *Diversity in college settings: Directives for helping professionals.* New York: Routledge.

Jordan, J.V. (1992). The relational self: A new perspective for understanding women's development. *Contemporary Psychotherapy Review,* 7, 56–71.

Jordan, J.V. (1997). Relational development through mutual empathy. In A.C. Bohart & L.S. Greenberg (Eds.) *Empathy reconsidered: New directions in psychotherapy* (pp. 343–351). Washington, DC: American Psychological Association.

Jordan, J.V. (2002). A Relational-Cultural perspective in therapy. In F. Kaslow (Ed.) *Comprehensive handbook of psychotherapy* (Vol. 3, pp. 233–254). New York: Wiley.

Jordan, J.V. (2010). *Relational-Cultural Therapy.* Washington, DC: American Psychological Association.

Kerwin, C., Ponterotto, J.G., Jackson, B.L. & Harris, A. (1993). Racial identity in biracial children: A qualitative investigation. *Journal of Counseling Psychology,* 40(2), 221–231.

Miller, J.B. (1976). *Toward a new psychology of women.* Boston: Beacon Press.

Miller, J.B. & Stiver, I.P. (1994). *Movement in therapy: Honoring strategies of disconnection.* Work in Progress No. 65. Wellesley, MA: Stone Center Working Paper Series.

Pearson, P. (2012). *Get out of the middle: Make your couples work harder than you do and get better, faster results.* Retrieved from www.thecouplesinstitute.com

Robinson, T. & Ward, J.V. (1991). "A belief in self far greater than anyone's disbelief": Cultivating resistance among African American adolescent girls. In C. Gilligan, A.G. Rogers & D.L. Tolman (Eds.) *Women, girls, and psychotherapy: Reframing resistance* (pp. 87–104). New York: Harrington Park Press.

Sue, D.W. & Sue, D. (2008). The superordinate nature of multicultural counseling and therapy. In D.W. Sue & D. Sue (Eds.) *Counseling the culturally diverse: Theory and practice* (5th ed.) pp. 29–45. Hoboken, NJ: Wiley.

Walker, M.M. (1999). Race, self, and society: *Relational challenges in a culture of disconnection.* Work in Progress, No. 85. Wellesley, MA: Stone Center Working Paper Series.

Walker, M.M. (2011). What's a feminist therapist to do? Engaging the relational paradox in a post-feminist culture. *Women & Therapy*, 2(1–2), 38–57.

Wang, W. (2012). *The rise of intermarriage.* Retrieved from www.pewsocialtrends.org/2012/02/16/the-rise-of-intermarriage

Wexler, B. (2008). *Brain and culture.* Cambridge, MA: MIT Press.

# 6

# SUPPORTING RELATIONAL GROWTH IN A SHIFTING CULTURAL ENVIRONMENT

## Therapy with Lesbian Couples

*Natalie S. Eldridge*

Working with lesbian couples has been an honored and rich theme of my psychotherapy practice over the past 30 years. Most of that time has been in Massachusetts, and includes the period of heated and open debate about same-sex relationships that resulted in the passage of the first state law legalizing marriage for lesbian and gay couples.[1] While work with any couple needs to make careful and ongoing assessment of the context for that couple, the contextual landscape for the lesbian couples I have served has been characterized by unprecedented, rapid and public shifts. These political and social shifts are one aspect of relational context, a key theme of this chapter.

Another theme shaping this chapter is one of relational movement and expansion. Just as Relational-Cultural Therapy (RCT) describes human suffering as an outcome of chronic disconnection or isolation (Miller, 1976), I also view most couples' suffering as arising from a sense of impasse, wounded isolation, or relational staleness. The goal in the therapy is to foster movement, shifting the relational dynamic in ways that allow for the dormant energies of each member of the couple to regain their capacity for relational growth. How the couple will grow is often unknown and unpredictable – it is the capacity for growth and the willingness to explore new movements that become the outcomes of the therapy.

Finally, the work described in this chapter reflects the influence of mindfulness practices as well as a grounding in RCT approaches to psychotherapy. Years of mindfulness meditation practice informs my awareness in sessions and colors the quality of presence I bring to the therapy encounter. I also frequently teach basic foundation practices of mindfulness to couples as a way to decrease reactivity and increase their capacity for awareness of themselves, their partners, and the relationship that lives between them. I pay particular attention to exploring how mindfulness states can be enhanced in the relational context of the couple's interactions (see Surrey, 2005 and Kramer, 2007).

## RCT Themes in Couples Therapy

Three RCT concepts to be highlighted in the application of RCT with couples work are: relational movement, waging good conflict, and the central relational paradox. Each of these interweaves with the others in the web of therapeutic work that is illustrated below.

### *Relational Movement: From Stuck to Resilient*

In working with couples, relational movement and resilience can be promoted from the very beginning of the therapy process. Couples typically come to therapy stuck in some impasse from which they cannot find a way to move. In this way, lesbian couples are no different than any other couples. Expanding relational possibilities in the therapy room often allows a greater clarity for each participant that dispels the original perception of the impasse. This sets the stage for each partner to find a way to move forward, to explore a different possibility. Building the conditions for movement in couples therapy involves creating a climate that allows for creative engagement, supported vulnerability, increasing resilience, and building trust in the possibility of change. For each member to come into authentic and growth-fostering connection with the other, it is important that the myth of "stand on your own" is addressed and that the couple begins to recognize and honor the vulnerability of each member. Rather than encouraging the myth of invulnerability, the RCT therapist helps the couple explore the notion of supported vulnerability. Both members have to come to terms with their own vulnerability and develop ways to make acknowledging that vulnerability safe enough for change to occur.

### *Waging Good Conflict: Balancing Safety and Authenticity*

Building the conditions for movement and creative engagement in couples therapy also means each partner must find enough safety in the new triad of the therapy relationship. This will include elements of "feeling safe enough" with the therapist and, also, feeling safe with one's partner in the new context of couples therapy. Talking about this openly creates a forum for discussing and promoting "safe enough" conversations in the couple's relationship both within and outside of the therapy room. Fostering safety includes a continuing assessment and discussion of the safety level each feels in the therapy process.

The pacing of the therapy is an area where I invite mutual input, with each member of the triad given permission to adjust the speed as needed by deferring a discussion to another session, returning to an unfinished issue, or raising a new concern. This agreement often goes a long way in increasing the sense of safety, after it is both discussed and demonstrated in action. Both members of a couple know that if a discussion feels unsafe, they can state their limits and honor their need to discontinue it at that time. Both members know that the topic will not be dropped forever but will be picked up again when both partners are less reactive and can be more truly responsive to one another's needs.

In waging good conflict, a parallel element to safety is authenticity, or speaking one's truth. I encourage participants to use "I" statements in discussing their concerns and experiences, and to move away from blaming "you" statements. In early sessions, I also encourage participants to only address their description of their concerns and feelings to me. This promotes a freshness in speaking as the speaker frames her concerns to someone without the history or response of the partner. This practice also allows the other partner to listen without the pressure of responding. By assuring the listener that she will have a chance to tell me her concerns, she is invited to remain in a listening mode while her partner is speaking to me. Authentic speaking is finding one's voice to describe one's experience of feelings, thoughts and memories. The capacity to listen, when well developed, includes the complex process of listening deeply to what the other person is expressing while also being aware of the feelings and thoughts that arise in oneself while listening. Authentic speaking and the capacity for careful listening are necessary prerequisites for productive conflict and lay the foundation for "waging good conflict".

This balance of safety and authenticity in RCT couples work creates the healing context for feeling "safe enough" to take new risks, while also offering resistance to the cultural pull for safety through disconnection and isolation.

### *Uncovering the Relational Paradox: Where Are We Trying Too Hard?*

Couples therapy is filled with examples of the "central relational paradox" (Miller & Stiver, 1997). The relational paradox construct is built on the acknowledgment that all people yearn for authentic, growth-promoting relationships. To the extent, however, that we have not been empathically responded to or have been neglected and hurt by important and powerful people in our lives, we develop strategies of disconnection. These are strategies that are in place to help us stay safe in relationships which do not welcome our full authenticity. In developing intimate, open and healthy relationships with our partners, we long for more complete sharing of who we really are. In therapy, too, we hope to be able to represent ourselves more and more fully. And we hope that we will be empathically responded to. This movement into fuller presence, or authenticity, is built on a necessary relinquishing of some of our strategies of disconnection; a process that always feels risky. It is important as a therapist to be extremely respectful of the clients' fear, sense of risk and vulnerability. Further, the greater the disappointment or injury in early important relationships, the more urgent is the yearning for connection. At the same time, the more crucial it feels to maintain one's strategies of survival (otherwise known as strategies of disconnection) in order to avoid the risk of even temporary disconnection.

This relational paradox places the clients in a bind. They yearn for connection, yet they fear the vulnerability necessary to create authentic connection. These dynamics inevitably surface in couples work and the therapist carefully honors both sides of the paradox: the yearning and the fear that operate to different extents and in different ways with the two people in the couple. As each person begins to let go of their strategy of protection, they may paradoxically move out of connection in order to maintain a sense of safety. Uncovering and naming this relational paradox can help the individuals in the couple move out of reactivity to a temporary disconnection, generate patience in the process, and open the way for deeper and more responsive engagement. This often involves a paradigm shift from an individual perspective to the relational perspective, or the "we", described in Chapter 2. The degree of stuckness in the presenting impasse is often related to how much effort is going into trying to "fix" the problem, with each partner "knocking her head against the wall" in a way that preserves the integrity of the wall.

### Building the Foundation for RCT Couples Work

Establishing a mutual level of safety in the therapy process is an initial goal for building a therapeutic environment for RCT couples work. I make this goal explicit, and we explore what will create a sense of safety in the therapy room for each of the three participants. A critical aspect of this is naming and discussing the power dynamics present in the room. Some of these power differentials can be lessened through discussion and by agreement, while others will remain inherent, though no longer invisible, throughout the therapy process. Increased transparency about power arrangements renders these dynamics less destructive.

Specific strategies for building this foundation are discussed below, followed by an illustration of the early sessions of my work with one couple.

*Equal access to my knowledge*: I begin sessions with what I know about each of them already to help everyone feel on equal ground. Perhaps one partner has called to set up an appointment so I will summarize the conversation: "I spoke with Anne on the phone to set up this appointment, we discussed fees and scheduled this meeting, and she mentioned you were in individual therapy with Dr Smith, who referred you both to me for couples therapy." I end by clarifying that this is everything I know about them so far. They can then correct or expand on my knowledge rather than wonder what I know or don't know. I also explain that their relationship is my client, and from that view, I rarely have individual sessions with partners in the context of couples therapy – which further equalizes access to what I know.

*Naming the risks*: I outline the inevitable risks in couples work. This includes the fact that the therapy has an uncertain outcome – though we will work together to set outcome goals that everyone in the room can agree on and work toward. I also note that many clients find couples therapy more scary than individual therapy in that there is someone in the room (one's partner) who can "tell on you" by presenting your behavior in a way you would never present it, or by disclosing something you didn't feel ready to disclose. It is my job to make the couples work as non-humiliating an experience as I can, while also predicting a level of vulnerability they may not anticipate.

*Honor relationship strengths*: Another intentional strategy is to bring in the strengths of the relationship from the start, rather than have the early sessions "problem-saturated." I might ask each to address questions such as "what do you appreciate about your partner?" or "what first attracted you to your partner?" This content roots all of us in what can hold the relationship through the disconnecting times.

*Demonstrate equal partiality*: I explain that my goal with them is to demonstrate equal partiality . . . not neutrality; I am not a judge, but "taking sides fairly." What is essential is that each partner feels that I understand her concerns, can validate her suffering, and can be fair in listening to each side. By consistently raising the question in sessions about whether both partners feel heard, assessing safety levels, and inviting concerns, I find I am informed more often when someone feels criticized or dismissed by me in the course of our work. Then I can endeavor to repair this hurt and move towards a more equal partiality, which further builds safety and resiliency in our triangle. Each time this happens, a process of reconnection and resiliency is modeled in the sessions, and the outcome is usually a more expansive sense of safety and faith in the process.

*Go slowly*: When a problem area emerges, I will acknowledge it, and label it as something we can get into when we all feel ready. If one of them brings it up later, or in more depth, I will ask whether this feels like an area we are all ready to address. If there is any hesitation or uncertainty about being ready, I typically will suggest they consider their readiness at a later session. Sometimes I am the one not ready, and I explain what might help me feel more ready.

*Developing the "we" language*: A final strategy I'll mention is developing a language of the "we" (Shem & Surrey, 1998; Bergman & Surrey, 1994). This often involves the paradigm shift from an individual perspective to the relational perspective, or the "we", described in Chapter 2. I clarify that the relationship is my client, rather than the individuals in the relationship. "How is your relationship today?" I might encourage a "we" consciousness by suggesting that their conflict be put in an extra chair, rather than being held between them. Sometimes the "we" is all of us: "we seem to be uncertain about where to move next."

## Anne and Beverly

*Session One*: Anne and Beverly, a lesbian couple in midlife, had been together about seven years when I met them in our first session. They report "having trouble dealing with anger and negotiating conflict." They describe the alienated disconnection they keep reinforcing with each conflict as a "knot." In addition to gathering information about the presenting problem, I ask each to tell me what she appreciates about her partner and what she hopes might change as the result of couples work. I listen for the relational strengths and the hopes each partner has for the future – the resources I will hold for them throughout the therapy. A deep love and respect each has for the other is revealed, as well as their recognition of their limitations in negotiating conflict.

*Session Two*: I begin by asking about their experience last session, particularly about how safe each felt and what concerned them. Anne speaks of feeling drawn by the calmness she felt from me, but raises concerns about whether I will be able to contain, or handle, the intensity of anger they can experience. When I ask what she fears might happen in the sessions, she says "that the anger just will not come up in session." Beverly says she had felt safe last session, yet speaks of her concern that the way she had described what she likes about Anne in the last session seemed different than how Anne had talked about her.

I hear that Anne is worried she won't feel safe enough with me (or will feel too protective of me) to let her emotions show, while Beverly worries that she already hasn't performed as well as her partner in some unclear standard she imagines I might have. I, in turn, worry that I will not find a way to work with them constructively and they will feel they wasted their time and their money. Aware of these fears or vulnerabilities in the room, I return my attention to my faith in the therapy process and in the strengths Anne and Beverly have already described. This shift in attention is a resilient movement, as I am moving myself away from fear by rooting back into my own faith in the process. This addresses the fears in the room with movement toward connection. I share with them my framework around couples work, seeking to build the conditions for enough safety among those in the room, including me, to allow a conversation about the problem to emerge in a way different than it gets experienced in their lives now.

I ask them each to talk about how she experiences the stuck place when they are in relational conflict, the place they refer to as their "knot". Beverly feels tight and tense, though she is often unaware of this until she feels her muscles relax when she moves out of the knot. This feeling is old and familiar for her. Before Anne, she has never been able to acknowledge it while in this stuck place. She has acknowledged it a few times with Anne, which has led to reconnection. She speaks of this giving her hope. Anne feels, when in her stuck place, "like a stone," unable to function or respond at all. What generally moves her out of this space is going to work, where others interact with her and she feels herself coming alive again, and senses her "goodness" as others respond to this in her. These are both examples of relational resilience, even if this movement isn't always functioning within their dyadic knot. I feel a surge of faith in the work we are embarking on together.

*Session Three*: Anne begins the session by raising the possibility of seeing me for individual therapy, as she had been looking, without success, for a good match for some time. She then expresses some jealousy, sense of exclusion, around Beverly's intense therapy work with her individual therapist, who had referred the couple to me. I am surprised by this request, caught off guard, and feel immediate resistance. But in an effort to "go slowly," I share my concerns about my capacity to work with her individually and stay completely committed to the relationship. I then suggest we all sit with the question until the next session.

*Session Four*: I get my first glance of the relational impasse in action, as they both come in angry. Beverly feels exposed by Anne's talking last time about the intensity of her relationship with her therapist. Anne expressed little in the session, saying she felt "whipped" by Beverly's anger and unable to feel safe. There is less listening going on in the room . . . I talk about safety, inquire how we might move together toward this, but little loosens. I name what I see, and "sit with them in their disconnection." I remind us all of their capacity for resilience, holding the relationship and my faith in them.

*Sessions Five/Six*: They report they didn't talk to each other for 24 hours after the last session, an unusual event. Beverly reports feeling better about the relationship since a reconnecting talk during the week. Anne is still harboring some anger about the last session which she isn't ready to discuss. In Session Six, Anne reports that they are doing a bit better, while Beverly disagrees. In the midst of some family of origin material, Anne suddenly flies into a rage around her sense of innate goodness being attacked by Beverly's anger, as it had felt in her own family. Beverly feels angry in turn, citing a message she feels from Anne that she shouldn't have the feelings she has, a message familiar from her own family experience. The knot was pulled tight, the anger at full blast. This is what no one had ever seen before; what Anne was concerned would not happen in therapy. Anne lets loose her rage, and the world doesn't fall apart. Beverly speaks her feelings and is not silenced. I am aware that by sitting with their disconnection, I am weaving a net that holds all of us in connection, with ample space for reconnection. I am reasonably at ease. I pay attention to breathing easily and fully through this sudden storm.

As sessions continue, they vary from comfortable connection to more tense conflict, but the conflict is coming into the therapy room more easily and with less fear. The knot really is loosening. They report their conflict between sessions as less frequent, and when it does occur, usually feeling terrible and followed by a reconnecting experience or conversation that leaves them with new insights to bring to the therapy work. Rather than despair about being caught in the knot, I hear more and more enthusiasm and zest from the process of loosening the knot or avoiding it pulling tight in the first place. Their relational images around the knot are changing.

This couple went on to deal with significant outside stressors that prompted continuing struggles around conflict. A metaphor of the relationship emerged as a ship adrift on a huge sea. With each storm it weathers, its strength and stability become more evident. As we ended our three years of work together, Anne and Beverly had learned to sail the ship, to set a course together, to rely on their differing skills to do the work, and to value the efforts to maintain the ship together. They had developed relational practices that came to assume the function of supported vulnerability and safe space the therapy hour had once provided.

Their relational growth was also my relational growth. My capacity for holding faith in the process was enriched and invigorated both at home and with other clients, as a direct result of my work with Anne and Beverly. This example of couples work from an RCT perspective involves building the conditions for movement and an ongoing relational resilience, consciously nurturing the relational skills already developed and recognizing and naming the obstacles to movement.

## Lesbian Relationships in Context

Therapy with lesbian couples is far more like therapy with other couples than different. Broad areas of typical presenting issues and intervention include: communication problems or impasses; differences in values and expectations around money, sex, parenting, or relationships with family of origin; and the impact of environmental stressors on the relationship. Still, there are unique contextual patterns that can emerge in working with lesbian couples that require the therapist to have a flexibility of perspective, and a base of knowledge, in order to respond authentically. The two dimensions illustrated here arise from the broader cultural contexts of heterosexism and patriarchy. The dimensions of race (Eldridge & Barrett, 2003) and class also have significant impact on couple dynamics, but are beyond the scope of this chapter.

### Coming Out in a Heterosexual World: Stages of Identity Development

Although norms are slowly shifting in pockets of Western culture, most children are raised in a family that assumes the children's heterosexuality. The coming out process for any non-heterosexual person in our society involves a developmental process of loss and reconstruction in the face of the cultural heterosexual assumption. While many specific identity development models have been offered in the literature, they all involve a movement from an internal assumption of heterosexuality to a growing awareness, varying stages of acknowledgment, acceptance, and perhaps to an affirmation of a non-heterosexual identity. This internal process is intertwined with an external and interpersonal process that includes behavioral exploration and experimentation, acknowledgment to others (disclosure), experience of various responses to disclosure, and seeking communities of support. As in any developmental process, the external experiences each influence and create context for the internal process, while the internal experience influences the external process.

The progression along this identity development process, with internal and external dimensions, is fraught with opportunities for shaming, denial, and violence. The confrontation with homophobia and heterosexual privilege is disempowering, while finding pockets of support and affirmation can provide welcomed relief and even be empowering. Strategies of isolation or chronic disconnection can be particularly well developed in both members of a lesbian couple, depending on their individual experiences with, and progress along, the development of an affirmative sexual identity. The chronic experience of hiding part of oneself, being "in the closet," can also be a challenge to experiencing and expressing oneself authentically. In these ways, the context of heterosexual bias and homophobia can contribute to the unique shape of a lesbian couple's dynamic.

It is an understanding of these sexual identity processes, and an assessment of each partner's experience with them, that provides the therapist with a glimpse into the dyadic tensions that become evident in couples therapy. These may arise from partners at different stages of this process, or choosing different ways to move through these processes. It may color the understanding of the family-of-origin influences on the couple. Even when lesbian identity development seems a non-issue with a couple, tensions can re-emerge when the couple faces developmental challenges such as becoming parents, having the choice to legally marry, or caring for extended family members.

A common scenario is the lesbian couple that has found great relief, support and sense of intimacy within their relationship that shelters them from the wider hostility of a heterosexist environment. They may have family members or co-workers who know of their relationship, but they don't have the community of affirmation that is needed to feel supported – safe enough – to address the scary issues within the relationship. The retreat to an "it's us against the world" stance can inhibit the capacity for relational growth. Couples therapy is often the first step toward a support system for the relationship, and I always work toward helping the couple to expand their circle of supporters (cheering section) for the relationship.

## Conceptualization of Marriage and Family Constructs

The national political and social context for same-sex couples has been changing dramatically over the past two decades. The legal realities vary considerably from state to state in the US, and even from locality to locality. The debate is a national one. On one side is a reification of traditional values, reinforced with religious doctrine and fervor, resulting in the passage of DOMA (the Defense of Marriage Act) in 1996. DOMA expressly defines marriage as the legal union of one man and one woman, and states that no state or other political entity is required to recognize a same-sex relationship treated as a marriage in another state. Furthermore, it codifies that the federal government will not recognize any same-sex marriage or union for the purposes of federal benefits (including social security benefits, filing of joint tax returns, or insurance benefits for government employees).

On the other side of the debate is the push for marriage equality, the right to civil marriage for same-sex couples. As of this writing, 48% of Americans live in a state (or city or county) that recognizes some form of legal same-sex relationships.[2] Ten states now recognize full legal equality, 11 states recognize some form of domestic partnership or civil union, and since 1993, all states have taken some position on marriage equality by either expressly banning it or recognizing some form of same-sex relationship. Currently, the state's marriage equality position is a prominent issue in at least 30 states.

Less apparent than the rhetoric about wedding bells and "I dos" has been the undercurrent of the "gayby boom," which has created much of the momentum for marriage equality. Same-sex couples, the majority of them female couples, have been raising children for generations. However, legal recognition of two same-sex parents for a child was not possible. Adoption laws required the biological mother, or the custodial mother, to forfeit her rights as a parent in order for another woman to adopt her child. In the 1980s, states began to allow second parent adoptions that permitted same-sex partners of an adoptive or biological parent to adopt without terminating the existing partner's rights. Thus, it is the legal recognition of the relationship between parent and child that is the predecessor to the equal marriage movement. The "best interests of the children" was the motivation, as expressed in this important 2002 statement by the American Academy of Pediatrics:

> Children who are born to or adopted by 1 member of a same-sex couple deserve the security of 2 legally recognized parents. Therefore, the American Academy of Pediatrics supports legislative and legal efforts to provide the possibility of adoption of the child by the second parent or co-parent in these families.
>
> (American Academy of Pediatrics, Committee on Psychosocial
> Aspects of Child and Family Health, p. 339)

Depending on state statutes, the right to marry provides both members of a married couple with the presumption of being parents of children born "after the legal marriage."

It is important to note that winning the right to marry has created considerable conflict within the non-heterosexual world. Many feminists view marriage as a tool of patriarchy, a heterosexual trap, especially for women. Most lesbians never thought they would have to struggle with the now legal option to marry, and the shift has left a profound confusion. At the same time, there is jubilation over winning the right to marry as a reflection of the feminist values of social justice and equal rights. It represents a movement toward greater recognition and privilege for same-sex couples and families, though without federal recognition, same-sex marriages are far from "equal."

## Cathy and Debbie

Cathy and Debbie, both in midlife, came to therapy five years into their relationship seeking to improve their communication capacities and to stop the sense of "drifting apart" that they had both been feeling for some time. Cathy was articulate in describing her longing for more genuine conversations with Debbie, frequently seeking to process things and frustrated that Debbie just didn't function that way. Debbie described herself as "conflict-avoidant," and wanted to learn to bring things up with Cathy in a more timely way, but got anxious about creating conflict. She also described herself as a caregiver and always busy "doing" something. In sessions, Cathy tended to talk about what she felt or worried about over the week, while Debbie tended to describe what they did, or what happened, since the last session.

They described other difference such as: Debbie is neat and concerned about tidiness, while Cathy is more "spread out" at home and doesn't seem to notice the clutter; Debbie enjoys going out and socializing, getting exercise, and wanting sex, while Cathy is a homebody and more introverted and sedentary in nature. They also each described a history of depression and anxiety, with Cathy still recovering from a severe depressive episode, and Debbie struggling with significant anxiety that she had at times medicated with alcohol. Debbie had been sober for 20 years, and had recently begun to experiment with "drinking safely." Cathy expressed considerable unease with Debbie drinking at all, and described her own history of growing up with an alcoholic parent.

Early sessions in this therapy served to highlight and articulate both the differences between them in style and perceptions, and how reactive each felt when her style was somehow seen as contributing to the other's hurt or frustration. Also apparent to me, and named in the therapy, was the underlying longing each felt to restore a sense of closeness and safety in the relationship. Sessions would some-times go in slow motion, as I interrupted a rising defensive argument by asking each to sit with their feelings and pay attention to their breathing and other bodily sensations. With practice, each became more able to tolerate this exercise, to notice their own feelings (and often associations), and to describe these in the session. Time after time, we used the familiar defensive impasse as a signal to pause, pay attention to what was going on inside, and acknowledge and share what was discovered. I would participate in this process as an image or metaphor arose for me that might help them articulate their own experiences.

For Cathy, this practice was intriguing, the slower pace welcomed, and the shift in focus still nourished her interest in processing the experience she was having. It also served to illustrate that her experience was one way to experience the relationship – not the only way. For Debbie, the exercise was more challenging, as slowing down the pace of the dialogue and sitting with the moment served to heighten her anxiety considerably. I would often prompt her directly and give concrete suggestions to help her articulate her experience while acknowledging how little practice she had had in this while growing up the eldest of several children in a somewhat chaotic family dynamic. Though Debbie sometimes complained that she was too often "on the hot seat," she also valued the sense of acceptance she experienced in the room for whatever she was able to share, and knew that she could take herself off the hot seat whenever she wished – which she frequently did. Cathy learned a great deal from listening to Debbie in a new way – a less defensive and less judgmental way – which allowed her to understand Debbie's "conflict avoidance" in a less personal way. Both were given specific suggestions for how to practice what we were doing in the session on their own. Debbie was good at this and would bring in a report on times she practiced this. Cathy eventually asked if she could take notes in session, as she realized she never remembered what the suggestions were during the week.

Three years into therapy, Debbie and Cathy began to discuss marriage. Their communication had improved, and they had pulled together to help each other deal with significant losses in each of their extended families. They were learning how to appreciate their differences and rely on their complementary strengths to nourish a stronger "we" that held them during uncertain times. They had negotiated Cathy's relapse into a paranoid depression, and Debbie's bout with alcohol, without pulling apart. Their capacity to communicate about the impact of these events on each of them, and their trust in their bond, resulted in greater resilience and recovery from these depths.

Cathy responded to the notion of marriage with a sense of constriction or being trapped, and would close down. While she didn't feel trapped in her relationship with Debbie, she began to recognize a connection with how she perceived her parents' marriage – an alcoholic stalemate. Debbie wanted a way to legitimize their relationship and to declare it more publicly. She was involved in a church community that valued same-sex relationships, and her experience of committed lesbian relationships, and lesbian families with children, was expanding. Debbie's family lived fairly near, often spent time with the two of them, and had accepted Cathy into the family. They had even asked Debbie about the possibility of marriage after same-sex marriage was in the news and became legal.

Cathy's family lived farther away and was less communicative in general. Though they knew about her relationship with Debbie, Cathy had never discussed the relationship with any of them. In digging deeper, it seemed that Cathy feared the judgment that she expected from her siblings on the prospect of her marrying a woman. She had also had a long-standing relational image of herself as "never married." Challenging this deeply held assumption was very unsettling for Cathy. Yet the increasing sense of space and movement in their relational dynamics decreased her fears about "what if Debbie starts drinking?" or "what if she leaves me during one of my depressive episodes?" Developing a joint understanding and agreement around Debbie's use of alcohol was a precursor to the vows they later wrote for their wedding, some two years after we began to discuss marriage in the therapy.

This couple illustrates the impact of social isolation in which there was little affirmation in the commitment they had with one another, even though some family was very comfortable and welcoming of them as a couple. Debbie's involvement in a religious community that actively affirmed the lesbian families in the congregation was a significant shift in her social context. Over time, this strengthened her resolve to authentically express her desire to get married despite her awareness of the conflict and immediate disconnection her truth would trigger. Cathy, more reclusive, did not attend the church services, but was still affected by the expansion of Debbie's world. Cathy's challenge was to face the fears of condemnation, and self-condemnation, that had prompted a split between her world with Debbie and her family of origin. By opening to the conversation, and the possibility of marriage, she began to mend that split and affirm the strength and depth of her relationship with Debbie by discussing their marriage plans with family.

As is often the case, family members who are unfamiliar or uncomfortable with same-sex relationships find ways to not be able to come to the marriage ceremony or celebration. This can be enormously hurtful, and is sometimes handled by not inviting family. I often encourage partners to identify who will represent their family at the ceremony. It might be one sibling, or an aunt, a grown child, or a friend or group of friends who are the woman's chosen family. The power of having witnesses and supporters on "both sides of the family" is often not fully understood until after the ceremony has occurred.

# The Effects of Social Context in Therapy with Lesbian Couples

RCT posits that power and the dynamics of privilege are formative in shaping individual development. Members of any marginalized group know the impact of shaming, the effort of the dominant power groups to isolate and silence the differing realities of the non-dominant groups. Marginalization and isolation are effective tools of disempowerment. Living in a heterosexist and homophobic culture places significant stress on lesbian relationships. Undoubtedly, strength and courage can arise in the face of these challenges. But depression, a sense of deviance, and the shame of feeling unworthy are also sequelae of social marginalization and oppression. These processes can underscore the ways lesbian partners connect with, and disconnect from, each other.

An understanding of lesbian identity development, as well as the historically oppressive and currently shifting political and cultural context, is an important perspective for the therapist in serving lesbian couples. These two processes reflect environmental realities that are often in movement for lesbian couples, that vary widely from couple to couple, and that need to be assessed and understood by the clinician and the couple together to promote optimal growth in relationship.

The increasing validation of same-sex relationships, particularly with legal recognition of same-sex marriage, is an important step toward eliminating social discrimination and moving toward social justice. Couples therapy with lesbians in this transitional period will undoubtedly echo the shifting values, increasing social acceptance and increasing appreciation of same-sex couples and families. This serves as a hopeful context within which to support the relational growth of lesbian couples at the same time that we foster essential social change, determined to bring about a larger movement toward social justice.

## Notes

1   *Goodridge v. Dept. of Public Health*, 798 N.E.2d 941 (Mass. 2003).
2   Marriage Equality USA (www.marriageequality.org/current-status-map), February 14, 2013.

## References

American Academy of Pediatrics, Committee on Psychosocial Aspects of Child and Family Health (2002). Coparent or second-parent adoption by same-sex parents. *Pediatrics*, 109, 339–340.

Bergman, S. & Surrey, J. (1994). Couple therapy: A relational approach. *Work in Progress No 66*. Wellesley, MA: Stone Center Working Papers.

Eldridge, N.S. & Barrett, S.E. (2003). Biriacial lesbian-led adoptive families. In L.B. Silverstein & T.J. Goodrich (Eds.), *Feminist family therapy: Empowerment in social context* (pp. 307–318). Washington, DC: American Psychological Association.

Kramer, G. (2007). *Insight Dialogue: The Interpersonal Path to Freedom*. Boston, MA: Shambhala Publications.

Miller, J. (1976). *Toward a new psychology of women*. Boston, MA: Beacon Press.

Miller, J. & Stiver, I. (1997). *The healing connection: How women form relationships in therapy and in life*. Boston, MA: Beacon Press.

Shem, S. & Surrey, J. (1998). *We Have to Talk: Healing Dialogues between Women and Men*. New York: Basic Books.

Surrey, J. ( 2005). Relational therapy, relational mindfulness. In C. Germer, R. Siegel, & P. Fulton (Eds.), *Mindfulness and Psychotherapy*. New York: Guilford Press.

# 7

# GAY MALE COUPLE WORK

## The Value of Individual and Group Therapy

*David M. Shannon*

## Relational-Cultural Theory (RCT) and Gay Couples

Relational-Cultural Theory (RCT) offers an important and unique lens with which to view the dynamics of gay male development as well as gay men's most intimate relationships. Where other theories and perspectives contribute frameworks and insights rooted in systemic, behavioral, family and psychodynamic processes (Johnson, 2004; Greenan & Tunnell, 2003), the Relational-Cultural model places the struggles, successes and growth of gay male couples clearly and explicitly in connection. By looking at gay men's connections throughout their lives, including with the dominant culture, we are able to recognize the unique strengths, challenges and complexities facing gay men as they grow and thrive in relationships.

Working with gay men on couple issues can be done in multiple treatment modalities. While the most obvious place to do this work is in couple therapy, valuable relational work does not necessarily involve both men in a couple being in the same room with a therapist. For a variety of reasons, not all individuals in relationships will want or initiate a couple therapy process. As a result, much of a couple's work can be done in individual treatment as well as group therapy. In this chapter, I will primarily be discussing the therapeutic couple work done in individual and group therapy. As a result of this formal, therapeutic work, as well as the work that they have done informally on their own and in connection with others, many gay men have been able to transform the pain and shame that is detailed below. They have been able to grow and heal in ways that enable them to experience rich and loving relationships.

Though laced with the strengths and resilience of gay men, this is a clinical chapter which is focused on relational struggles and difficulties so that they, too, may be healed and transformed.

## Cultural Shame

It is important to locate the reality of gay male coupledom in a larger cultural context. Both consciously and unconsciously, gay men in intimate relationships are impacted by the sociopolitical realities in which they live. Although we live in a time where there are increasing civil rights protections and victories for LGBT (lesbian, gay, bisexual and transgender) people across the United States, the extent of those protections and victories varies quite a bit from state to state, city to city and municipality to municipality. The ever-present realities of heterosexism and homophobia must be recognized and acknowledged. Heterosexism involves the subtle, yet clear privilege and power that are unearned (McIntosh, 1988). Laird & Green (1996) define homophobia as "irrational fear, prejudice, and willingness to discriminate against lesbians and gay men" (p. 4). The ever-present realities of heterosexism and homophobia, manifestations of a power-over model (Miller & Stiver, 1997), have a trickle-down effect; the legacies they leave for gay men impact all parts of their lives and nowhere more profoundly than in their most intimate relationships.

As Niolon (2011) notes, the stress and strain of institutionalized prejudice makes itself known in almost every area of a gay couple's life. Decision-making around housing, employment, healthcare, traveling, financial planning, religious participation and child-rearing is affected. Gay men must carefully consider their choices and negotiate their involvements so as to manage stigma and minimize harm and discrimination to themselves as individuals and to their relationship. Implicit—and oftentimes explicit—in this cultural prejudice and discrimination is the belief that gay relationships are less than heterosexual ones and therefore not worth the standard protections afforded other relationships. Their relationships, they are told, are unrecognized and unrecognizable, less than, unacceptable and unworthy. What is transmitted by this legal discrimination, then, is a strong sense of society's disapproval and cultural shame.

## RCT and Gay Male Development

### Gender Socialization, Homophobia and the Gay Boy

All young people are socialized with clear gender expectations. Although some assert that our society is evolving and becoming more flexible, most would agree that children are still subject to age-old messages about what it means to be a "healthy", "normal" and "acceptable" boy or girl. These messages have profound implications for relational growth and development.

For the average boy, the message is clear, firm and often unyielding: to be a "healthy" male means to be able to function autonomously, separately and powerfully so that he can demonstrate his self-sufficiency, strength and sexuality. To be a "normal" male means to not make mistakes, want support or ask for help so that he can project his power, independence and invulnerability; to be an "acceptable" male means to embody stoicism and disconnect from his emotional self to survive, compete and, more importantly, achieve and excel.

This socialization has grave implications for men's presence in relationships. Society's historical notions of maleness and masculinity stress males' power and ability to assert control in all aspects of their lives including their connections with others. As Bergman (1991) notes, most boys are taught about connections with an emphasis on them*selves* and perhaps themselves in relation to other people (especially via points of comparison and competition). What is lacking is an emphasis on the fluid and dynamic *process* of the relationship between people. In order to be the healthy, normal and acceptable male described above, boys are taught how to distance and disconnect from themselves and others, as well as the very active and engaging process of connecting and relating.

Gay boys have been raised as most other boys have; at the same time, there are often dynamics that are unique to their experiences. Most gay men describe how they knew, from a very early age, that something was different about them. Though at the time they may not have been able to identify this difference as having anything to do with sexual orientation or identity, they were clear that it set them apart from other boys. Many gay men do in fact report that they were aware of being attracted to other males when they were very young. Some also say that they were more sensitive and gentle than other boys. Many report that they were not as athletically inclined or interested in many hobbies or recreational activities as other boys. Others remember that other people seemed to be almost preoccupied with them and disappointed in them; they recall being evaluated and told that they were not as good as "normal" boys.

Sadly, these differences—observed, evaluated and judged by both self and others—have often been seen as negative and wrong. Most, if not all, gay men remember receiving early messages about what it means to be gay. Many gay men say that they learned from these early messages (delivered by their families, faith communities, teachers, friends, media and politicians) that their differences were in fact problems. Throughout the years, homosexuality and all things "gay" have been associated with being unnatural, disordered, deviant, sick, strange, weak, isolated and undesirable. Some people say that they don't remember hearing any explicit messages about what "gay" meant. This silence, in and of itself, is a message. One gay man remembered a dinner table conversation as a teen when his father began talking about a female cousin's girlfriend. While serving dinner, his mother simply said, "Ssh" to the father, shutting down all conversation. The message to this growing gay teen was, "We don't talk about gay things. It's *that* bad."

The homophobia and heterosexism described above generate biases and perpetuate stereotypes. Additionally, these messages become what Patricia Hill Collins (1990; cited in Jordan, 2009) describes as "controlling images". These images, created and proliferated by a dominant culture, become dictates for how people are seen by others and, naturally, have implications for how people are viewed and experienced in relationships. Similarly, they are fed to individuals and oppressed groups themselves and impact how those people see and experience themselves and each other. *The Sick Homosexual, The Deviant* and *The Lonely Gay Man* are but a few of the controlling images created and transmitted by and through our culture. The implications for relationships are profound and will be explored in detail below.

## *The Birth of Shame and Isolation*

Societal messages about homosexuality and being gay become more complicated for male adolescents who begin to feel—through the hormones surging through their bodies and the emotions they begin to experience—that they are gay. They begin to notice the very natural pull to other boys. Where heterosexual adolescents are permitted and even openly encouraged to explore these feelings via dating, gay adolescents often have limited support, if any support at all. Many gay men recall having this burst of feelings and not knowing what to do with it. Although most did not get explicit guidance and support to explore intimacy and their identity, they did get clear guidance nonetheless in the form of the early messages described above. The key message was to not be gay *at all costs*. Gay boys remembered what they had been told: that homosexuality and being gay meant *unnatural, disordered, deviant, sick, strange, weak, isolated and undesirable.* More importantly, the controlling images, visions of what it means to be connected to others, became further internalized as homophobia and shame.

Many gay men speak poignantly of feeling exposed when they were younger. They describe the frequent commentaries and judgments from others as contributing to a pervasive experience of self-consciousness. They thus began to move through the world believing, because they were repeatedly and vehemently told so, that they lacked worth, value, respect and honor. And, for those gay boys and for legions of gay boys before them, this became *felt* as badness and worthlessness. Shame was born in gay boys.

In this way, and as part of their learning about society's views on being gay, many gay boys also learned that their differentness meant vulnerability— a vulnerability that, as Jordan (1989) describes, in an unsafe world, is "an invitation to possible danger" (p. 3). Many gay men tell stories, their life stories, of their differentness being met with scoffing, slights, exclusion, isolation, harassment and violence. Their differentness, and thus their very selves, were met with relational ruptures, disconnections and violations.

Jordan (1989, p. 6) summarizes the experience of shame:

> While shame involves extreme self-consciousness, it also signals powerful relational longings and awareness of the other's response. There is a loss of the sense of empathic possibility, others are not experienced as empathic, and the capacity for self-empathy is lost. One feels unworthy of love, not because of some discrete action, which

would be the cause for guilt, but because one is defective or flawed in some essential way.

Many gay boys, then, were taught that they were not worthy of connection, and this became internalized and felt as shame.

### The Central Relational Paradox, Strategies of Disconnection and Authenticity

In order to protect themselves, and in many cases in order to literally survive, many gay boys learned that they needed to conceal themselves. When gay boys received the messages described above about what it means to be gay, and when their shame and anxiety intensified, they learned that they needed to keep more and more of themselves out of connection in order to stay in connection. This central relational paradox became a relational guide and gave birth to strategies of disconnection (Jordan, 2009). Many gay boys were repeatedly shown that their sensitivity, gentleness and interests, the ways that they connected with others in the world, were sources of suffering. Feeling the very natural pull to be in relationship with the people in their world, they also felt and experienced the danger and threat in those relationships.

Many gay men learned to protect themselves by disconnecting from parts of themselves in order to connect with other boys. They may have learned to disconnect from their feelings in ways that denied, repressed, suppressed and otherwise concealed—consciously and not—all the new and natural (and wonderful) ways they felt sensations in their bodies. They may have disconnected their feelings from their day-to-day, visible way of living. They may have learned how to visibly have friendships with other boys while secretly fantasizing about having sexual relationships with those same boys. In this way, they may have split their sexual feelings from their emotions. Their sexual feelings were felt as dangerous; in other words, they were dangerous insofar that they became *expressed*. So, many gay boys learned to not express what they felt as a way of protecting themselves and maintaining safety. And they learned to disconnect from what they wanted, and what they needed, to live full and vital lives.

Gay boys may also have learned to hide and disconnect from the pain of relational betrayal and isolation. Gay boys who have faced the ruptures and violations described above—and by mosts account there are many—tried to make sense of both their treatment at the hands of hostile others and the subsequent shame that they felt. Many boys became confused (Heyward, 1989) and, in attempting to understand what was happening, turned inward. They may have blamed themselves, worried that they did something wrong, considered changing themselves or simply ruminated over mistreatment that was impossible to understand and reconcile. In these ways, they continually learned to move to an internal place while, at the same time, creating distance from their feelings and their sense of vulnerability. They may have turned away from their internal pain and toward the external pursuit of being the nicest, the smartest, the most helpful, the most successful and "the best little boy in the world" (Tobias, 1998).

This relational template of hiding and secret-keeping therefore dictates that they keep parts of themselves out of relationships. They may have learned to be quiet, to shut up, to shut down, to fake it, to mask it, to become invisible and to fly under the radar. They may have also learned to dress it up, to become bigger—in personality and in appearance—to stand out, to excel, to convince, to prove and to perform. In essence, they learned that who they were and how they were in connection to others were not good enough; they learned that they were unacceptable. They learned shame: "a felt sense of unworthiness to be in connection, a deep sense of unloveability, with the ongoing awareness of how very much one want to connect with others" (Jordan, 1989, p. 6).

Thus, many gay boys, now men, learned that they needed to be inauthentic in the name of safety and connection. They learned that they needed to be certain ways—and more importantly, that they needed to *not* be certain ways— if they were going to survive in the world. They soon realized that their parents, siblings, classmates, neighbors, religious leaders, extended family and strangers on the street would hurt, hate or otherwise reject them if they really knew them. Thus, they began to withdraw, create distance from others and disconnect from relationships. Some also learned to hide, keep secrets and turn inward. Though they may have remained connected to family members, peers and others, their whole selves remained outside the scope of a healthy and honest relationship. And, in the midst of this 'to connect, I must disconnect' paradigm, they often felt great anxiety, which often leads to a greater experience of isolation and shame.

### *Isolation and Turning away from Connections*

This turning inward, along with the anxiety, hiding and pretending, can evolve into a pronounced and pervasive *turning away* and *separating from* and, rather unconsciously and in pursuit of protection and safety, *moving toward isolation*.

Isolation amplifies and expands one's sense of inadequacy, difference, anxiety and felt sense of wrongness (Jordan, 1989). Many gay boys, having been overly visible to others and their evaluations and judgments, learned to question their very essence and doubt their thoughts and feelings. This can lead to a deep and pervasive sense of disempowerment and difficulties and even inabilities to bring oneself fully into relationship with others (Jordan, 1989; Miller & Stiver, 1997). Specifically, they may have lost or been deprived of knowing how to talk, listen, ask questions and show themselves to others.

The relational implications and images become quite clear. Many gay boys grow into gay men who consciously think, and perhaps more importantly, consciously and unconsciously feel and act in ways that reflect the following beliefs:

96

- To be in relationship means I must hide, create distance and pull away (Jordan, 1989).
- To be connected to others means I must show only certain parts of myself.
- In order to show only parts of myself and feel OK with that, I must disconnect from my feelings.
- To disconnect from my feelings, I need to shut down, numb out or change how I feel.
- In order to disconnect from how I feel, I need to be on guard for anything and anyone who stirs my vulnerability, who taps into how I feel.
- To be in relationship and connect with others means I need to disconnect from my feelings—from my pain and shame—by eating too much, by looking a certain way, by drinking and using drugs to excess, by having sex, by being the smartest, by being the nicest, by being the star, by . . .

### *Biased Messages about Gay Relationships*

The cultural shame created by heterosexism and homophobia sends clear messages to all people and, as discussed above, to gay men in particular. The gay male couple hear these messages keenly and in specific ways that impact their relationships. Though many gay male couples protect themselves, each other and their relationships through the buffers of supportive families, friends, cities, neighborhoods and employers, not all are able to create these worlds. And even if they are able to do so, this cultural shame sometimes makes itself known through internalized homophobia that shows up in a particularly unique and tailored way for the gay couple.

Many gay men recall the clear messages they received when they were younger about what it means to be a gay *person*. What was often absent was what it means to be in a gay *relationship*. The silence and invisibility around this is both striking and telling. The widespread stereotype of The Lonely Gay Man is a controlling image and code for a man who lives his life in isolation; it dictates that the gay man lives apart from any significant, lasting emotional, sexual and romantic relationship with another man and apart from the support and acceptance of others. The messages are clear for gay couples: intimate relationships between men do not exist; intimate relationships between men, even if they do exist, do not warrant mention or discussion because they don't last in any visible or meaningful way. And, if they do manage to last, they are unacceptable and less than heterosexual relationships.

What the gay men in relationship hear and see, then, is that their relationship, which feels solid and good and healthy, is not those things at all. In addition, their relationship (often not even seen or recognized as a relationship by others) is not sustainable. And, to make it last, they must fight against all odds. Both gay men in relationship and single gay men sometimes feel society's lack of support (at best) and expectation of failure (at worst). Odets (1998) addresses this cultural power play when he describes the reality of gay men

97

receiving more support over the last 25 years for dying rather than living, thriving and growing in loving and healthy relationships.

### Hiding in Relationships with Male Partners

The cultural shame that the dominant culture has instilled in gay men via messages about what it means to be both gay and in a gay relationship has a deep and lasting impact. As previously discussed, many gay boys grow into men who have learned that survival and relationships with others must be rooted, to various degrees, in secrecy, hiding and silence. Vulnerability is to be avoided. Sharing thoughts, feelings and self is seen—and, more importantly, felt—as dangerous and threatening. The experiences and behaviors described above, coupled with the isolation of inauthenticity, often lead to greater feelings of shame and worthlessness. And this cycle—one filled with anxiety and hyper-vigilance—continues.

The relational challenge is clear: men who, when they follow their deepest emotional, physical and sexual longings, wish to connect with other men often come face to face with their sense of shame. Gay men also report that other boys and men were often the ones who transmitted cultural messages of maleness and masculinity to them. Likewise, other boys and men were often the ones who sanctioned and punished gay boys through the hurling of anti-gay words, judgments and often violent behaviors. And even if this never happened, the threat of it happening was ever-present. Thus, the one he desires and deeply wants to connect with, another man, is also the one who hurt him when he was younger. This deeply longed for other becomes the one who he has hid from and, rather unconsciously, must continue to hide from in order to protect himself from the dangers and terrors of connection.

### Relational Strengths

Gay men are survivors of historical oppression and warriors for personal freedom. Most have developed relational strengths and abilities born of their suffering. The core of these strengths is the realization, and conviction even, of the power of connection due to the pain of disconnection and isolation (Jordan, 2009). Many gay men describe having a special affinity for the underdog and others who may have struggled, like they did, against all odds. This is a deep compassion comprising true kindness and understanding. In order to feel this deep compassion, many gay men have developed a sense of empathy and an ability to tune in and be sensitive to others. As scanners of safety born of their own need and desire for survival, many gay men are natural observers. In addition, they have become considerate in the truest sense of the word. In order to move toward greater connections with others, they have needed to consider both themselves and others' responses to them. These skills, of tuning into and considering another in relationship, are critical components of any mutual relationship.

For generations, gay men have created a web of friendship and support networks that have sustained them. Due to the cultural bias previously described, gay men have had to, in secretive and undercover ways, create and nurture their relationships. They have developed skills at reading cues and communicating in subtle and non-verbal ways that met both their needs and the needs of their newfound connections. Related to this, they have helped create a thriving culture that has helped support and deepen these connections. Gay men have also often been known and honored for their sense of humor. Many describe honing this through their survival skills. Their ongoing observations of others and self, along with the need to deflect hostile attention and win the support of others, have led them to nurture this sense of humor which, in turn, often allows them to weather relational struggles, repair ruptures and reconnect with those they love.

Odets (1998) speaks of the "tenacity and courage so many [gay men] bring to *becoming themselves* – to forging lives, including relationships, that express who they really feel themselves to be" (emphasis in original). Through coming out and claiming their sexual identities, gay men have reshaped their regard for themselves. Moreover, they have reconnected with what they feel, what they want and what they need. As many gay men have understood and embraced their identities, they have moved from a place of deep disempowerment to conviction and pride. This has often been translated into healthy assertiveness and a desire to be seen and heard. Many gay men have nurtured the ability to speak up for both themselves and others. This desire to have an impact, coupled with the felt sense of others' impact on them, is at the heart of relational mutuality.

In these ways, the stage is set for gay men to enter into healthy relationships. Through their coming out processes, they have moved from places of internal and external isolation and disconnection to repair and authentic connection. The hallmark of gay men's sexual identity development is mindfulness. Their desires and abilities to be aware of their deepest feelings, to acknowledge and honor them, without judgment, are mindfulness in action. These are the same skills that gay men bring to the inevitable joys, challenges and stumbles of loving and growth-filled relationships.

### *Psychological and Relational Impact of Cultural Shame on Gay Male Relationships*

What is the day-to-day psychological and relational impact of this larger, pervasive cultural shame for the gay men who have formed a relationship and seek to connect intimately?

As detailed above, many gay boys have not had opportunities to safely and openly learn the skills of intimacy. They have not been able to develop ways to effectively flirt, approach, date, talk, express, listen, negotiate sex, experience rejection and navigate intimacy in ways that other young people have.

Essentially, they have been deprived of opportunities to be seen and to be authentic by fully representing themselves (Miller & Stiver, 1997). The result is many gay men who feel that their development has been interrupted and stunted by a pervasive cultural bias. One gay man spoke about his upset at finally learning how to feel confident and not shameful as he negotiated dating in middle age. He described not learning as a young man how to be rejected as part of the dating process while knowing that he was "not a bad person" when he was rejected.

Second, the cultural expectation of failure for gay male relationships may enter gay men's psyche as an expectation of disappointment (Odets, 1998). In addition to messages about men (i.e. all males) needing to be independent, separate, self-sufficient, stoic and non-emotional, society sends messages about men in relationships (usually meaning heterosexual relationships). Given these expectations and messages, many boys grow into men who may not know how to be in mutually supportive and empathic relationships. Related to this, the prevailing belief is that men are motivated mostly by sex and, as a result, have difficulty being sexually faithful and devoted partners. Gay men reap the spoils of both of these prevailing stereotypes and expectations. Specifically, the teach-ing is that men cannot be emotional, faithful, supportive or connected in relationship. Some gay men may not have confidence that they can find another man with whom they connect; they may worry that a potential partner (or themselves) cannot maintain closeness in a relationship. They have been taught that, if and when two men come together, there is inherent distance. Gay men may date and have relationships with men, yet a cloud of cynicism and hopelessness may surround them and affect how they engage those men. They may feel angry, bitter, depressed and alone, and these feelings may become self-fulfilling prophecies by the ways they think and act.

The coupled gay men who have been told that their relationship will fail may leave their relationship prematurely when struggles begin; they may misread very common and expected relational ruptures as violations requiring the end of the relationship rather than as expected conflicts that require repair. This, in turn, may reinforce their expectation of disappointment. At the same time, the gay male couple may feel societal pressure to stay together beyond when they should for fear of fulfilling—in a way that seems very public and exposing—society's expectations of them. One gay man spoke about his sense of utter failure after the end of his relationship. He did feel sad, angry, hurt, rejected and a host of other ways that most people feel after break-ups. What seemed to reverberate most with him, though, was a sense that he had somehow failed, in a very core and personal way, because his relationship ended.

Third, many gay men describe how their struggles with internalized homophobia show up in their sexual relationships with the men with whom they are partnered. It is important to stress that internalized homophobia, though experienced and felt by gay men as shame, is the clear result of our culture's bias and prejudice. They experience and feel this shame not due to

100

any intrinsic, individual pathology, but rather due to society's pathological messages about being gay. Some gay men have spoken about how they have not integrated their rich and loving emotional relationship with their partner with an open, communicative and enjoyable sex life with him. "Dirty", "bad", "dark", "deviant" are words some men have used to describe how they view sex (in general) and, specifically, sex with their partners. Odets (1998) frames this challenge as one related to contamination: many gay men, wounded by homophobic messages about gay sex as "dirty" and "bad", want to protect the men they love and thus struggle to integrate sex into their emotional relationships.

This sexual dilemma is another manifestation of the central relational paradox. We often disconnect from ourselves when we feel we must divorce parts of ourselves that have been sources of rejection and isolation (Najavits, 2002). In other words, we learn that we need to keep more and more of ourselves out of connection in order to stay in connection (Miller & Stiver, 1997). Gay men may employ strategies of disconnection by setting aside that part of themselves. One's sexuality, feelings, longings and desires become separate not only from one's mental and emotional self, but from one's most significant, loving and potentially healing relationships. Though the ongoing experience of coming out begins to repair this, the individual gay man may carry his specific, sexual strategy of disconnection into his relationship with another man who also engages his own strategies. In addition, society often reduces gay male relationships to being primarily about sex and often about sex alone (i.e. just sex). Our dominant culture thinks about and presents a controlling image of gay men as singly focused and hypersexual. What is often left out of these depictions and views of sexual orientation is the reality that attraction—both same-sex and opposite-sex—is complex, varied and multidimensional. Gay men describe their attraction to other men as emotional, mental, biological, physical *and* sexual (not to mention all the other ways that we are attracted to people that are unnameable, but certainly knowable and felt).

## Treatment Implications: Individual and Group Therapy

Multiple treatment modalities can help support gay men and their most intimate relationships. Couple therapy is an obvious choice as both partners are present in the same room, displaying the strengths and limitations of each individual as well as the dynamic couple. This modality is limited, however, in that not all individuals in relationships will want or initiate a couple therapy process. As a result, much of a couple's work can be done in individual treatment (supported by periodic sessions with partners) as well as group therapy. In this section of the chapter, I will primarily be discussing the therapeutic couple work done in individual and group therapy. Individual work clearly gives men

101

opportunities to discuss relational ruptures and their roles and responsibilities. More importantly, though, individual work can deepen men's emotional experience of themselves, their therapists and the dynamic connection they co-create with their therapists. By experiencing, revealing and sharing their emotional vulnerability in connection with their therapists, men have experiences of mutual empathy where they and their therapists are moved and impacted by each other; they see and, more importantly, begin to feel and deeply know that they matter and that others matter to them (Jordan, 2009). This process of growth and respect in connection can be amplified in group settings where men actively experience relational movement in connection with other men (Jordan, 2009).

Gay men, like all psychotherapy clients, initiate therapy with a variety of presenting issues including depression, anxiety, trauma and abuse, and a host of compulsive issues. Relational issues, both past and present, underlie many of these presenting issues and are certainly critical to a client's healing, recovery and health.

Both individual and group therapy allow gay men to create, build and continually shape alive and unfolding relationships while observing and intentionally nurturing this process. With therapists as their guide and partners, men grow in their abilities to *feel* the vitality and acceptance of a vulnerable, healthy relationship, reshape relational images and move into greater authenticity while deepening intimacy skills. As therapists connect these experiences and skills back to their primary relationships, men are able to practice with their partners and experience felt differences in their most important relationships.

The heart of gay men's relational healing and transformation is their movement toward authenticity (Downs, 2005). The very real and mutual relationships they co-create in therapeutic encounters—with therapists and fellow group members—give them opportunities to be visible and to continue to reveal who they are over time. These ongoing experiences of connection provide moments where respect and trust are felt and shared, mutuality is experienced and clarity, zest, worth, movement and a desire for additional connections are born and nurtured (Miller and Stiver, 1997). Through these moments, they are able to learn skills, reshape early relational images and strategies and feel the healing power of healthy connections.

### *Reshaping Relational Images*

In individual and group therapy, gay men have opportunities to form new relational images. By being seen, accepted and not judged by his therapist, the gay man begins to experience vulnerability in connection. The therapeutic connection gives both him and his therapist an experience of mutuality in vulnerability. They are able to actively engage in a fluid process where they not only affect each other, but those impacts are honored, felt and spoken by both people. Therapeutic moment after therapeutic moment help to create a new relational image that ultimately allows the gay man to face the shame he feels born of homophobia. Instead of being judged, shunned and violated, the gay man begins to experience and feel safe in his vulnerability. As he does this more and more, he grows in his ability to risk being seen, as he knows and feels that he will be met, held and accepted in those risks. These experiences, explicitly noted time and time again by him and his therapist, accumulate to counter the messages born of his shame. He is told, he sees and, more importantly, he begins to feel more and more that there is nothing wrong with him. He is valuable and important. His thoughts, words and feelings have worth. He is capable of love and connection. This forms the foundation for further growth that is fostered in the therapeutic relationship and serves as a model for all dyadic connections, most importantly his most intimate relationships.

In group therapy, gay men are able to deepen this work with their peers who share the desire to connect in more authentic ways. This modality allows men to break the isolation of struggling in a relationship by coming together to connect with other men who want to grow in their abilities to be intimate. Most significantly, perhaps, the group process invites men to tune into and tend to multiple, dynamic relationships. Mutuality is created, negotiated and challenged as men partner to talk about their lives, reveal more and more of themselves, discuss how and why they continue to hide and keep secrets and share the impact that they have on each other. These empathic possibilities are navigated and ultimately, in all their complexities and messiness, relationships are created: gay men name how they feel when they move away from isolation and into the vulnerability and power of connection.

Specifically, how do their relational images and expectations of what it means to be part of a couple change as a result of the new relationships built in individual and group therapy? Gay men learn that being in a relationship no longer means that they must hide, create distance and pull away. Rather, they learn that they can risk, reveal and, with great vulnerability, trust and move closer to those they love. Being connected now means that they can learn to show and present more and more of themselves to their partners. Learning how to do this also shows that they can (and in fact must) connect to their feelings and to their wants and needs. They slowly learn that they no longer need to be vigilant, angry and on guard in relationships. Instead, they experience vulnerability in connection and break the link between vulnerability and violation. In relation to this, gay men learn that, in experiencing vulnerability with another, they can feel more, express those feelings to their partners and experience what it feels like to be cared for.

### *Facing Vulnerability*

Getting in touch with one's vulnerability and responding to it, both internally and in relationship with another, is at the core of both gay men's therapeutic work and their robust and healthful connections with other men. The cultural use and abuse of power and control of gay men and their relationships leaves many men both *feeling* and *being* vulnerable. Vulnerability is the reality for all people; we all feel pain and sadness, gain and lose in all sorts of ways, get sick, age and eventually die. And all of this happens to the people we love, too. However, gay men, like members of any oppressed group, experience added vulnerabilities. The cultural shame discussed above leaves a legacy of shame, anger and anxiety for many gay men.

Personal and relational healing for the gay man, then, requires work centered around feeling, revealing and responding to one's vulnerability in safe and healthy ways while also working to claim both personal and community power. The core source of healing is relationship. Connections with their families, friends, partners, therapists and fellow group members are recognized as transformative, healing opportunities. Expectedly, the central relational paradox is at the heart of this work. Gay men, having experienced cultural and relational trauma, can easily feel anxiety, fear and even terror in connection and thus move to protect themselves by hiding and disconnecting. At the same time, their sense of longing and desire to connect is strong and instinctual. Healing, then, requires men to face, accept and share their vulnerabilities without hiding from others or protecting themselves in unsafe and unhealthy ways.

The therapeutic process of accepting one's vulnerability is continually unfolding. For many men, an important initial first step is showing the therapist their various strategies of disconnection. By revealing these strategies, many gay men slowly reveal themselves and enter more fully into relationship with another who sees and accepts him. Many of the strategies that gay men employ are compulsive in nature. Many gay men in therapy discuss how they use drugs, alcohol, sex, food, money and work as ways to tend to their vulnerability. They describe leaning into those behaviors to feel pleasure, stop feeling pain or to not feel at all. More importantly, they describe how these compulsive strategies disconnect them both from themselves (their feelings, thoughts and day-to-day realities) and from healthful and close connections. In trying to protect their senses of vulnerability, they essentially keep more and more of themselves out of relationships by secretly engaging in compulsive behaviors that continue to block, distort and veil their authentic selves. The ongoing process of honoring and letting go of historical strategies requires mindfulness of emotional and physical states as well as increased skill development in holding and bearing all of their feelings related to their vulnerability.

It may be useful to consider this work in the context of Stan. (Note: all cases presented are composite stories; identifying details have been altered and protected.) Stan entered individual therapy to help him deal with coming-out issues. His partner, John, who was open about his sexual orientation with family, friends, and colleagues, was getting increasingly annoyed with Stan's slow and tentative process in disclosing his identity. Stan, feeling pressured by John, began to withdraw from him as he felt both anxious and angry. He also had begun to secretly spend more and more time looking at online porn sites and chat rooms, and he was considering meeting and having sex with some of the men he had met in them. He came to therapy open (if not enthusiastic) to the idea of looking at these issues as he said he loved John and didn't want to lose him. And he knew he would if they couldn't work through these issues.

As the therapy progressed, Stan and I together explored and unveiled the relational images that guided the ways he connected with others, especially John. Having grown up with a depressed mother who was continually humiliated by his alcoholic stepfather, Stan noted that he learned to loudly and actively defend and protect his mother while staying especially vigilant for the ongoing potential for chaos and abuse. He also observed, rather matter-of-factly, that he was very different outside his family; he was not nearly as loud and visible in his personal life. He had gone to Catholic parochial and high schools and had received clear and bold statements about the "evils of homo-sexuality". He never let on, he said, that he was gay. Although never directly targeted for being gay, other boys were and, "I got the message. Loud and clear. I couldn't be gay. And if I was, I sure as hell couldn't let them know." Just as impactful, he said, were the classroom lessons about how gay people were disordered and immoral: "When the teachers began talking like that, I felt like I was under a spotlight. I even began to sweat and get a little light-headed." Together, we were able to see how he learned to connect by protecting and defending others while hiding himself. Rather ironically, he hid himself by becoming bigger and more visible. In his family, in order to protect his mother and hide his own fear, he often grew loud. In school, he became the smartest, the award-winner, and the ideal Catholic boy who garnered attention and praise, all the while hiding his strong feelings of excitement, anxiety and shame about his attraction to other boys.

Stan and I were able to see and honor how these templates worked quite well for him: they kept him connected to his family and his school communities, and they helped nurture his independence, competence and achievement-oriented self. At the same time, we noticed how they were not serving him well with John. Not only was his continued hiding straining their relationship, but Stan wasn't communicating his anger and fears to John. His role with John, he said, was to love and protect him as he did his mother (though we wondered if John needed his protection). So, he did that in a number of ways, but he never directly expressed his simmering anger and fear. Rather, he withdrew from John and moved closer to what made him quickly and more easily feel accepted and relieved: online sexual encounters. This behavior furthered a cycle of shame and deepened his feelings of worthlessness and anger at himself, John and the larger world.

Through the process of therapy, Stan and I were able to notice and name the vulnerabilities that he faced and felt throughout his childhood. He said he had never done that before; he *knew* what his childhood was like, but he never felt it in the ways he was feeling it now. He became a bit more in touch with the role shame played in his life, and he increased his ability to identify and name the shame when he felt it. More importantly, we highlighted the importance and the value of sharing these vulnerabilities with John. Revealing himself—his thoughts, feelings, childhood and compulsive behaviors—to me was a huge and radical step for him. We noted that together, and I was able to show him, through my facial expressions and words, the impact that he had on me. We also were able to be with each other in that mutuality, naming its impact and power on us both. Perhaps more importantly, we connected our experience together to the rest of his life and, in particular, to his life with John. To have the life and relationship he wanted, he would need to stretch and make himself even more vulnerable by sharing and showing himself—in all his glorious, human messiness—to John. This remains his work, our work together.

## *Acknowledging the Trauma of Cultural Shame*

Acknowledging the trauma of cultural shame allows gay men to understand their experiences, find a sense of community and become free of its legacies. In group work, gay men gather not only to talk about the details of their day-to-day lives and struggles, but also to name, in ways that have often gone unnamed, the realities of their lives. In one gay men's psychotherapy group, I will frequently root discussions of shame, secrecy and coping through compulsive behaviors to homophobia. While stressing and accepting their personal responsibility, group members also have opportunities to reflect on and feel the impact of the power-over model of homophobia and heterosexism throughout their lives. Members of the group often grow thoughtful and quiet during these conversations in ways that are different and deeply emotional. They express appreciation for having the opportunity to be together to discuss what they say they don't talk about very often. Framing discussions in these ways allow gay men to locate the source of their suffering in a cultural, relational trauma. Together in their vulnerability, they are able to feel shame, express anger and name their anxieties born of homophobia. More importantly, through the group therapy process, they are able to locate sources of healing, relational repair, growth and freedom, in building connections. These connections they describe are ones where they can be seen as real and human; their authenticity is both invited and encouraged by the relationships they form in group. In these ways, they are able to shift the power paradigm to one that is shared among them in their mutuality.

## *Practicing Skills of Intimacy: Mutual Empathy,*
## *Care-Giving and Care-Receiving*

Individual and group work also creates moments where gay men can move beyond facing their vulnerability and toward mutuality. This mutuality allows gay men to learn about and practice care-giving and care-receiving. The experience of chronic disconnection that many gay men experienced and felt naturally has the effect of not knowing how to feel vulnerable *and* connected;

many men were not afforded the opportunities to be met in their vulnerability with kindness and care and instead were isolated. Similarly, they were then not provided relational opportunities in which they felt both safe and skilled in giving that same care.

In individual and group therapy, gay men are able to learn and practice skills of intimacy including defining, creating and honoring their sense of safety, pacing their involvement, stating and negotiating boundaries and navigating feelings. Through their growing relationships with their therapists and fellow group members, they are afforded regular opportunities to listen to others, ask questions, respond both verbally and non-verbally, speak with empathy, deepen understanding and compassion for others, use humor as a means of joining and pacing, and struggle, challenge and engage in conflicts. These skills create alive relationships where men and therapists alike can learn to, perhaps slowly and carefully, fully show and reveal themselves, thereby moving into greater and greater authenticity.

This emotional skill development is perhaps some of the most valuable work for gay men in individual treatment and proves to be one of the more valuable skills he brings to his primary relationships. As noted above, some of the most important strengths of gay men who come out are their awareness of their very natural and counter-cultural feelings, the courage to honor them by speaking them aloud and acting on them through building community and connections that respect and nurture their sexual identities. Using this as a model—their awareness of their feelings and the honoring of them—can assist gay men as they become more emotionally skilled and sophisticated. Many gay men need the encouragement and reminders of their proven track record as they learn to identify their feelings (often first in their bodies) of sadness, longing, anger, anxiety, grief, powerlessness, helplessness and shame. This mindfulness—a mindfulness born of coming out—then allows them to have experiences of feeling those feelings without needing to push them away, hide, protect themselves, keep them secret or lash out at others. Perhaps more importantly, the therapeutic relationship built with their therapist allows them to reshape relational images and note the felt differences.

In group therapy, participants form real relationships with each other in which they can also learn and practice skills of intimacy. While discussing their life challenges, they listen to, encourage, guide and learn to trust each other. At the same time, they may disregard, fight with and hurt each other. These unique and complex relationships serve as a training ground where men can rewire some of the legacies of their socialization born of cultural shame. They learn to give kindness and care through listening, inquiring and responding (Hartling, Rosen, Walker and Jordan, 2000), asking questions, expressing concern, following up week-to-week, gently challenging, honestly disagreeing and expressing feelings. They also learn to receive care through speaking, speaking up, being seen and heard, being remembered and considered, tolerating disagreement and feeling care and love. Each of these postures—

giving and receiving care—requires of gay men an openness and vulnerability that they have long protected through some degree of hiding.

In addition, an important care-receiving learning for gay men centers on the development of self-empathy (Jordan, 1989, 2009). After being met with so much judgment and disregard, many gay men do not know how to treat themselves with kindness; they often have not had connections that nurture self-compassion and self-care. In fact, they may only know how to meet their pain and vulnerability with the same degree of harshness and abuse that others subjected them to. Thus, some of the self-care work involves transforming men's self-harm (including the range of compulsive behaviors as well as other self-abuse) into gentleness, patience and acceptance of themselves.

In one long-term gay men's intimacy group, members were discussing the recent addition of a new member. One member, Paul, gently raised his concern that, with the group size having increased, his needs would not be met; he worried that he would not be able to speak up and be heard in the group. Moreover, he was scared that he would slide back into his previous way of being in the group when he joined four years earlier; he was worried that he would be silent, feel hidden and become isolated and forgotten. As his fellow group members inquired more about his concerns, they began to respond by sharing their own worries. The therapist wondered with the group if their worries were familiar and reflected other relational struggles they experienced in their lives. A few nodded sadly and began speaking about what it felt like growing up as gay boys. This was a familiar theme to them, as the group had often spoken about the legacies of growing up gay. Paul nodded, describing that he and his boyfriend of seven months often fight because Paul feels continually disappointed, unsupported and frequently frustrated in the relationship. These feelings, he explained, were felt throughout his childhood when he had to hide his sexual feelings from his classmates at his private, all-male boarding school. Another member, Thomas, spoke about what he saw as a familiar role in relationships, namely that as protector and caregiver. He spoke about how he often feels sexually rejected by his husband of six years and that he doesn't feel like he can say verbally and directly to his husband that he wants to have sex; it feels like giving up some type of control.

As they often did, group members responded with questions and stories of how they had felt similarly in their relationships (which were a range of long-term partnerships and more casual dating relationships). The therapist simply and quietly observed that they seemed to feel vulnerable in those moments. Members nodded and agreed, and Thomas became tearful describing how he often goes to bed feeling hurt, rejected and angry. He also noted that he doesn't share these feelings with his husband and recalled how disconnecting from his feelings (and from others) was a familiar and prominent relational theme for him, in part due to his role in his family as well as what he felt like he needed to do as a gay boy in middle and high school who was harassed for not fitting in with other boys.

The therapist asked Thomas how he was feeling in the moment, and he noted feeling sad and angry. The therapist wondered if he felt vulnerable, too, as he was sharing not only the details of his sexual struggles, but also his very real and present feelings as seen in his tears. He nodded that he did, and that it felt good to him at the same time as his fellow members were listening to him and identifying with his struggles. The therapist also noted how the group members were asking him questions, responding to his vulnerability with their own and looking supportively at him. He nodded and said that he noticed and felt their concern and support; he felt heard and understood. The group ended with members returning to Paul's worries about the group size and wondering how to address it. The therapist observed that, in many ways, they were addressing it by encouraging Paul to share his nervousness and inviting Thomas and the others to explore and grapple with how to speak up about their wants and needs—namely, face their vulnerabilities, reveal themselves and authentically represent themselves in their relationships with each other.

The following week, Thomas shared that the previous week's group process inspired him to show himself a bit more fully to his husband. He decided that he wanted to more directly and clearly give voice to what he wanted from and with his husband. He reflected that the previous week's group, along with other group experiences he had, taught him that he could perhaps take more risks with his husband by not censoring himself or keeping parts of himself—namely his desires, fears and anger—hidden. He expressed that the group had given him another experience of being real and seen and vulnerable and imperfect, all ways that he has learned that he wants to be with his husband, too. He laughed while explaining this, noting that I had made some mistakes in the group's conversation and had gotten in the way at times; he explained how my skills, but perhaps more importantly, my stumbling, helped create a space where he could stumble and be vulnerable, too. He described having a conversation with his husband who expressed that he shared Thomas's desires of sexually connecting more regularly. Jim, another group member, then began talking, wondering about how he could stretch himself as he periodically moves closer to and then quickly away from dating.

## Special Dynamics

There are specific issues and dynamics that are sometimes present with gay male couples that deserve special attention. Although they are beyond the scope of what is presented here, they do merit acknowledgement and further exploration and discussion.

### *Therapist Identity*

In thinking about working with members of different cultural groups, therapists often wonder whether they need to share certain identities and life experiences

109

with their clients. With regard to working with gay men around couple issues, natural questions arise: "Would a gay male couple benefit from working with a gay male therapist?" "Do gay men in therapy for couple issues need to work with an LGBT person regardless of sex or gender identity?" "Can heterosexual therapists provide culturally competent care to gay men?" These are all legitimate and thoughtful questions and, naturally, there are no easy answers. What is clear is that gay men receiving mental health care—individual, group and couples treatment—need and deserve to work with a clinician who is both familiar with and sensitive to LGBT issues.

As discussed above, the cultural shame born of homophobia and heterosexism wields great power and influence in the relational worlds of gay men. Many would thus assume that gay male therapists would be a natural fit to provide care and treatment to other gay men. In some cases, this is accurate. For example, a gay male therapist who has done his own internal and relational work around the impact of cultural shame in his own life may be especially attuned to those issues with his gay male clients. He would then be poised to co-create healing moment after healing moment with his clients, allowing and encouraging them to reveal their vulnerability and reshape relational images of all kinds (i.e. relational images of men, of other gay men, of dynamic, non-sexual relationships with other gay men, etc.).

However, a gay male identity does not guarantee this sensitivity and competence. Sensitive and competent care is care that reflects a deep understanding of the nuances of the effects of that cultural shame. Moreover, competent care is care that allows for, invites and challenges men to explore and feel the effects of that cultural shame. Some LGBT therapists can do that work brilliantly; others may fall short due to their own counter-transferential blind spots. Similarly, some heterosexual clinicians may skillfully guide and accompany gay men in their work, providing particularly powerful cultural healing moments; others may not have any awareness of what they may be missing. The clearest and best answers to the questions posed above will be gleaned from talking candidly with gay male clients, at the onset of treatment as well as routinely throughout the course of treatment. At the heart of these conversations is the core of Relational-Cultural Therapy; the process of considering and negotiating these questions—regardless of the identity of the therapist—calls forth mutual empathy, respect and the empowerment of gay men in relationship.

### *Intimate Partner Violence*

Intimate partner violence has been found to occur at similar rates in heterosexual and gay male communities: reports indicate that 1 in 3–5 gay men experience domestic violence (Cruz, 2003; Gay Men's Domestic Violence Project, 2012). As a result, all clinicians who work with gay men individually and in couples need to be skilled at assessing for violence as well as intervening in safe, effective ways. It is critical that clinicians, as well as police officers, court personnel and medical professionals, be mindful of the stereotypes and controlling images of gay men which may lead to biased assessments. The images of *The Sensitive Gay Man*, *The Weak and Passive Sissy* and *The Educated and Sophisticated Gay Man* often render men in violent relationships—both victims and aggressors—invisible. Many people believe that sensitive, sophisticated gay men are more evolved than other men and would thus never resort to violence. Others believe that men whom they consider gentle, sweet, passive or effeminate would never act violently. Thus, men in relationship with each other are sometimes seen as not having the problems that some heterosexual men do (namely with the power-over model of patriarchy). Others may assume that two men together, who have been socialized in a power-over structure, will naturally resort to violence, and there is not much that can be done to rectify or resolve that couple dynamic.

Clearly, these controlling images serve to isolate men in violent relationships and prevent critical and often life-saving interventions. Many men engage strategies of disconnection and keep the true nature of their relationships hidden and secret. Furthermore, when the nature of those relationships is revealed (e.g. through 911 calls, the issuing of restraining orders), it is often difficult to accurately assess who is the primary aggressor and who is the victimized partner. Clinicians working with gay men, individually as well as in couples and groups, would benefit from skills in assessing and intervening to help maximize safety.

### Non-Monogamy

Many gay male couples decide to structure the sexual parts of their relationships in ways that are non-traditional, inventive and creative. These couples choose to open their relationships—in myriad ways and designs—to having sex with people other than and/or in addition to their primary partners. This decision-making process requires a good degree of structure, sophistication and complexity. It would be valuable to illuminate and explore the relational images of each man in the couple in order to understand more fully the motivations and expectations of such restructuring. Many gay men approach this process of negotiation with an openness and vulnerability that moves them closer to authenticity.

An obvious risk is that one or both partners may leave parts of himself out of the process, thus compromising not only his authenticity and fullness but also the authenticity of the structured relationship. For example, one partner may not be honest about wanting a non-monogamous relationship for fear that his partner will be angry, hurt or rejecting of his desires. He may therefore leave his desire unspoken while acting it out in secrecy. Still other couples who actively engage in detailed conversations about rules and guidelines may veil their wishes about specific rules and sexual practices for a number of reasons. Conversations about sexual structures in relationships could be framed by

111

naming the central relational paradox. Prioritizing connection and healthy conflict while honoring and acknowledging various strategies of disconnection could guide often difficult and complex conversations. In doing this, the core skills of mutual empathy—care, inquisitiveness and responsiveness—are built and utilized. And, most importantly, the men in the couple bring more of themselves into their relationship.

### Sexual Trauma, Power and Anger

In many respects, the cultural shame transmitted to gay men via heterosexism and homophobia represents a form of sexual trauma. Relational ruptures and violations give rise to feelings of threat and fear, which, in turn, create a host of affective, cognitive, behavioral, physical, spiritual and relational consequences. Many aspects of these traumatic experiences have been described above. What hasn't been mentioned, but deserves acknowledgment, is the broader relational trauma histories of gay men. In addition to the sexual trauma detailed above, many gay men report histories of childhood physical, sexual and emotional abuse as well as adult experiences of rape, assault and intimate partner violence. Any therapeutic work with gay men—individual, group or couple—must involve an initial assessment as well as a routine inquiry/assessment of these traumatic experiences. Multiple layers of trauma and its effects will impact the relational healing and recovery of gay men.

Related to this, further exploration of the power dynamics in gay male relationships is indicated. Due to gender socialization and homophobia, issues of power are often explicitly named and more subtly struggled with in gay male relationships. A detailed analysis of how power-over and power-with dynamics (Jordan, 2009) show up in the day-to-day interactions and negotiations with gay men is warranted. A particularly important part of this analysis would involve a closer look at how anger is felt, expressed and used in the context of vulnerability as both protection and punishment by men in relationship with each other.

## Conclusion

RCT offers a distinctive, powerful and useful perspective with which to view the dynamics of gay male development as well as gay men's most intimate relationships. Although many gay couples may not enter couple therapy, valuable couple work can be done in both individual and group therapy. Through naming, exploring and healing cultural shame, both therapists and their gay male clients can engage in a process informed and enriched by RCT. Gay men are able to recognize and navigate the central relational paradox in their lives and, by facing their vulnerability and reshaping relational images, move from isolation and towards both greater authenticity and connection in their relationships. In these ways, gay men demonstrate their resilience, creativity and strength as they heal, grow and thrive in connection.

# References

Bergman, S. (1991). Men's psychological development: A relational perspective. *Work in Progress*, No. 48. Wellesley, MA: Stone Center Working Paper Series.

Cruz, J. M. (2003). Gay male domestic violence and reasons victims stay (Synopsis written by Rus Ervin Funk, MSW, Center for Women and Families, Louisville, KY). *Journal of Men's Studies*, March, 11(3), 309.

Downs, A. (2005). *The velvet rage: Overcoming the pain of growing up gay in a straight man's world.* Cambridge, MA: Da Capo Press.

Gay Men's Domestic Violence Project (2012). *A service provider's guide for working with gbt victims and survivors of domestic abuse.* Retrieved from http://gmdvp.org/guide-service-providers

Greenan, W. E and Tunnell, G. (2003). *Couple therapy with gay men.* New York: Guilford Press.

Hartling, L., Rosen, W., Walker, M. and Jordan, J. (2000). Shame and humiliation: From isolation to relational transformation. *Work in Progress*, No. 88. Wellesley, MA: Stone Center Working Paper Series.

Heyward, C. (1989). Coming out and relational empowerment: A lesbian feminist theological perspective. *Work in Progress*, No. 38. Wellesley, MA: Stone Center Working Paper Series.

Johnson, S. M. (2004). *The practice of emotionally focused couple therapy: Creating connection.* New York: Taylor & Francis.

Jordan, J. (1989). Relational development: Therapeutic implications of empathy and shame. *Work in Progress*, No. 39. Wellesley, MA: Stone Center Working Paper Series.

Jordan, J. (2009). *Relational-Cultural Therapy.* Washington, DC: American Psychological Association.

Laird, J. and Green, R. J. (1996). *Lesbians and gays in couples and families: A handbook for therapists.* San Francisco: Jossey-Bass.

McIntosh, P. (1988). *White privilege and male privilege: A personal account of coming to see correspondences through work in women's studies.* Report No. 189. Wellesley, MA: Wellesley Center for Women.

Miller, J. B. & Stiver, I. (1997). *The healing connection: How women form relationships in therapy and in life.* Boston: Beacon Press.

Najavits, L. M. (2002). *Seeking safety: A treatment manual for PTSD and substance abuse.* New York: Guilford Press.

Niolon, R. (2011). *Issues for same sex couples.* Retrieved from http://psychpage.com/family/library/gay-lesbian.html

Odets, W. (1998). Some thoughts on gay male relationships and American society. *Journal of the Gay and Lesbian Medical Association*, 2(1).

Tobias, A. (1998). *The best little boy in the world.* New York: Ballantine.

# 8

# EVOLVING SEXUALITIES
# FOR THE COUPLE

## Integrating RCT and the
## Sexual Health Model

*Meg I. Striepe*

This chapter brings together Relational-Cultural Theory (RCT) and the sexual health framework for working with couples in therapy. This integrative developmental approach helps clients gain greater awareness of their sexual history and fosters the couples' mutuality while supporting positive change in their sexual relationship. The RCT perspective offers therapists a lens to see what relational dynamics lies beneath presenting sexual complaints. More often than not, couples' sexual complaints are about their need for connection and not about sexual functioning. By fostering deeper connection in their sexual relationship the goal is for clients to feel at home in their bodies and increase their authentic capacity to connect sexually and emotionally. Typically, couples seek counseling looking for an outcome such as more frequent sex or mutual orgasms and are unaware of how a chronic pattern of disconnection has affected their sexual functioning.

The RCT process of using relational images (RI) is an effective way for the couple to modify their sexual expectations and bring more flexibility and aliveness into the sexual connection. Both partners will discover qualitatively more pleasure experienced in connection with a sexual partner as a function of intense sensate experiences, joy in joining with and exploring experiences together, excitement in having fun, pleasing the other person and knowing he/she wants to please you, (Jordan, 1997). With RCT the larger sense of the pleasure of connection and mutuality is seen as the couple give themselves over to each other and the relationship. This involves a kind of mutual surrender to a larger union, a temporarily diminished self-consciousness and decreased awareness of the other as separate. This is the rhythm of human passion and sexual synergy; the health of the connection is supported by mutual empathy and authentic presence.

## Human Sexual Response Cycles

Most of us have been trained and culturally conditioned to assess sexuality based on the human sexual response researched by Masters and Johnson (1966) in the 1960s. Their research identified physiological changes primarily of the autonomic nervous system along with phases of sexual response including excitement (arousal), plateau, orgasm, and resolution. Kaplan (1974) later added a desire phase, which for couples is often the phase when they experience disconnection and avoidance, that is the "getting going" or initiation phase. Low sexual desire is the most prevalent sexual issue among women today (Basson, 2002; Working Group for a New View of Women's Sexual Problems, 2002). While providing important information, the advancement of qualitative and quantitative research on the human sexual response led to sexuality being medicalized. It also reinforced the performance model of achieving orgasm, with heterosexual intercourse as the gold standard (Tiefer, 1996). Masters and Johnson's (1966) individualistic, physiological model set the criteria for the DSM sexual dysfunctions and paraphilias (American Psychiatric Association, 1994).

Given the cultural bias that sexuality is primarily about performance and orgasm, most clients come in with the conditioning that they "should" be sexual in a certain way and that they are deficient or broken if they cannot achieve "sexual success" as thus defined. When couples are constantly working toward orgasm, they miss the experience of sexual connection for the pleasure it can provide. As the therapist introduces a relational sexual health framework it is important to notice what comes up for the couple. The therapist may provide examples of pleasure beyond orgasm, thus expanding potential "successful" sexual repertoires and encouraging couples to attend to their own and each other's specific experiences of pleasure. Couples are often hesitant or have trouble trusting the idea that being sexual is primarily about connecting, not about achieving a physical goal. The quality of their connection is the primary determinant of satisfying sexual engagement. But unless people are in crisis or significant relational pain, they sometimes lack awareness of the importance of attending to the health of their connection. I once had a couple ask, "What is connection?" Couples need to feel safe enough to ask these questions and explore this new territory. And they often need help in learning how to connect sexually.

## Sexual Health Model

It is helpful to give the couple a definition of sexual health, particularly as it defines aspects of intimacy; and it is important to have this model in hand to help offset the cultural sexual messages that we are bombarded with daily. It is also important to work on aspects of connection that the couple can practice. The sexual health model is an approach to sexuality founded in accurate knowledge, personal awareness, and self-acceptance, where one's behavior, values, and emotions are congruent and integrated within a broader sense of self. Sexual health involves the ability to choose to be intimate with a partner, to communicate explicitly about sexual needs and desires, to be sexually functional (to have desire, become aroused, and obtain sexual fulfillment), to act intentionally and responsibly, and to set appropriate boundaries. It also depends on paying attention to and caring about the needs and responses of one's partner. Sexual health further has a communal aspect, reflecting not only self-acceptance and respect, but also respect and appreciation for individual differences and diversity, as well as a feeling of belonging to and being involved with one's sexual culture(s). Sexual health includes a sense of personal confidence, personal attractiveness and competence, as well as freedom from sexual dysfunction, sexually transmitted illnesses, and sexual assault or coercion. Sexual health affirms sexuality as a positive force, enhancing other dimensions of one's life (Coleman, 1997; Robinson et al., 2002; Rosser et al., 1995: WHO, 1975).

After introducing this framework, I have couples take a deep breath and ask them what they noticed in hearing the definition. The definition is comprehensive and often can feel overwhelming. As therapists we are in a position to help couples identify together where they are in their sexual development and bring awareness to the ways they can grow together. It is not unusual that a couple has never shared their sexual histories or ever reflected on their own sexual development. Sometimes there is resistance to exploring sexual expectations; the couple may be looking for a medical fix or for the "identified patient" or powerless person to step up and be sexual. In this dynamic we can see how the personal and political are entwined. Just as sexuality can be a part of healthy development and flourishing connectedness, it can also be problematic and contribute to problems in connection. We can be neglected (not receiving what we need to develop well), shamed (our sexuality makes us bad and leads to disconnection); the negative impact of sexual conditioning needs to be identified and worked with therapeutically.

The therapist needs to be prepared to speak through the silence and remind couples that it is not unusual that they have not received the sexual information they need. It is courageous for a couple to seek help at any point in their relationship. Sexuality work is powerful; helping the couple find a way to move out of disconnection and build connection, step by step, is at the core of the process.

## Relational Sexual History Taking and Relational Images

The starting point with a couple is to listen to their description of their sexual connection and help them begin to recognize the cultural influences and messages they have received about their sexuality. Relational images (RI) are the inner constructions and expectations about relationships that we each create out of our experience in early relationships (Miller & Stiver, 1997). Cultural beliefs have an impact on our sexuality in many ways, including the family of origin belief systems and the larger cultural context in which the family was embedded.

## Vignette: Mary and Joe

For example, 52-year-old Mary grew up in an Irish Catholic family where sexuality was silenced. Not only was sex not talked about, there was limited touch from the parents to the children. Mary does not remember being hugged by her parents or being tucked into bed. Mary talked about how she learned to be self-sufficient. In therapy, she recalled a negative relational image of herself as a young girl curious about her changing body and seeing the Pope, dressed in bright red, looking down at her in dismay; she felt shame. A sense of unworthiness spread to many areas of her life. Subsequently she experienced shame each time she felt a positive sensation in her clitoris. Over time she disconnected from sensations in her clitoris in an effort to free herself of the shame. As a woman she does not experience any feeling in her genitalia, including during childbirth: "I just wanted the baby out and safe." She felt shaky remembering how alone and scared she felt in her body.

Mary's relational images of marriage were also characterized by disconnection and shame. She remembered seeing her mother turn the other way when approached by her father for affection. Today, Mary has two children; however, she cannot "let go" sexually. It is evident that she becomes paralyzed by shame. In her shame she feels an impulse to hide, to pull away; she does not feel lovable. This leads to a place of isolation and self-blame, hardly conducive to emotional or sexual connecting. She is scared that she is doing something wrong with her husband. In the therapy, identifying RI helps construct steps to change her expectations, including the belief system she learned as a child and the emotional disconnect that happens in her body with her husband.

In the context of the couples work, for the first time Mary takes a step and speaks to what she experiences internally. Initially her voice is stifled, shaky, and restrained; she looks young and scared as she shares. Her husband appears strong and clear in the context of therapy, wants his wife to be free of the burden. He looks at her empathically. He does not shame her. This provides an opening for her to connect differently with her sexuality and her husband. The therapist witnesses powerful and freeing moments like this when couples are empathically connected and the connection goes deeper while an old sexual relational image shifts. Relational therapy heals shame by reestablishing a sense of empathic possibility. Empathy also goes far in healing relational neglect and/or abuse. In the context of couples work a deeper healing of old relational injuries can occur.

In couples work the therapist learns to follow the growth of the couple, allowing them to pace the unfolding of intensity. Both have opportunities to tell their stories. In this case, as Mary adjusted to hearing her own voice and felt more connected sexually she was able to see and touch her husband more fully in day-to-day connections. Joe received more relational support as Mary was more available physically and emotionally. Her look of disapproval and avoidance of being sexual had left him feeling rejected and disempowered. In therapy, Joe got in touch with how he felt unlovable and isolated when Mary did not respond to his desire to be connected. He identified his relational image of growing up in a family where the man's job was to be the provider, and he felt he was failing and undesirable. Joe discovered that it was not all up to him; he was able to hear and see Mary as desiring him and that she was not dis-approving of him. As the sexual dynamic changed, Mary gained a sense of zest and clarity about how she valued and loved Joe's ways of taking care of the family and wanted him to receive her empathy. Joe recognized that he had been living in a disconnected way and was relieved to have Mary's empathic connection.

---

Even when the couple presents as being clear about their sexualities and their conflicts—for example, wanting to have more frequent sex—it is not likely that a behavioral approach such as scheduling time together or progressive sensate focus will lead to greater mutuality. Assessing their sexual history and identifying their relational images of connections and disconnections will provide important information about what is interfering with their sexual mutuality. The following questions (taken from Program in Human Sexuality Questions for Reflection on Sexual Development, n.d.) are a guide for reviewing sexual development.

1. The messages I received about sex from my mother(s) were . . .
2. The messages I received about sex from my father(s) were . . .
3. I thought my parents' sexual relationship was . . .
4. The first time I looked at my genitals I thought . . .

5. I received my most positive sex messages from . . .
6. I received my most negative sex messages from . . .
7. The first time I masturbated I felt . . .
8. The first time I menstruated I . . .
9. When I was a teenager I thought my body was . . .
10. When I was a teenager I wanted to look like . . .
11. My first sexual experience with another person was . . .
12. The first time I had sexual intercourse I felt . . .
13. The first time I had an orgasm I . . .
14. I think my sexual fantasies are . . .
15. The best sexual experiences I've ever had were . . .
16. The worst sexual experiences I've ever had were . . .
17. When I'm nude I feel . . .
18. My feelings about masturbation now are . . .
19. My feelings about fantasy now are . . .
20. My sexuality is _____.

## Cynthia and John: A Case Vignette

Cynthia and John are in their 50s and have two children, aged 14 years and 12 years. They both reported a history of enjoying being sexual together and today are willing to work on their sexual relationship. They reported that with the challenge of raising kids they fell out of their weekly pattern of having sex on the weekends. As much as they tried to get going again, they kept feeling like they were failing and a wall of resentment was building. They both viewed the other person as not doing enough. In telling me, they both shifted to a tired and exhausted place where they felt alone. I observed the shift and how they looked isolated and alone.

The effect of chronic disconnection, including disconnection from oneself and lack of perceived mutuality, was apparent. Their sexual routine had kept them connected although it was in an unspoken way. The disappointment of not being sexual was a cumulative effect of desiring connection and feeling voiceless to say, "I want you" or "I need you." Both Cynthia and John had learned independence in their families of origin and had done well with an "I can do this myself" mantra. Today, they were dedicated parents and had made their children's upbringing their top priority. As a therapist you might find yourself thinking, "Do I even bring sexuality up?" Again, having a sexual history guideline provides a needed structure.

119

The sexual history taking revealed that Cynthia and John both grew up in families that were loving and supportive day to day; but at home they were left on their own to learn about sexuality. They both received sex education in school; the quality of the connection in the room changed when they claimed sex was "no big deal"; I noted, to myself, that their disclaimer felt adolescent-like (e.g. "I'm cool with it"). They mostly learned about sexuality in the context of peer relationships. During high school, Cynthia liked having a boyfriend and getting attention. She felt she lucked out because she did not feel forced to be sexual; although she also wasn't sure she wanted to be sexual when she was. She continued to have the RI that as a woman it was her job to please the man. John felt comfortable dating and mainly had a high school sweetheart that idolized him and took care of him. John said he just did what he thought boys did when dating, and remembered being looked up to because he had a girlfriend. Today he noted feeling uncertain and uncomfortable seeing how he had sex in an unknowing way. As John gained clarity that he had no idea how it was for his girlfriend, he sought connection with Cynthia. He was troubled because he was uncertain about how Cynthia feels about being sexual.

With the developing mutuality in therapy, Cynthia and John noticed more empathic connection with themselves as well as each other. They realized that as young people they had been left alone to figure out what to do in sexual relationships. However, at this point in their development they had hit the wall of being self-sufficient; they began to grasp their own developmental history of neglect. In particular they felt the sadness of not knowing sexuality as relational; this included being aware of sexual needs and being able to act intentionally in response to one another. They had both come from good enough families; they had received emotional support and did not have histories of significant physical, emotional, or sexual abuse. They both progressed through life following a typical sexual script that included numerous relationships and doing what they were supposed to do. It was evident based on their descriptions that although they enjoyed being sexual and orgasmic together, it was more going through the motions rather than feeling alive and connected sexually. They were on a path of feeling burned out as a couple. They both responded positively to my connecting to them as a well-intentioned but significantly burned-out couple.

Conducting a sexual history can be done in a relational way. My sense in doing this with Cynthia and John was that the disconnection was twofold: not knowing their own sense of sexual pleasures and the disappointment and aloneness they felt in relationship. Relatively early in the work, I decided to talk about masturbation to get a better sense of their development and information about their connection with their own bodies. Initially it was awkward and quiet in the therapy when I brought up masturbation. I reassured them that this is a topic I routinely ask clients about and it's normal to feel awkward. There is a teaching point in the field that often comes in handy; that is, that 99% of people masturbate at some point in their lives; the other 1% lie. My connecting with them in a lighter, humorous way helped, including my sharing that I had not talked about masturbation with my parents or friends before my training.

In talking further, neither one of them had known masturbation as pleasurable and found the topic to be embarrassing. John masturbated for tension release but had not shared this before with Cynthia. Cynthia shared that she really did not like looking at her body and would never have time to masturbate. Fortunately this couple had a level of relational resilience that allowed them to engage in sexual development that moved them toward mutuality, "openness to influence, emotional availability, and a constantly changing pattern of responding to and affecting the other's state" (Jordan, 1986, p. 1). Sexually this translates into finding a language they could share to be sexual, including knowing their own bodies, being open to masturbation and not feeling neglected by the other. Their mutual empowerment was palpable and they appreciated that they were not being told what they were "supposed" to do but, for instance, that they had the choice to masturbate or not. Cynthia shared that she noticed feeling turned on by John's encouraging her "to take time for you". She wanted to discover more of her sexual initiative and what she called aggressive sexual energy. John responded with wanting to unwind and relax with her. I noticed they sounded more energetic and looked more relaxed, with a different sexual connection in place.

## Shame and Sexuality

RCT emphasizes that in growth-enhancing relationships people take mutual responsibility for the relationship and provide the means for each other's development (Jordan, 2010). The combination of RCT and a frame of sexual health helps us track relational sexual growth in couples work throughout the lifespan (Daniluk, 1998). Currently in psychology there is an emphasis on attachment (Ainsworth et al., 1978; Bowlby, 1973; Lyons-Ruth et al., 2009) and how relationships in early development impact brain development during childhood (Schore, 2003; Siegel, 2001). Not yet described in detail is how newborns are touched and loved and learn to self-regulate (Schore, 2003) as part of sexual health. As a sexually shame-based culture we are not comfortable saying out loud "This is sexual development." As we saw with John and Mary, many aspects of sexuality are silenced. For instance, few people are comfortable talking about masturbation; there is a sense of badness, shame, unworthiness that comes up for people when they are asked about this topic.

Shame drives us into isolation and that leaves us all alone with our questions, our body sensations, our self-exploration. While we need to help kids see that masturbation is a private activity, we do not need to shame them into self-blame and isolation about their natural curiosity and responsiveness to pleasurable sensations. Repressive values unfortunately still pervade our cultural stance on any sexuality that does not have the Good Housekeeping stamp of approval.

## Helping Health Providers Address Sexual Development

A current emphasis of the sexual health summit (Coleman, 1997) is to educate health practitioners on how to address sexuality as part of their practice. For example, there is often a disruption in sexual growth as kids mature into preadolescents because as adults we are at a loss for what to say or how to respond to our children's sexual growth spurt that is not only physical but emotional and cultural. Part of growing up is living with the energy of curiosity, which includes the exploration of sexuality and sexual identity. Commonly, parents as a couple feel at a loss or anxious about how to help their maturing child develop sexually. They may bump into their own losses of not having received information or support, what they needed at different points in their sexual development.

Therapists often help clients repair lapses in their sexual development. Through a sexual health lens the therapist will see the quality of connectedness of a couple and how it changes as their sexualities are addressed. Couples can be great at talking about what they don't do sexually or what they want to do; it's a type of comfort zone and is easy to join in as a therapist. Couples have difficulty initiating change because it is hard to deal with stuck patterns. As the therapist introduces a change, the couple's bodies may shift, their voices change and eye contact may alter. Just as the therapist tunes into these sometimes subtle changes in the couple, it is important for the therapist to be aware of his or her own reactions as well.

Comfort with one's body starts early—some would argue with conception on a cellular level (Lipton, 2008). My background in human biology and chemistry supports my interest in thinking not just at the macro level but also at a microscopic level of cellular aliveness, for instance. The rhythm of development starts in the uterus, including sensation. (For a view of how neonatal behavior is organized at an early sensate level, prior to birth, I recommend viewing the PBS video of a fetus masturbating (Nilsson, 2001). Human touch creates connection and is necessary for healthy emotional development; this supports sexual development.

Children of all ages touch their bodies for pleasurable sensations. Children do not experience the sensations or thoughts associated with adult orgasms. Parents' own disconnect with bodily pleasure and stigma of masturbation may interfere with being able to see the child's behavior as normal. The sexual developmental trajectory of children receiving and experiencing touch in the service of self-regulation is not yet well researched or documented. Supporting sexual development in couples work involves helping them tolerate and get comfortable with their body sensations and knowing their sexual anatomy (Dodson, 1987).

There is an important connection for each individual between pleasure and pain. Part of sexuality work is helping people differentiate pain. I once worked with a male athlete who developed the mantra of "mitochrondia not hypochrondia". It helped him settle into noticing different sensations in his body while being sexual and helped him recognize that he was safe inside, i.e. he did not need to shut down. As an athlete his level of rigorous training and mental focus had disconnected him from noticing sensation, positive and negative. His partner was feeling resentful and hopeless about ever developing a warm, loving connection with him. As this athlete learned to approach his partner, the partner initially felt scared of an intensely competitive performer "coming at him for sex". It took time and practice for this couple to not compete and become collaborative sexual partners. It helped to include shared sensory experiences such as music, massage, and a choice in when to be sexual.

## Fostering Connection, not Disconnection, throughout the Lifespan

As adults we forget that children do not initially experience shame and disconnection when they are seen self-pleasuring or masturbating. Therapeutically, it is important to ask about masturbation, especially since children are often actively shamed or reprimanded if they are caught masturbating or if they bring up experiences of bodily pleasures and the parents are the couples we see. The "punitive" adults may be shame-filled themselves in a culture that is intolerant of self pleasuring and sexual curiosity. Often parents simply don't know how to respond to evidence of their children's sexual interest. Parents appreciate learning how normal it is to masturbate; it helps them if they have a way to respond to their child's emerging sexuality. For example, a parent might say: "I know it feels good to touch your body that way and it is also a time to be in private space, like your bedroom". Parents describe the benefit of having confidence in being able to feel more positive about masturbation. This allows them to appreciate the ways their children are finding to connect with their bodies. The implications of a less shame-based reaction to sexuality for children's overall development are enormous.

## Keeping the Connection in Adolescence

RCT helps us appreciate the ongoing need for connection through adolescence as maturing children experience body changes and discover new relational interests. Adolescents have needs for intimacy, tenderness, nurturance, and deeper involvement in relationships, especially with peers. The shift from shaming their sexual connectedness to honoring it changes their sexual development. Imagine the 12-year-old girl who is standing tall and proud of her budding breasts and shape or the 13-year-old boy with peach fuzz who can use his deepening voice strongly and sound different from his peers. With the support of parents as a couple who are clear and empathically connected there is less shame and less chronic disconnection that would cause adolescents to go more inward, to a lonely and painful place.

With acceptance and support from parents, adolescent sexuality can serve as the foundation of developing relational mutuality. Movement towards relational mutuality can occur throughout life, through mutual empathy, responsiveness, and contribution to the growth of each individual and to the relationship (Jordan, 1986, 2010; Miller & Stiver, 1997). An absence of shaming, and acceptance and respect for the adolescent's natural curiosity and developing sexuality contribute to sexual health and relational development. Acceptance of the budding adolescent also eases the degree of relational tension parents deal with. Parents who can see and accept their child's sexuality are free from trying to control their child's growth. RCT helps us see that children continue to need a connection through adolescence.

## How Do We Think about Boundaries?

Couples often ask about how "to do" boundaries with each other or their kids. The concept of boundaries is defined and applied in many different ways in the field of psychotherapy. Feeling safe (working with boundaries) is crucial to sexuality work. But it is important to clarify the construct of boundaries, as it often carries connotations of separateness (safety in separation rather than safety in good connection). RCT suggests that what many call "good boundaries" refer to safe, clear interactions in which all people involved can expect to be respected and empathically responded to. RCT refers to these as growth-fostering relationships in which there is mutual benefit. How do we work to build connectedness and ensure a personal sense of feeling safe and authentic, i.e. being able to say what we think, feel and sense, trusting that we will be listened to and not disregarded or judged? As an ongoing guide in couples work, I think about the couple as a connected system. In the therapy we not only talk about creating safety and clarity (boundaries) but describe and play with how the couple lives with their personal sense of space and orientation in their bodies.

As we have noted above, a key time in development of sexuality and gender identity is adolescence. When therapists look at adolescent development we often focus on this as a time of separation and establishing boundaries. We think about the adolescent needing space and the parent needing space from the irritabilities of the adolescent. In only emphasizing the need to separate and differentiate we may miss how much the adolescent continues to need connectedness, not just with peers but with family as well. The combination of being pushed toward separation and what may be experienced as parental withdrawal (frequently in the face of confusing messages from the adolescent) often leaves the adolescent vulnerable to shame ("What's wrong with me?" "How could anyone possibly love me?") Addressing shame with an empathic other ( parent, mentor, friend, therapist) brings us back into connection rather than leaving us feeling what Jean Baker Miller called "condemned isolation" (Miller, 1986).

## The Story of Maria: Moving toward Connection, Not Shame

Twelve-year-old Maria decided to take on making lunch for her brother and friends who are 10 years of age. After making the mac & cheese, she served the boys and received negative remarks of "Yuk" and "This is it?" Maria, who was also hungry and wanted to eat, became upset with the comments. She left the room and started to cry. Her mom, who was nearby, inquired about her tears and the daughter shared that she chose to make lunch instead of play outside (a relational gesture to the boys) and now the boys were being mean. The mom might have reacted to her daughter's distress about this disconnection and lack of appreciation by thinking something like "What drama my girl is having over mac & cheese." This would further disconnect the girl from her emotional experience. It would also set up the dynamic of the mom taking the boys' side.

Taking a page from RCT, the mom might take a more relational route. She might, instead, honor her daughter's pain of not being seen or responded to in a positive way and empathize with her disappointment and frustration that her efforts were not received positively. Mom could say something like, "Oh I know so well how disappointing that can feel . . . to put your heart into making some-thing for a meal and then have it trashed. I also get upset when that

125

happens. You have probably seen me upset that way." Mom might make a face or get quiet or make a noise of frustration—errggh. Maria feels validated and understood, mom feels connected instead of critical of her daughter. Mother and daughter might even move on together to problem solve about how to let the brother know that Maria felt disappointed. For instance, they might talk about what the daughter could say: "You know I took time to make this meal just for you and although it might not be your favorite I would like to receive some appreciation." It is a different message to the girl than "You are a drama queen" or "Toughen up and don't let relationships bother you."

This is also a poignant example of the gender power imbalance that can arise with boys and girls when relationships are not mutually respectful. In this case it could have taken the form of gender power dynamics: boys should expect to be taken care of by girls (an entitlement power position) and girls shouldn't be so emotional (drama queens, too sensitive) or expect mutuality. Quite a different lesson was taken away from these interactions when connection was at the center. In taking the "drama queen" route, Mom would have overlooked the shame that was creeping into her daughter. Maria needed to be seen, and needed her mother to see exactly what was happening from her perspective; she needed to feel mom's empathy with her and thus feel connected with mom. At the same time the boys needed to get feedback about their impact on Maria and learn to be attentive to ways they could be invalidating. Both Maria and her brother needed to find a way back to reconnection, feeling heard and responded to by one another.

You might be wondering: How does this example of mac & cheese apply to sexuality? Sexuality is about connectedness and not about separateness. How do women of all ages let others, but especially partners, know what they would like and not like? How can they trust they will be heard and responded to? How can both men and women speak their needs safely? And where do they typically experience the most vulnerability? To assure authentic, mutual sexuality, we must help clients build mutual, respectful relationships. But finding our voice and bringing it into relationship occurs in many different ways for couples. And our capacity to speak authentically is partly determined by power arrangements and gender.

In the mac & cheese example, with support, Maria was able to find her voice, to say to these particular boys and her mother what she thought, felt, and saw. Eventually she will access this voice to address her needs and feelings with future partners. Her ability to say: "I made mac & cheese for you and it hurts my feelings when you do not even try it before you bad mouth it" may one day allow her to speak up about her sexual preferences and need for connection.

In a culture where white male privilege prevails, girls learn early on to accommodate to boys and become silent; Jean Miller (1986) noted: "Women are supposed to be the quintessential accommodators, mediators, the adapters and soothers" (p. 125). They often feel bad when their experience is not honored, but they tend to self-blame ("What's the matter with me?"). This path of culturally prescribed accommodation stunts girls' growth relationally and sexually. Ultimately a pattern of dominance and subordination does not lead to satisfying or mutual sexual engagement.

---

## Vignette: Finding Empathic Responsiveness

Isabel is a 27-year-old strikingly beautiful woman who is very successful in her career. She came to therapy to treat low sexual desire. In the process of taking a sexual history it was identified that as a young girl she really enjoyed being active outside and playing, mostly with her older brother and peers. Isabel had always had athletic poise and she felt good about her body, proud of what she could do.

As Isabel described her memories of playing with the boys and physical feats, her posture improved, her face brightened, her voice was proud and full. A shift happened when she retold what happened when she was 12 and she was circled up with the boys to play baseball. In selecting teams, one boy pointed to Isabel and said, "She can't play. She has titties." Isabel was immediately shamed and fled to find her mother. Her mother heard the story and said, "He is right, you are too old to be playing with the boys. You have breasts." Isabel was shamed again and inside felt as if the life had been sucked out of her. As she shared this with me I observed her chest fold in and head hang low. Today she is hit by shame when she tries to connect with her body whether it be physically or sexually. She can sense her body fold inside and she detests seeing herself in the mirror. Isabel is unable to take in the attraction her husband feels for her. She can masturbate but finds it more of a release of tension and a sign that she is trying rather than a source of pleasure.

In the couples work, Isabel was able to tell her husband about the incident and how ashamed she felt. Her husband responded empathically and even playfully in validating how her family of origin does not see her for who she is and that her mother continues to be critical. The possibility of allowing shame to be seen by and empathically responded to by a partner is a powerful aspect of relational healing. Connection repairs emotional neglect and contributes to sexual growth.

Mutuality further developed as Isabel's husband shared that a younger part of him was shamed for expressing his sexual attraction. They both experienced much needed healing in this connection, and their adult ways of connection improved.

---

## Vignette: Exploring Disconnections

When there are significant differences in sexual desire, therapists need to sensitively explore the sources of disconnections. When the occurrence of childhood abuse and neglect is part of the story, it is not necessary to unburden all affected parts before a couple can be sexual. But it is always important to proceed carefully and to be responsive to each individual's needs and limits. Often the "presenting complaint" may not accurately or fully represent the core issues that need to be explored.

Brian and Nancy came in to work on having sex more often. Initially they talked in such a way that it seemed Nancy was the one who had sexual hang-ups, including not liking her body. Nancy quickly saw herself as the problem. (Note: women are more likely to self-blame.) This is where therapists would often make the assumption that Nancy needs to work on body self-esteem and on freeing herself to think and be more sexual. With careful listening, it emerged that Nancy's body disconnection was in response to Brian's hypersexual connection. When more details of their sexual patterns were looked at, it was understandable that a younger part of Nancy was feeling overwhelmed by the sexual power of Brian, who as a boy masturbated to regulate his hyperactivity.

In the relationship Brian was demanding that Nancy have sex with him nightly to fall asleep. Nancy did not have the sexual experience to recognize that many people would find this level of sexual engagement overwhelming, and she believed it was her job to please Brian, to accommodate to his needs, thus ignoring her own level of desire or sense of limits. As she began to appreciate the driven and disconnected nature of his sexual need, she could empathize with his need for release but also respect her own need to pay attention to her sexual rhythm. Although there was no evidence of sexual abuse in this couple, his almost compulsive sexuality often left Nancy feeling unseen and left alone.

## Building Safe and Satisfying Connections

Full sexuality involves knowing and being known, being open to the impact of the other person, a desire to join, to give and receive love. There is a sense of safety and freedom in the connection. In relational sexuality we move out of a power/control mode and into empathic responsiveness and honoring the needs of both people (Jordan, 1997). It can be a place of great joy and affirmation. It can, unfortunately also be a place of disconnection and isolation. In working with couples' concerns about their sexual relationships it is important to attend to the quality of relatedness that is the context within which the sexuality flourishes or withers.

Because sexuality is such a very private experience for most people, it is never easy for couples to ask for help in this realm. The therapist's attention to safety and to the quality of connection in the couple is essential to the positive movement of the therapy. Relational-Cultural Theory provides a necessary framework for appreciating the importance of connectedness and the sexual health model provides an extremely helpful perspective for better understanding the couple's sexual and relational development. Combined, these two approaches support therapists in their efforts to help their clients develop loving and mutually responsive relationships.

## References

Ainsworth, M.D.S., Blehar, M.C., Waters, E., & Wall, S. (1978). *Patterns of attachment: Assessed in the strange situation and at home*. Hillsdale, NJ: Lawrence Erlbaum Associates.

American Psychiatric Association. (1994). *Diagnostic and statistical manual of mental disorders, 4th ed. (DSM-IV)*. Washington, DC: APA.

Basson, R. (2002). Rethinking low sexual desire in women. *British Journal of Obstetrics & Gynecology*, 109, 357–363.

Bowlby, J. (1973). *Attachment and loss, Volume II: Separation: Anxiety and anger*. New York: Basic Books.

Coleman, E. (1997). Promoting sexual health: The challenges of the present and future. In Borras-Valls, J.J. and Perez-Conchillo, M. (eds), *Sexuality and human rights: Proceedings of the XIIIth World Congress of Sexology*. Scientfic Committee: Instituto de Sexologia y Psicoterapia Espill, Valencia, pp. 25–29.

Daniluk, J.C. (1998). *Women's sexuality across the life span*. New York: Guilford Press.

Dodson, B. (1987). *Sex for one: The joy of selfloving*. New York: Crown.

Jordan, J. (1986). The meaning of mutuality. *Work in Progress*, No.2. Wellesley, MA: Stone Center Working Paper Series.

Jordan, J. (1997). Clarity in connection: Empathic knowing, desire and sexuality. In Jordan, J. (ed.), *Women's growth in diversity*. New York: Guilford, pp. 50–73.

Jordan, J. (2010). *Relational-Cultural Therapy*. Washington, DC: American Psychological Association.

Kaplan, H.S. (1974). *The new sex therapy*. New York: Brunner/Mazel.

Lipton, B.H. (2008). *The biology of belief: Unleashing the power of consciousness, matter, and miracles*. New York: Hay House.

Lyons-Ruth, K., Dutra, L., Schuder, M.R., & Bianchi, I. (2009). From infant attachment disorganization to adult dissociation: Relational adaptations or traumatic experiences? *Psychiatric Clinics of North America*, *29*(1), 63–86.

Masters, W.H. & Johnson, V.E. (1966). *Human sexual response*. Boston: Little, Brown, and Co.

Miller, J. (1986). *Toward a new psychology of women*. Boston: Beacon Press.

Miller, J.B. & Stiver, I. (1997). *The healing connection: How women form relationships in therapy and in life*. Boston: Beacon Press.

Nilsson, L. (medical photographer) (2001). *Life's greatest miracle* [DVD]. Available from www.pbs.org/wgbh/nova/body/life-greatest-miracle.html

Program in Human Sexuality (n.d.). *Questions for reflection on sexual development* [handout]. Minneapolis: University of Minnesota.

Robinson B.E., Bockting, W.O., Rosser, B.R.S., Miner, M., & Coleman, E. (2002). The sexual health model: Application of a sexological approach to HIV prevention. *Health Education Research*, *17*, 43–57.

Rosser, B.R.S. (1995). *Know sex or no sex: The need for sexual health promotion in HIV prevention*. Plenary presentation at the Society for the Scientific Study of Sex Midcontinent Region Annual Conference, Minneapolis, MN.

Schore, A.N. (2003). *Affect dysregulation and disorders of the self*. New York: W.W. Norton.

Siegel, D.J. (2001). *The developing mind: How relationships and the brain interact to shape who we are*. New York: Guilford Press.

Tiefer, L. (1996). The medicalization of sexuality: Conceptual, normative, and professional issues. *Annual Review of Sex Research*, *7*, 252–282.

Working Group for a New View of Women's Sexual Problems (2002). Part 1: A new view of women's sexual problems. In Kashak, E. & Tiefer L. (Eds), *A new view of women's sexual problems*. New York: Haworth Press, pp. 1–8.

World Health Organization (1975). *Education and treatment in human sexuality: The training of health professionals*. WHO Technical Report Series 572. Geneva: WHO, pp. 5–33.

# 9

# STRANGERS IN A STRANGE LAND

## Men in Relational Couples Therapy

*Randy Markey*

## What Brings Couples to Therapy?

When a couple comes for therapy, they are always in some kind of crisis. This is not a generalization; this is, in my experience, a maxim. Well over 75% of the time, one of their common ways of dealing with the crisis, coping with the crisis or understanding the crisis, or sometimes a combination of those things, is to blame their partner for the crisis. In the case of infidelity, for example, with one partner "cheating" on the other, it seems rather simple to do. There is a party that injures and a party that is injured, and that is the end of it. But there are a few more things going on, because nothing happens in a vacuum.

It's a lot more complex than that. Relational-Cultural Theory (RCT) seeks to look at marriage through lenses that haven't always been used, and as a result, couples therapy using RCT is quite different. Here is the how and why of it.

When men and women come to therapy with problems, their problems exist in a social and cultural context that needs to be explained and reframed in order to use RCT effectively. What people usually mean when they use the word "communication" is "talking out loud to each other about feelings." I will accept that as a working definition to begin with.

Since couples want to be able to "communicate better" it is important to recognize that they can't communicate better if they don't recognize that they communicate differently.

This chapter will deal primarily with heterosexual couples therapy in America. It is important to make those distinctions when discussing RCT for several reasons. The first reason is that gender is only one of several factors that impact the way marriage is experienced, and by extension the way therapy is experienced. It is quite rare that cultural factors are addressed in psychotherapy, and even rarer that gender differences are addressed in ways that impact the full nature of their contribution to the relationship, both positive and negative. There are also issues of power—physical, economic, and gender role power—that are always a part of a marriage, and of any interaction between men and women; and are expressed in many different ways by each person in the relationship. These issues contribute visible strengths, and invisible detriments, sometimes things that are unaddressed, sometimes things that the partners are utterly unaware of, but always something that is affecting the relationship.

John Gottman has made a career out of the study of marriage. For over forty years he has scientifically studied how couples make relationships work. His work is primarily with straight couples, but he has also done work with gay and lesbian couples. He wrote that there are four sure predictors of marital failure. He calls them the Four Horsemen of the Apocalypse. They are: criticism, contempt, defensiveness, and stonewalling (Gottman, 1999). The reason they are important to an understanding of how men operate in marriage is that perception of criticism (for example, men hearing the message "you aren't doing your job") can lead to a feedback loop that is extremely destructive. This is often true when the man's perception doesn't match up to the wife's intention. We then are faced with something I call the Telephone Game. Here is how that works.

Remember the Telephone Game we played as children? A dozen kids sat in a circle, and one kid started with a secret she would tell the kid next to her. The trick was, she would say the secret into his ear as fast as she could, and he would do the same to the little girl next to him. No matter what the little boys and girls heard, that is what they would repeat to the person next to them as fast as they could. When the last boy told the first girl the telephone message, she generally laughed, and told the entire group what her original message was, and what the message was when it arrived back to her. "I love to play with my dog" becomes "My uncle lays on a log" very quickly when it goes through 12 kids. And really, that is a mild variation.

When you put the Telephone Game into a marital situation, and you add the gender factor, some very important things happen. Men and women put decidedly different values to different words. On the main, women find that talking about feelings is a much more valued form of interaction than men do. Women are more comfortable in that region, and more socialized to "live" in that region.

So a couple comes in for therapy, and the husband is immediately red-faced. The wife looks at me and her eyes start filling with tears. Stephen Bergman, in the book he wrote with his wife, Janet Surrey, calls the man's feeling "relational dread" and describes it as " a sense of failure, shame and paranoia. A sense of exposure" (Shem & Surrey,1998). Bergman goes on to say that the "relational impasse" that occurs when men feel exposed creates "an inability to express ourselves, despite a desire to".

"What's going on with you guys today?" I ask.

"I am NOT going to talk about last night YET AGAIN because it's going to be all about blaming me for doing something I already told you I was going to do."

Frank and Joanne have been down this road before. A facilities manager for a large corporation, Frank is a very nice guy who loves his family very much. When Joanne feels sad, or seems angry or upset, Frank genuinely wants to help. He wants to figure out what will make it better, do that, and then consider the issue over and done with. The problem with that is, as I have said to Frank on multiple occasions, this isn't a math problem. If it was as cut and dried as a math problem, or an issue with a building that he has at work, all he would have to do is fix the leak, and then it would be done.

Alas, when people have feelings, it isn't like a building leaking. For Frank and Joanne, like everyone else in the world, these kinds of interactions bring conflict, and conflict raises all sorts of reactions—emotional, mental and physiological. For Frank, when Joanne is upset, particularly with him, he immediately feels a sense of failure and defensiveness. It takes him out of relationship, and moves him into a sense of deep, deep shame. For Joanne, it isn't experienced that way at all. In fact, his sense of shame and failure is a surprise to her, and the two of them begin to "spin out" in a spiral of misunderstood reactions to each other that takes them far away from the initial issue, and farther and farther apart. Using the small example above, simply bringing up the issue makes Frank feel awful, and yet it is the only way through the mire of misunderstanding for Joanne, AND for the two of them.

## The Gendered Stress Response

Until recently, stress research has put forth as truth that when we are stressed, we either fight or flee; in extreme stress, we freeze. This theory (the fight or flight response to stress) has been part of bedrock psychological theory for decades. Several years ago, the renowned stress researcher, Shelley Taylor (2002) and her graduate students noticed that all the research on responses to stress was done on males. When this research was replicated on female subjects, a different response was discovered. The females showed what Taylor labeled a "tend and befriend" response. Female albino rats engaged in mutual grooming, as did female macaque monkeys. Human females reached out to make contact with friends or family. Connected with this response is the release of the hormone oxytocin, now often referred to as the "affiliative hormone".

Taylor discovered this very interesting physiological difference between how men and women deal with stress. With stress, the oxytocin hormone, nicknamed the "tend and befriend" hormone, is essential to the survival of the species. That is, in the most dangerous circumstances, the woman's response is *towards* her fellows, *towards* the community, *towards* caretaking in a highly personal and interpersonal way.

The "fight, flight or freeze" response (driven by different hormones and neural circuitry) also had its place in the survival of the species. It was the task of men to hunt and build and protect. Women could not do that while pregnant or breastfeeding, and so men, physically, were tasked with that job. As such,

133

they had to know when and how to fight, both with each other and with their prey. They had to know when and how to leave. They had to be able to be decisive and quick about how, when and where to go when in harm's way. Taylor's research confirmed that stress responses were mediated by gender—socially, biologically and neuronally (Taylor, 2002, 2006).

Our bodies, our minds, and emotions are intimately connected to each other and to how we interact in the present. The fact that little boys are taught to "man up" and "big boys don't cry" is no accident. It is an artifact of a time just prior to the Industrial Revolution when, if a boy cried, his family was in extreme danger. When all is said and done, for a little boy to learn to keep his emotions in check is urgent. Of course, in America in the 21st century, there is nothing explicit about this; but we can use this as a backdrop for thinking about how people in heterosexual couples differ from one another. This difference is a potent starting point, particularly in understanding how men experience relationships.

Let us return to the Telephone Game. When you don't know how the "telephone" works, you may make assumptions about what is happening on the other end. By that I mean, maybe all the words you have said haven't gone through. Maybe the words haven't been understood the way you've said them. Most importantly, maybe what you said was interpreted differently by the listener than what you intended the meaning to be. In my personal experience with couples there is nothing more common than couples who make assumptions about the meanings of their words, and couples who disconnect (more about disconnection later), around not reading emotional cues or not interpreting them correctly. Assumptions, misinterpretations, and not understanding the necessity to reinterpret your spouse are the three things that most often lead to communication difficulties.

## How We Take Care of One Another

Men do not typically initiate the therapy experience. Lately I have been getting a lot of telephone calls from men, but on the main it has been because their wives have pressured them about calling for help, not because they wanted to make the calls. Again, I am generalizing. I have gotten calls from men, but it is the minority case. When men are brought into marital therapy they have a frame of how they look at it. Being "brought in" certainly helps maintain the frame that they have, but they would quite probably have that frame anyway. There is a lot of guilt, shame and defensiveness that men bring into coming to therapy, and that is before they even open their mouths. Let's start at the beginning.

As a very small child, I have a memory of seeing my grandfather (who was only five feet tall) stick his finger into my father's chest and say quite forcefully "An unhappy wife has a bastard for a husband." I was four years old, and that is one of the earliest memories I have. They were standing outside my parents' bedroom where my mother was once again locked inside, crying and deep in the throes of a clinical depression. Of course, I didn't know that at the time. What I knew was that my Grampa was telling my Dad something about making Mom happy. What I knew was that Dad had a look on his face that I had never seen before—he looked really sad. Today I know he was really defeated and ashamed. I filed away the words Grampa said, even though I didn't know what they meant. Now I know what they mean. They mean that my Dad was responsible for my Mom's feelings. They mean that my Dad was an absolute failure. They mean that for the rest of my life, if I was in a relationship with a woman and that woman was unhappy, I had to fight to make her happy because, believe me, from the earliest and most impressionable time in my life, I knew that her happiness was my responsibility.

For many men, just as going out to "kill the wooly mammoth" was their job in the days of caves, caring for the happiness of the family is their responsibility today. It's just a little complicated by the fact that they generally have no idea what "happiness of the family" really means. It's also complicated by the fact that it is a fallacy to think that any one person can be "responsible" for another person's happiness. Here is what we know. In order for a fetus to survive in utero, a woman's body must feed it. In order for a woman and her newborn child to survive, if she is not working herself, she needs to depend on someone or something else to help her. In a heterosexual marriage, a man holds himself responsible for the physical survival of the family because his physical assistance is needed. In the history of the species, it has been a fact until very, very recently. This great change in the way we experience things as a family unit is a very recent occurrence. As such, our bodies (and I am referring WAY beyond just conception, pregnancy, childbirth and child rearing) have not caught up to the fact that women occupy different places in society than they once did. How does this relate to couple therapy and to men's experience of couple therapy?

These differences, based partially in biology, are still in place for very good reasons, and function to affect different stress reactions that still remain when men and women interact over things as seemingly unrelated as financial problems, division of tasks at home, sex, intimacy, sex as opposed to intimacy, and most importantly, how a couple communicates about any given issue.

When a couple comes into my office and says that communication is the issue, they are spot on. Communication is definitely the issue. All the other issues stem from the inability to understand each other. And we return then to the different tasks that men and women have, and how these primary tasks inform the way the partners communicate.

We can look at couples therapy in several different ways. Most people look at couples therapy (particularly men, but quite often women too) as a place to go where they can find SOLUTIONS to their problems. John Gottman (1999) says that the goal of conflict resolution is a VERY BAD IDEA. Here is why. Gottman has found that 70 percent of all marital conflict goes unresolved (and remember, this is after studying tens of thousands of marriages over 40+ years of research). Now that is good news and bad news. The reason it is bad news is that the way that MEN look at conflict tends to be as a win/lose proposition. It is also a truism that many, if not most, couples therapists have used "conflict resolution" as one of the tools of couples therapy.

The focus of couples therapy should be "Learning to live together with unresolved conflict". Now THAT is why all the stuff back there about physiology and the Telephone Game is so important to how men and women experience couples therapy. Because if we start with a goal that can't be reached (resolving conflict), then we are already at a losing proposition before we even start the game. The first thing we want to do is make sure that we are fighting for the same thing. That is where RCT comes in.

## RCT with couples

Freud and his students first studied the mind and the processes that contribute to healthy mental and emotional development. One of their first tenets was that healthy adulthood included the movement towards independence, with the growth of a stronger ego and greater internalization of superego functions (Freud, 1920). Ensuing psychodynamic theories, often arising out of Freudian models, posited separation–individuation as the hallmarks of maturity. This psychoanalytic model became accepted as fact, as psychological health. The problem was that it didn't take account of many factors that were endemic to women's experience. The result was that completely healthy women were often seen as unhealthy, less mature, and more neurotic when compared to this Freudian model of psychological health.

In 1976, after years of living with a template that did not simply ignore women but misrepresented and pathologized their needs, Jean Baker Miller, a psychiatrist in Boston, wrote a book called *Toward a New Psychology of Women*. Among its revolutionary concepts, perhaps the most important one was this: Men were seen as maturing by means of individuating, by becoming independent individuals, by mastering their internal drives. For Miller, and the group of women who wrote and theorized with her (Jordan et al., 1991; Jordan, 2010), what characterized women was that they grow and change in relationship, throughout the lifespan.

There are a number of reasons that this is important to know, and why this is a crucial jumping-off point for a couples therapy that is based in RCT. Women typically enter into couple relationships with an interest in understanding the different facets of the relationship. They bring a depth of understanding with them in ways that most men neither understand nor utilize.

RCT places the cultural context clearly at the core of individual development. Jean Baker Miller gives an excellent example of cultural context, using the workplace and a comparison between how a man and a woman react to getting a promotion.

When Mary got a well-deserved promotion, her initial reaction was to feel weak and helpless in the face of the formidable task; she was convinced she was totally incapable of doing the job (Miller, 1986). The more she held on to the old image the more afraid she became; these fears were not based in reality. Mary was, in fact, completely qualified for this job. John, by contrast, getting a similar kind of promotion, equally well deserved, had a very different reaction. He was pleased and proud, and immediately went to get his new business cards made. And then he developed some fairly severe physical symptoms; characteristically he didn't talk about them (Miller, 1976). Miller makes two points about this. First she says that John's wife knew exactly what was going on, even if John didn't. Second, she said that John's wife could never bring it up directly as a stress problem related to his job; it would have to be indirectly related to their diet. Why? Because any direct acknowledgement of his neediness would upset the power structure. Both husband AND wife must buy into this collusion in order for it to continue.

For couples, we must consider the power differentials that exist between the two members of the couple; if we do not illuminate the power issues, we leave the couple without important and significant tools with which to view their relationship. As couples explore their differing ways of using and experiencing power, they can endeavor to change the dynamics, so that their relationship becomes more equal, or at the very least more transparent. For many couples, simply knowing that power is an issue, and seeing it in a neutral, non-blaming way, has revolutionized the way they look at their marriage.

## Power and Privilege: Visible and Invisible

Men have unearned privilege. White people have unearned privilege (McIntosh, 1989). The middle class or the upper class have privilege that the poor do not have. Heterosexuals have unearned privilege that gay, lesbian, bisexual, and transgendered people do not have. The real questions for couples are how these privileges affect their relationships. Since you cannot know what you don't know, and most people really don't even look for this kind of issue, it is hard if not impossible to see its effect.

Issues that become important to both partners may at first seem to be about communication but very often involve difficulties around power differentials as well. When couples really understand that, and can deal with both things, seeing their marriage on both levels, the way they interact with each other is changed dramatically.

Jim and Sue have been married for eight years and together for 14 years. Jim is a certified public accountant in a large corporation. Like many men, he sees problems as things to be overcome or fixed, and although he really loves his wife, he feels pretty strongly that once they have "solved the problem" Sue should just "get over it."

Of course, Sue feels quite different about it. Sue is an executive administrative assistant who is used to working at a very organized job at a very high level, and has an expectation that her husband will not only listen to her feelings about the things she needs, but that he will WANT to listen to her feelings about what she wants and needs.

These differences in needs and expectations are more than just communication differences. They are also more than just socialized differences, although that is a large part too. First, the social difference is that women put great value in understanding feelings as an integral part of the experience of interaction, as an integral part of relationship. Men have much more focus (again this is a generalization) on seeing relationship issues with a utilitarian outlook. This is not to say that men don't experience feelings or have an awareness of them. Rather, what is important here is that when problems arise, men have much more of a tendency to look at them in terms of how to come to resolution rather than sharing attendant feelings.

This can, and often does, create what RCT calls a "disconnection." Again, though, RCT comes through to save the day in ways that typical couples therapy may not. In the sense that men very often are looking at "resolution" (that is, answers to problems) and women look more often at process (that is, sharing of feelings), these problems in communication can be seen as ways that people come to understand each other's world views. Neither has a moral valance, neither is right or wrong; in fact, both have values in different ways.

The important thing to note is that when people think and experience the world in a particular way (particularly the dominant culture), they have an expectation that the rest of the world shares that thinking and feeling and experience of the world. Often a difference in experience of the world is met with great surprise. Sometimes it isn't met at all. Sometimes, tragically, it is met with contempt or even violence.

## How Culture and Couple Intersect

What psychotherapy has failed miserably to bring into the consulting space for decades is the effect of culture on relationships. Jean Baker Miller and her cohort of women felt strongly that an understanding of the impact of gender, as well as race and economic status, was intrinsic to an understanding of relationships (Miller, 1986; Miller & Stiver, 1997; Jordan et al., 1991; Jordan, 2010, 2011). Their theoretical context was the feminist movement, and the politics of making a new psychology was fully recognized by these theorists (Robb, 2007). What that meant was that they were going to have to address power differentials, because to leave them unaddressed was to leave the existing power arrangements unexamined and thus holding sway. Without this acknowledgement of power issues, equality between individuals in a couple would be impossible.

But why would a dominant culture see their dominance as a problem? If they don't feel that their dominance is anything but benevolent, then they focus on the benevolence and truly fail to see the dominance as problematic. I write that as a white, upper middle-class, college-educated, able-bodied American male. There is not a woman in the world that does not experience fear out in public in the night time. Men do not know that, aren't aware of the universality of that experience. The dominant culture is not aware of many experiences of the non-dominant groups. That is part of the privilege of dominance; others have to pay attention to and respond to your experience, but you do not have to respond in kind. The reason that this is crucial to consider is that it is not a piece of clothing that you can take on and off at your leisure. It is a permanent piece of life; it is the skin of the subordinate culture. They, whether they are women, or the poor, or the otherwise disenfranchised, are always aware of their "one down" position. They are always thinking of it, thinking from it, dealing and experiencing from it and about it. There is no piece of their experience that isn't informed by their "place" in the world.

So very often, in the context of a couples therapy, men expect to dominate without thinking, and women are dominated without considering the impact of the domination. Once a woman "dares" to have an opinion, or make a point, or try to change the direction of a marriage, one of the undercurrents that seems to come up very often is that it really isn't her place to make that move. It doesn't seem to matter whether or not her income is primary to the family, or whether or not his idea is rational. What matters is that he is the man and she is the woman. This is not something that is normative only in very sexist couples. This is something that all heterosexual couples I see struggle with. The man AND the woman are struggling with the issue of power in ways that can be completely mystifying to everyone involved.

One very important reason this struggle exists is that these power issues haven't been seen as power issues. Instead they have often been seen as issues of domain. Men weren't really "supposed" to have domain over matters in the house, like decorating and division of labor for chores inside the home. Until recently, women, classically, have had little to no say over financial matters, and certainly never have had the final decision-making power. It was a rare home indeed where the decision-making power over budgets, over how and where money is spent, was a shared and conscientiously decided thing.

This dynamic originated with the physical strength of the man, and the childbearing responsibilities of the woman. It was underlined in cultures where women were traded like chattels, or used for economic, social and political gain in marriage. Following the Industrial Revolution, those kinds of transactions became less and less possible, and so the cultures that still made them were almost always cultures that were not industrialized. Still, the social and religious positioning of women as a disempowered class of people remains to this day a fact of life to some extent in every culture in the world.

## Vignette: Jim and Sue

So we return to Jim and Sue. They come into the office, and Sue has that look on her face. It is a look of anxiety, of annoyance. Jim looks guilty and angry. I feel ready to go.

R: So what's up, you guys?

S: I ask him to do one simple thing, one simple thing for me, and he can't do it . . .

J: You know what, that is just not true, I don't see why you have to tell Randy that like I refused, or like I am incapable.

S: Well, you ARE, Jim. I just asked you to take out the trash, and you act like I am asking you to move around the whole world.

J: *(glares at her and pauses)* Look, if you are going to tell the story, at least you can tell it right. It wasn't like that at all.

S: Fine, well then what was it like?

J: She always seems to pick the exact worst times to ask me to do something. Look, she comes in, sees that I am watching the hockey game, asks me to take out the trash, and then starts yelling at me that I never help her with anything.

S: I didn't yell at you . . .

J: You DID yell at me . . . and can't you see that I am watching the hockey game? Damn, Sue, it's not like the trash can't wait for a few minutes . . .

S: You know what Jim? I never ask you to do anything, and when I do I always have to wait for you . . .

R: OK, stop here for a minute. So you each want to do something, right? *(Jim and Sue both nod.)* And does anyone feel like they are being heard? *(They both shake their heads no).* OK, so Jim, what does Sue need to know about the hockey game, about the time that you spend watching sports? What does she need to know that you think maybe she doesn't know?

J: Hmmm. I guess she needs to know that it really does help me unwind. It really does make me feel a little better. You know, sometimes . . . (not a lot, but a few times), it is a way to bond with the three-year-old. Mostly, it is a way for me to just unwind. I don't want her to think that it is just a way for me to escape from her and from the family, because it really is something I enjoy watching . . .

S: Great, that's fine. But you know, you ALWAYS get to do what you want to do. I'm stuck here in the house, and I have to answer the boys whenever they call; I am a complete prisoner to their wishes, Jim . . . and it's like you don't even know that.

*J:* I know that . . .

*R:* Hold it, hold it, we are going to try this a different way . . . listen to her a minute . . . I am going to ask her a really different question here, okay? *(to Jim)* Watch this. *(now to Sue)* Sue, when Jim doesn't take out the trash, or doesn't take it out in a timely fashion, what does that mean to you? How does that make you feel . . . really?

*S:* It . . . well . . . it's almost like he doesn't care about us.

*J:* *(interrupting)* After all I do . . .

*R:* Sssh, listen to this . . . it's really really important.

*S:* It's our home, you know *(her eyes are shiny with tears)* . . . and I think he doesn't really know how important that is to me.

*J:* *(He IS really watching now, and his hand slides over to hers)* Jeez Louise, I thought it was just the trash . . . I . . .

*S:* Well, it IS just the trash, but it's OUR trash, it's OUR HOME . . . you know? And I need you . . . your help . . . it makes me feel like you don't respect what I do . . . what I NEED . . .

*J:* *(Starts to say something and I shush him again)*

*(Long silence)*

*R:* What is the difference Sue, when you say it this way?

*(Another long silence)*

*S:* It's not really the trash at all, is it? I don't feel heard. He knows I appreciate his work *(Jim starts to talk and I cut him off again: "Don't worry, we'll get there too")*. I just want him to know what the trash, what taking out the trash really MEANS to me. It's like, when he doesn't take out the trash, it feels personal . . .

*(Now I can see that Jim really SEES her . . . is really getting it.)*

There is a saying, a maxim in RCT that says that we listen one another into voice. This refers to the fact that we develop and grow and become who we are in relationship. But it also has a literal meaning: I believe this may be especially true for women, even when they don't understand that they are being silenced or don't have a voice, or when they don't think that the situation is very important. I believe that this is true of men even if they don't perceive themselves as particularly pushy or entitled relative to what they feel may be considered stereotypically entitled. A man must be willing and able to listen to a woman, and a woman must be willing and able to be listened to until her voice is heard. A man then must be able and willing to understand and react to what he has heard. It is REALLY hard to do this.

*R:* OK, Jim.

*J:* Gosh . . . honestly I had no idea *(He is really kinda startled)* . . . I want to listen . . . I . . . didn't understand . . . how could I know? I had no idea that the trash was that important to you.

*R:* Hold that thought . . . hold it right there. See there are two very important things going on here, and I want you both to see and hear and feel them both, but there is a whole lot going on here, so just listen for a minute and relax. This is going to sound weird, but I think you are going to absorb more of this with your bodies than you are with your brains, so just bear with me for a minute and take a deep breath and listen. *(pause)* Ok? Jim, I am going to use a phrase from feminist psychology, and when I say it, Susan is going to vigorously shake her head yes, as if she heard it a million times before and she agrees passionately, even though she may never actually have heard it before. You, on the other hand will probably have no idea what I am talking about. Ready?

*R:* Sometimes the only way for a woman to effectively communicate with a man is to be listened into voice. *(Susan begins to nod vigorously. Jim looks at me, puzzled.)* See? I am a genius.

*(They both laugh, and the tension breaks a little . . .)*

*R:* The reason a man doesn't know that a woman struggles to be heard (or doesn't have a voice) is because he always has a voice. *He assumes* that she always has one too. See, our work here is to break down assumptions. (Again, this harks back to power.) There are people for whom this discussion is very appropriate in an overt way. The politics and the economics of power are a really good match for the people that I am talking to. It is always germane to the conflict; ALWAYS, but it isn't always appropriate to talk to a particular person about the depth of the politics or the economics. Sometimes, just talking about the immediate impact on each other and the immediate advantage that men bring to virtually everything is more than enough. In point of fact, we are often addressing unearned power and politics without naming it that way. For many people, talking about politics and power makes their eyes glaze over. They don't want to get all philosophical in the context of couples therapy. Once they can see that there are other ramifications to their dilemmas, sometimes they will show an interest in the wider implications.

## The Circle of Connection: Connect, Disconnect, Repair, Reconnect

I want to talk about two things: One is connections, and the importance of changing the prototype of connections; and the other is assumptions. Most people think of connections as linear; that is, you are either connected or disconnected. It's kind of like an on–off switch. In relationships, if that is true, and if that is a principle around which you build success and failure (another paradigm that is really destructive), then relationships are doomed most of the time. Go back to Gottman's science and remember that most conflict doesn't have "resolution" and remember that if we think of "connection" as successful resolution, then we are truly doomed.

Now, here is the good news. RCT, which is based on healing connections, throws the notion of linear connection out the window and replaces it with something far more fascinating, far less punishing, far more process-oriented, and of course, far more complex. Here is how that goes.

Suppose every time there was a disconnection, instead of just goodbye, *tout finis*, it's over, see you later, there was this flow. Jean Baker Miller posited that a disconnection in a healthy interaction could be followed with a *repair* and then *a reconnection*. That means that all healthy connections are circular, not linear. They move around a constant circle of connect–disconnect–repair and reconnect, with each component having all sorts of iterations.

Now remember, because women seem to be more likely than men to "catch on" to this, my experience is that it is a little more difficult for men to grasp this easily in couple therapy. First I lay out a specific picture that describes relational theory in male terms. What I talk about here is the "dead end argument" as opposed to the capacity for open-ended change. What I talk about is the capacity for everyone to "dig themselves out of holes." What I talk about is "deal-breakers" and "non-deal-breakers." Men have to know that arguments aren't about "making points," at least not for women, at least not most of the time. How many men would be stunned that the major point of the trash conversation was about feeling respected and really heard? He still has to take out the trash, but his attitude about it is utterly different given his understanding of her needs.

Here is the other part about that which is equally important. As soon as Susan knows she is heard, we begin to talk to her about how she said what she said about the trash.

R:  If you knew that Jim understood the significance of the trash to you, would that change the way you talked to him about it?

S:  I don't know what you mean.

J:  See . . . goddam . . .

R:  Hold on . . . this just means that you guys have a disconnection around meanings, not around intention . . .

143

*J:* What? *(Susan looks at me quizzically.)*

*R:* You just want the goddam trash out, right? And particularly now, knowing that you are totally heard, with great love and affection, the two of you are running on all cylinders (here comes the important part): not only do you not want to hurt him, or lash out, or anything like that, but you want to keep that sweet connected part going while you ask him to do this thing.

*S:* Yeah, well I don't want to kiss his butt for doing a simple chore *(power differential)*.

*R:* I know, I know, and let's remember power here. You shouldn't have to kiss anyone's butt to do anything. You do want to keep the nice vibe going, yes?

*S:* Yeah.

*R:* And let's stipulate that what you think of as a simple reminder comes across as a bit . . .

*S:* I am not very nice when I ask.

*J:* Yeah, that.

*R:* So let's change the goal. The first time I asked you, Sue said the goal was to get the trash out and Jim said the goal was to watch the game. What if, knowing what you now know, Jim, about how and why the trash is important, your new goal is staying connected. And remember . . . you can be annoyed or upset or whatever and still be connected, because you repair and come around the circle. Susan has already changed, see, and so have you. You know what I think? Jim, you look at this as a win or lose proposition so you think that if you get up from the game, or if you feel like you are being "controlled" by Susan, then you have somehow lost. Susan, if you feel like you are being dissed, then you are invisible and your needs aren't being met, yet again. And you know what the worst part is? Neither one of you knows that this is how the other one is thinking. So what we do is change the way you are thinking so you both want the same thing, see?

The relationships that men have at work are competitive and hierarchical, and seem to exist only to benefit the company. There is personal anonymity that ignores anything that interferes with making money. Everything of any importance is determined by the use of power and manifest by a hierarchical structure. Everything from salaries to parking places to corner offices is determined by the use of or the opportunities derived from power. When a man, in that atmosphere all day, comes home to an atmosphere that demands a complete change of thinking, acting and relating, he is asked to do two things that are extremely difficult.

When a woman is at work, she is almost always a stranger in a strange land. Either she is a secretary or some low-level employee, she isn't treated well, and she has to deal with low pay; or if she is an executive, she has to deal with people who think a woman who is an executive is not acting like a woman because she is being bossy in ways that aren't feminine. If she is more collaborative in style, people complain that she is "changing things" even if it's productive. She has to deal with the fact that she has had to change some of her core values to function in that world or she has sacrificed things that she feels ambivalent about, like having delayed or sacrificed (children, family, whatever) in order to have a successful career. (Again, this is extreme generalization.) When she does have a family, her challenge is this.

Can she be authentic? Can she be authentic in both venues? The question is the same for both husband AND wife who "want it all" so to speak. Again, back to an important distinction I wanted to make.

When a woman comes home from a stressful day at work, she wants to reach out, to make contact, to talk. Under stress, oxytocin may in part support this movement toward connection (Taylor, 2002). When women are under stress they love to pick up the telephone and call their girlfriends and talk about it. They also, when under stress at home, can't wait for their husbands to come home so they can talk to them.

Given the same set of circumstances, a man walks in from a hard day at the hierarchy, and does he want to talk about it? Not usually. His stress response may throw him into fight, flight or freeze mode. Remember, this isn't his fault. He has been under extreme stress all day, and this is not just because he is at a job, it is because this is how a male-dominated society has set up the workplace. It is hierarchical and competitive, whether he is on the top and is fighting to stay there, or is on the bottom and either fighting to get up the ladder or depressed and angry because he is constantly reminded that he is not an alpha male. These messages contribute to chronic stress. So when he walks in the door and his lovely and beautiful and beloved wife, the mother of their children, wants to talk about it, he just doesn't have a whole lot to say. It's fight, flight or freeze. Again, this isn't every case every time. But when I explain this to troubled couples coming in to see me for couples therapy, it really resonates.

It is from that destructive and soul-tearing atmosphere—a place of armor and grindstones—that a man returns home to a marriage. There his wife and family make a completely different set of requests (that really feel like demands) on him. Now let's go back to intentions. A wife intends to reach out to her husband. Often her intention is loving ("Hi sweetie, how has your day been?") sometimes her intention is functional ("Hey Jimmy, will you take over the kids for a minute, I have been doing this all day and I could sure use a break"), but a common thread that I hear is that men very often feel "attacked" at the door.

The two important things are "attacked" and "at the door." The reason they are important is that couples do not understand the role of the stress hormones AND the importance of looking at this relationally. When men and women understand that what men are going through is a sense of attack (not at all what women intend); they can modulate the encounter. The crucial aspect of the intervention I make is this. The entire reason the couple moderates the encounter is NOT so the "woman takes care of the 'poor baby husband' who comes home so tired and upset from work." It is so the two of them can create and maintain and sustain an effective and loving connection based on understanding and acknowledgement of their physiological and psychological needs. And that is the theme of their show.

The husband, then, has space and intention to be able to say "I am aware that you have been with the kids all day, and that you need a break. Give me 10 or 15 minutes of 'down' [sometimes playfully called 'cave'] time and I will be able to decompress a minute and help you the way we both know is good for ourselves and each other." (Of course it NEVER goes like this.) I like to use a lot of broad humor when talking about it, and most of the couples I work with appreciate that. I call it "cave time" and most of the couples really appreciate the metaphor. It really takes very little time for men to "decompress" in these stressful situations. When I prescribe 10 minutes (more or less) of cave time, and suggest to the wives that they leave the guy alone, it is usually met with rolled eyes, and with the suggestion that I am "on the man's side." More often than not when they return, both people talk about how the "cave time" works for them as an antidote to feeling as though they are stuck at the door at the end of the day.

It also works in conflict, when couples get to a point where the men can't (or won't) talk in ways that the women seem to need them to. A common complaint I hear is that "he just doesn't talk to me when I want him to" or "we can't talk about feelings." Emotions, particularly vulnerable feelings, are not exactly a premium on the battlefield, or in the workplace, or while killing the wooly mammoth. Guys just do NOT know how, do not have much comfort or facility with emotional vulnerability. We want to please you, though, so we look into our computers, our experiences, our life lessons for ways to talk about feelings, and this is what we find. First, men who talk about their feelings aren't "real men." Second, you must make your wife happy at all costs.

The other part of that is that women don't know about these conflicting messages, because we also have the overlay of "never let them see you sweat" or see your vulnerability. Most men I know, most men I treat, do one of three things with that. They shut down completely and talk about their tools or their car, or change the subject so that their wives can talk about THEIR day, which is easy enough because women will do that. But when it is really tough, or essential (a sick child, a death in the family, why did you stay out late last night?), a man's ability to move into the affective realm is almost always overlaid with shame and embarrassment, and it is almost always expressed with anger. Why? Most men, like me, have one way or another absorbed a message that if your wife is upset, it is YOUR fault. This is a message, it turns out, of immense power. I have tried on various occasions to introduce that concept to men in therapy, with almost universal failure. What I say instead is that fault, blame, responsibility are non-starters. I use humor, again, to ask the following question.

*R:* How does it make you feel if you really believe that it is your fault that Sue feels bad?

*J:* God, it's just awful.

*R:* Well, what if it wasn't your fault?

*J:* That would be better. *(Sue glares at him.)*

*R:* Listen me out, Sue. What's important here is that no one can control you like a puppet. *(She glares at me. I'm thinking that is a good sign.)* If he is responsible for whether or not you feel good or bad, then you are just a nice little Stepford Wife, and he gets to call all the shots, and nothing you do or say has any consequence. But . . . (here it comes) if the TWO OF YOU decide to be influenced by each other . . . that changes everything. You have an opportunity to share every part of this, to look for ways to be equal, and to acknowledge mistakes as opportunities, even when you mess up.

*S:* This does NOT sound easy.

*R:* Well, what would you like?

*S:* *(sigh)* . . . I think I just want to know that he wants to try . . . he doesn't always . . . he . . . doesn't always want to try.

*R:* And what do you want him to know?

*S:* I want him to know that I am trying. That I want to be here. That I am not the enemy . . . it's like everybody is the enemy.

*R:* Ha! . . . Well, marriage certainly isn't for the faint of heart. The thing is, I really don't think men and women are from Mars and Venus. I just think we are from earth, both very different and similar. But I think we want the same things. And remember what I told you about connection. The most important part of the circle of connection is repair and reconnection. Here is why. We have to anticipate and acknowledge that every good marriage, every good relationship is going to have disconnections of one kind or another. The key is learning how to have safe disconnections where you don't fault each other or punish each other for misunderstanding or miscommunication or making a mistake. Things happen all the time, and the idea of having ways to move through them that strengthen a relationship is what this is all about. Repair and reconnect in a stronger more resilient way. Got it?

## Conclusion

Relational-Cultural Therapy, once thought of as a model best suited for working with women, has evolved into a theory that works effectively with both women and men. In addressing issues of power, the importance of context—the ongoing need, experienced by all people, for connection—is highly relevant to couples therapy. Couples do not exist in a vacuum; they exist in a sociopolitical context. This context sets different expectations for men and women and those expectations inform every heterosexual couple. Often these larger cultural dynamics are left unexamined or unnamed, leaving the members of the couple feeling personally at fault for the suffering the couple is going through. RCT allows the couple to grasp how many of the miscommunications are culturally determined; it also provides a neurobiological template for understanding some of the differences that men and women bring to the couple.

Therapists working with RCT must develop awareness not only of their clients' gender and power issues but of their own as well. In working from disconnection to connection, therapists too must examine their own biases, relational shortcomings, cultural immersion, including the effects of their own gender socialization. The couple comes to therapy looking for change, movement, growth, with the hope of developing a more satisfying, robust and zestful relationship. The therapist arrives with the hope that he/she can contribute to the growth of the couple. RCT provides a model that acknowledges that both couple and therapist will grow in these interactions, that all growth is mutual.

# References

Freud, S. (1920). *Beyond the Pleasure Principle*. Standard Edition, trans. J. Strachey, Vol. 18. London: Hogarth Press.

Gottman, J.M. (1999). *The marriage clinic, a scientifically-based marital therapy*. New York: Norton.

Jordan, J., Kaplan, A., Miller, J., Stiver, I., & Surrey, J. (1991). *Women's growth in connection*. New York: Guilford.

Jordan, J. (2010). *Relational-Cultural Therapy*. Washington, DC: American Psychological Association.

Jordan, J. (Ed.) (2011). *The power of connection*. New York: Routledge.

McIntosh, P. (1989, July/August). White privilege: Unpacking the invisible knapsack. *Peace and Freedom*, 10–12.

Miller, J. (1976). *Toward a new psychology of women*. Boston: Beacon Press.

Miller, J. (1986). *Toward a new psychology of women* (2nd ed.). Boston: Beacon Press.

Miller, J. & Stiver, I. (1997). *The healing connection: How women form relationships in therapy and in life*. Boston, MA: Beacon Press.

Robb, C. (2007). *This changes everything: The relational revolution in psychology*. New York: Farrar Strauss.

Shem, S. & Surrey, J. (1998). *We have to talk: Healing dialogues between men and women*. New York: Basic Books.

Taylor, S. (2002). *The tending instinct: Women, men and the biology of our relationships*. New York: Henry Holt.

Taylor, S. (2006, December 15). Tend and befriend: Biobehavioral bases of affiliation under stress. *Current Directions in Psychological Science, 15*, 273–277.

# 10

# MOTHERHOOD AND MARRIAGE

## Naming the Work

*Kumkum Pareek Malik*

This chapter proposes that a woman's ongoing work of motherhood is often not an understood or supported aspect of her marriage. It is hoped that couples therapy can become a safe place where a woman's work of motherhood can be acknowledged and supported.

The work of motherhood is often invisible. It is also not a valued part of dominant discourse (Coll, Surrey & Weingarten, 1998). This chapter aims to make the work visible so that it can be named within a couple's work on their marriage. It is important to make the work of motherhood visible as it contributes to the robustness of a couple's relationship with each other: not only is her work as a mother a major preoccupation for the woman, it also occupies huge amounts of her physical and emotional resources, and is a major organizing principle for her life choices.

Marriage in this chapter refers to a heterosexual marriage. Of course, this is not the only form of marriage, nor is marriage the only family unit within which children are raised. The clinical cases presented in this chapter are from the author's work with mothers within various stages of a heterosexual marriage, including separation and divorce from such a marriage. In the absence of other, equally relevant information from other kinds of marriages, the material presented in this chapter should be considered applicable within the context of a heterosexual marriage.

Relational-Cultural Theory (RCT) (Miller, 1976; Jordan, 2011) will be used as the theoretical frame to study the work of motherhood, particularly its impact on a couple. RCT enhances the process of making the work of motherhood visible. When this is not done, a chasm can open up within the marriage that only deepens with time, since there is disconnection rather than connection (Miller, 1988).

All case composites will highlight the actual work that a mother does. The first one will name the physical work of motherhood that is invisible and devalued. The second one names and elaborates on the emotional work of motherhood. The third one highlights difficulties in couples therapy when neither the therapist nor the couple has a language for the ongoing work of motherhood. Mothers themselves often do not see their work as "real" work, and have difficulty placing value on it. It is more common for them to call it "love," and to downplay the work and skill that goes into such love.

The cases will highlight how a mother's physical and emotional resources are clearly being consumed by the work of motherhood. Yet, as mentioned above, she is quick to downplay her work. It is common for mothers in my practice who work from 5.30 am to 12 am every day, to have difficulty falling asleep because their brains do not have permission to let down. They normalize the demands on them, still believe they are not doing enough, and feel guilt and inadequacy about themselves as mothers. It is as though a mother is forbidden to say that these are impossible hours and inhumane demands: as if saying this reflects badly on her as a mother and as a person, and casts doubt on her love for her children. This seeming prohibition and the tendency to discount her own work needs to be understood by a couples therapist, and a mother encouraged and supported to talk about her daily work, instead of brushing it off as "something all mothers do."

## Controlling Images of Motherhood

The theoretical construct of controlling images (Collins, 2000) can be helpful in comprehending some of these observable behaviors, especially the apparent contradiction between the huge physical and emotional labor expended by a woman on behalf of her childen and her worry and guilt about not doing enough, her ongoing concerns about being a good mother, and her sense of personal inadequacy around her motherhood work.

A controlling image (CI) is an image or series of images about a group that define how that group is perceived by others. For example, CIs about the "good mother" are of a mother who is selfless, ready to suffer, always available for her children. Such images control the cultural imagination about what mothers should be like, and the socially permissible realm of possibility for mothers.

CIs are generated by voices outside the group, usually by voices that exercise dominant power in society. They serve to maintain the status quo and are based on stereotypes. When the real experience of a group member (a mother who is frustrated because she has to stay up five nights in a row to tend to her sick child) departs from the CI (she should be able to ignore her own needs because she should be totally concerned about the child's suffering, and the child's needs), that difference is defined as deficiency. The individual (in this case, the mother) begins to feel personal inadequacy and shame, which makes it very difficult to share her experience with others. The individual comes to believe that there is something intrinsically wrong with her, because her experience is not fitting in with what a good mother is supposed to feel. This makes it risky for her to share

150

her experience. Emotional isolation as well as a silencing of the real lived experience occurs, strengthening the power of the CI as the only "truth" about that experience or about that group as a whole.

The dominant CIs about motherhood in this culture are that motherhood is easy and "natural" for a woman, that it is intrinsically fulfilling, and that it should be a joyous experience. There are at least two results of the controlling images of motherhood. First, there is an absence of support for the actual work of motherhood. This makes perfect sense, given that motherhood is not imagined as work: it is supposed to be a fulfilling and joyous state. What supports could be needed for a natural, easy and fulfilling way of being? Support is therefore deemed unnecessary.

Secondly, there is incomprehension about how and why motherhood can generate stress. So any stress is downplayed and minimized. Again, given the CIs, this is a logical stance. How and why should an easy, natural and fulfilling state be stressful? The implication is that motherhood should be effortless, something that women do easily. Real work is more commonly associated with work in the public sphere: work that is visible, has a commonly recognized value, and is accorded respect.

## The Stresses of Motherhood

Thus, when a mother talks about feeling stressed, the unstated assumptions are that she is making a big deal about nothing, or that she is not doing something right, or that she is doing something wrong. As a consequence, any stress arising from the "non-existent" work of motherhood is labeled as a problem with the woman, rather than understood to be a result of the demands of the work itself. There is also a societal silence about the fact that mothers do this work for most of their adult life without being accorded respect or acknowledgement. A woman who is a mother will spend 18 plus years doing constant work that is considered non-work. This is an area of a marriage where a couples therapist can open up the silence, and encourage sharing as well as respect for the work.

## Naming the Physical Work of Motherhood

As mentioned above, mothers have difficulty naming their work as real work, and are apt to be dismissive about its value. The following case composite presents such an example and highlights the work. It is hoped that when a mother is helped to name her work within a couple's therapy context, the couple can be helped to address the underlying anger, resentment and depression that often accompanies devaluation and minimization.

Mina is the mother of three children. She came to see me for depression, and reported that it had been building up over time. After her third child, Mina had decided to stay home, after almost 10 years of working as a lawyer. The demands of her work and the needs of her three children became irreconcilable, even when she tried working part-time.

As part of this decision to stay home, Mina told me she is now fully responsible for doing all the work of making a home and raising the children. However, when asked to list her work, Mina had difficulty doing so, saying vaguely that she did what all mothers do, and that she probably does not do as good a job as she should.

A therapeutic intervention was made. Mina was reassured that this difficulty of listing her work of caring as real work is common with mothers; at the end of a day of constant labor, a mother often cannot say just what it was that she did all day. The culture she lives in does not value the work of caring as work, and she has learned to dismiss it or minimize it, even while she is doing it. In addition, the controlling images of motherhood being a joyous and fulfilling role silence and prohibit a woman from accessing her own experiences that are different: that motherhood is real, constant work, and that it is often challenging, tiring, and repetitive. Mina reported that she felt tongue-tied, unable to represent her own experience within the therapeutic relationship. This mirrored what she was experiencing in the world about her work as a mother.

The exercise of naming is important for the therapist and the husband to witness in a couples therapy setting. Within an individual therapy setting, it proved very powerful. Mina, in response to her therapist's request, agreed to be mindful of what she did each day, listing each thing that she did, even if she thought it was "not really work."

After several weeks of keeping notes, here is what emerged. The list is almost too long to read, which is the point. It comprises real work done every day. Each day, Mina is responsible for all the meals and snacks. This includes planning them to ensure that the family's nutritional needs are met, shopping for them, making the meals and the snacks, laying them out for the family, and cleaning up after them. Mina is also responsible for gathering up the laundry, doing the laundry, folding and putting it back, cleaning the house, and cleaning the bathrooms. Her work includes daily pick-up, daily putting away, and daily finding anything that is needed and cannot be found, as well as shopping for whatever is needed in the house, or for clothing the children. All maintenance work for the home, such as house repairs, technology needs, seasonal chores in the house and the yard, maintaining a garden, plumbing issues, problems with appliances, heater and air conditioner malfunctions, and any other requirements for creating and maintaining a home are also her responsibility.

While she is doing all of the above, Mina is also responsible for the children's daily needs. She wakes them up each day, ensures that they are dressed and fed, and then drives them to and from school, and to and from the daily evening activities; three different schedules in three different locations each evening, organized amid making dinner, feeding the children, cleaning up after the meal, while also making sure all homework is done. She supervises homework every evening, and most often, helps all three children with it, including their attitudes to it, their moods at the end of the day, and their learning styles. She makes sure all school supplies are available, keeps track of the letters and notices sent from school about activities the children will be involved in, the permission slips that need to be monitored and signed for these activities, getting the supplies for said activities, and rearranging her day with no notice to support these activities. She is responsible for keeping up a relationship with teachers, intervening whenever something is not working for the teacher or the child.

Each evening after the children go to bed, Mina puts the remaining food into containers and stores it appropriately for another use, washes the cooking pots and pans, loads the dishwasher, cleans the kitchen, prepares next day's lunches, and makes sure school clothes and supplies are ready: this necessitates going through each backpack to ensure there are no notes from school unreported by a child, all homework is packed, outfits are washed and ready with accessories such as socks and shoes, along with weather-related outerwear. While Mina is doing all of this, she is also scanning her mind about what she might have forgotten and what she should be doing next, while she is also checking her email and returning phone calls. She will then pay bills, and worry about money.

Despite all her work, Mina feels vulnerable because she does not make money; she feels she is not doing "real work." This underlying vulnerability is caused by the invisibility and lack of legitimacy in our society for her work of motherhood. It is an unnamed trigger, and can trigger all other worries without warning, resulting in "I am not doing enough," "I should do more," or some other variant of anxiety, guilt, or self-blame. Mina will then put more effort into whatever she is doing, with a nagging imperative to ease everyone else's life just a little bit more. As long as something needs to be done, Mina will feel responsible for getting it done. Serving the needs of others has become Mina's primary avenue to self-worth and purpose.

Naming her work, and having her therapist as a witness for her work, made Mina realize that she was constantly working, and that this work was necessary for children to thrive. This realization eased her self-criticism that she was not doing real work or was making too much of the work. She also realized that she did this work in isolation. The most painful part of her isolation was that her closest friend, her husband, did not recognize what she was doing. Mina's husband often gets home late at night. By then, the living area is picked up and looks nice, the children have been bathed and fed, and next day's lunches have been made. He is usually very tired, but does not ask Mina if she is tired too. When she talks about her day, his mind often wanders, and Mina feels she is talking about unimportant details that he couldn't be bothered with. Thus her experience in the relationship mirrors what she has experienced in the culture: her work of motherhood is not important. Her husband is also simply mirroring what he has learned in the culture outside: motherhood is easy and natural for a woman, Mina has the easier time of the two; she is comfortable at home while he is out there doing real work with real stresses.

Another aspect of Mina's work that directly impacted the couple's life as a social unit is the family's social connectedness. Mina manages relationships with the parents of her children's peers, organizing play dates for the children, informal dinners with the parents, and contributions of the family to the school's need for volunteer efforts. She also manages the family's relationship with their religious and cultural heritage. They are Jewish, and it is very important to them that they raise the children with strong awareness of, and connectedness with their heritage. So Mina spends regular time and effort to develop a relationship with their temple. She makes sure to organize her and the children's time such that they can go there consistently: the children go to Hebrew language and Jewish culture and history classes, in addition to their regular school and school-related extracurricular activities. Mina also makes time to volunteer at her temple, thus creating a community for the family.

## The Devalued Work of Caring

Mina was helped by the therapist's intervention about the role of the culture in devaluing the work of caring. She began to understand that both she and her husband had internalized this low value on a mother's work, and began to work at naming her own work and seeking respect for it within her marriage. The experience proved to be very empowering for her, and she reported that her husband felt a sense of relief that she had a specific request from him, rather than unspecified anger.

Mina's decision to seek therapy was triggered by an incident with her husband. He remarked on the status of the unfinished basement, piled high with "get to it someday" boxes and stacks: surely Mina could get to this in her free time? Mina reported to me that she had exploded, screaming at her husband that she worked longer hours than he did, was always tired, and felt that no one saw how much work she did on behalf of each person in the family. She had made the choice to stay home for the sake of love, she said. She had not expected to feel invisible, and had not anticipated the slow draining away of her self-esteem. A couples therapist could make a significant intervention at this point, helping the couple communicate rather than blame and withdraw from each other. Mina has exploded not because she is "irrational," but because the gap between her inner experiences of motherhood and the lack of naming and acknowledgement of them has become simply too wide for her to negotiate. Her isolation and depression can be lessened when her partner, with the help of the therapist's intervention, "sees" her work for what it is (Miller & Stiver, 1997). When the mother lists her work, opportunities will open up for noticing and acknowledging the work. Small concrete ways of doing so can be suggested. For example, the daily task of ensuring that there are meals on the table can be acknowledged. When the children talk about activities they are engaged in, such as dance or tutoring, Mina's efforts to make them happen can be acknowledged. Similarly, noticing her mood and exhaustion level at the end of the day, and asking her what was stressful for her, can be suggested. This is an effective intervention on many levels: it allows the couple to check in with each other, it opens up space for the mother to share her experience of mothering, and it also provides the husband with a platform for giving concrete acknowledgement for work done in the course of his wife's day. This intervention exemplifies RCT's theoretical construct of relationships as action (Surrey, Kaplan & Jordan, 1990).

Becoming parents often affects a marriage in unexpected and powerful ways. Both partners can take quite some time to adjust. The major part of parenting is still done by the woman. By actively intervening to name this, a couples therapist can help a couple acknowledge this safely, while also helping them to understand the labor and skill required by the mother to do the work of motherhood, and then helping them to renegotiate the unwritten rules of support between them.

It is often helpful to provide language. Most couples are helped when they can see that the work requires a high degree of constant attention to the children by the mother: attention that must simultaneously weave between the differing needs of children who may be far apart in age, temperaments and capacity to manage their needs. Mina's work of love requires the skills for anticipatory as well as ongoing empathy; the ability to be attuned such that she can be present for each child with a differentiated responsiveness. Her cognitive and affective experience is constantly oscillating and zigzagging between the needs of each child, the daily maintenance work for her family, and the interfacing between each child and the outer world. On one hand, it is like having three bosses; each making simultaneous, equally urgent demands, with little capacity to monitor themselves, and requiring responses that are pressing and time-sensitive. On the other hand, while she is juggling and titrating her capacity to register, understand, and respond to these three bosses, she is also responsible for single-handedly running the entire company. Her work is without fixed hours. Children's needs do not arrange themselves neatly along a nine to five schedule. They do not switch off when mom is tired, it is late, or she is juggling other pressing demands. Additionally, she is doing a job where there are no feedback sessions, no mentoring, no coaching, and no "team" that meets regularly for companionship and encouragement. The only feedback a mother gets is when something goes wrong. She needs acknowledgement, respect and support from her husband in order for her to continue to love him over time.

A couples therapist can play a significant role in shifting the dynamic in a marriage around the wife's work of motherhood. Too often, clients report that the couples therapist "babies" the husband, rather than expecting him to shift unhelpful behaviors. Work that is deeply demanding of the wife's physical and emotional resources needs to be accommodated within the shared reality of the couple, and a couples therapist is in a position to help them do so.

## Naming the Work of Caring

The next case example highlights the impact on a marriage when the woman is aware of her work of motherhood, tries to explain it to her husband, but runs up against the societal silence and incomprehension around the work of caring being non-work. Sometimes a husband may not understand that caring is real work, that it requires skill as well as effort, and results in exhaustion as well as other emotions such as frustration, impatience, and worry. In other words, the work of empathy is real work, often requiring paying attention to the needs of the other person(s), and deserves validation and support like any other demanding work.

Alisha came to see me for ongoing depression, alternating with anxiety. At our first meeting, she described herself as "reactive," even when she did not *want* to be. She reported that she worried a lot. Her marriage of 11 years had settled into an uneasy status quo. She was angry with her husband but could not say why. When not angry with him, she felt guilty about feeling angry. Overall, she rarely felt happy or joyous, even though, according to her own analysis, there were no obvious reasons for her to feel unhappy. This caused additional guilt, which then turned into increased efforts to be happy and pleasant. Invariably these efforts failed, and she felt depressed or anxious in a restless kind of way.

Alisha worked full-time along with her husband Paul, managing their consulting business. By her own definition, this work was fiercely demanding and the marketplace unforgiving. They had two children, ages six and three. If you were to meet Alisha during a school gathering, she would strike you as a smart, articulate and successful woman.

As part of the initial evaluation I began to gather details of her day. Like many women, Alisha tended to underplay most of her work as a mother. For example, she described her day something like this: mornings began with getting the children off to school and day care, then she worked all day at the office, then the children were picked up by her, and then came dinner and then whatever else needed to be done in the evening: baths, office work, etc.

In contrast to this bland recital, Alisha had no trouble describing the details of her day at her business: the fragmented demands of difficult customers, the juggling of time for service delivery versus business creation, the constant attention needed for managing the employees, as well as myriad other issues that she faced each day.

I remarked that it seemed that the children somehow just got to school from their beds, and then disappeared when they got home. Dinner just appeared on the table, and the children magically reappeared. They then automatically ate whatever was put before them. Somehow, after that, they were asleep in their beds. And the housework, laundry, errands, cooking breakfast and dinner, cleaning, managing the finances, I asked? Who did all of that?

Reconstructing Alisha's day as a mother and the work that went into it took several tries. At first Alisha was hesitant. She felt she would bore me, or that I would judge her as making too much of what every mother did every day. I reassured her that I needed to understand the details of her day. Then she became anxious: upon exploration, it emerged that she felt vulnerable about being judged. It became clear that Alisha felt she fell short of her own ideas about a "good mother" many times. Life was so rushed, with so many stresses: she felt she short-changed the children.

An intervention was made, validating her concerns. Alisha reported feeling very validated when I shared that most mothers I work with felt just like she did; no matter how much they did, there was always something left undone, or something they felt had not been done well. She was startled and very curious when I named the role of the culture: the impossible expectations that exist about the "good mother." If children need something, we expect a mother to do it, regardless of whatever else she might also be doing. I further explained how we internalize the values of the culture we live in, and that our standards for what is normative are for the most part an unconscious process. Understanding and absorbing this intervention shifted Alisha's belief that her feelings reflected a personal shortcoming of hers. When Alisha felt secure that I would not be judging her, here is what emerged.

Each day began with Alisha getting up earlier than Paul, so that she could shower and get ready before waking up the children. She then went individually to each child's room. In her six-year-old's room, Alisha would call the child's name (Bunny) to wake her up. On a good day, she would smile as the child opened sleepy eyes, while bending down to kiss the six-year-old, murmuring "good morning" while holding her close. On a stressed morning, she would be aware of the need to manage the tone of her voice, of not rushing the child too much, and controlling the effect on her of the pressure of time. She told me she was not always able to do all of that. Regardless, Alisha's work as a mother began with waking Bunny up. The six-year-old would get out of bed and begin the daily ritual of heading to the bathroom.

Alisha would then proceed to her three-year-old's room, sit on the bed, and gently call for her to get up. She told me that this younger child (Peanut) tended to be fussy in the morning, so Alisha tried her best to manage her own impatience and stress levels while waking up Peanut. On a good day, she usually stroked the child's face and forehead while waking her up. The three-year-old opened her eyes to mom's face smiling and murmuring endearments, along with prompts for her to get up. Often, Alisha would pick up the sleepy child with much laughter and kisses exchanged, and head towards the bathroom.

Once in the bathroom, it was necessary to enter into negotiations with Peanut around who would open the toothpaste tube, who would spread the paste, turn on the tap, and so on; such negations were necessary, Alisha explained, since Peanut was at the stage when she wanted to do everything herself. It required Alisha to anticipate what Peanut needed, slow herself down, and exercise patience; again, Alisha was quick to own that this was not always possible, but she felt very pressured to make the waking-up ritual a warm and pleasant start for the children's day.

Next came the stage of undressing and then dressing for the day. This could go smoothly or it could take time, like it did that morning, said Alisha, with a new-found confidence that her work as a mother would be understood and respected. Today her three-year-old had insisted that mom leave the room: the child who could not find or pull on a pair of socks unaided wanted to dress all by herself.

After this had been dealt with (and mom allowed to stay in the room), Alisha faced her younger daughter's decision to wear a pink mini skirt over the blue jeans that she absolutely had to wear that day. It was a good morning, so Alisha was able to distract and cajole Peanut to wear just the blue jeans. The pink skirt, it was agreed, would be much better with the pink socks and the pink shoes which Peanut could wear as soon as she came home from school, when she could also dress up her doll in exactly the same way.

At the same time that Alisha was involved in these delicate matters, she could hear Bunny in the other room, dressing by herself. Keenly aware that Bunny might feel left out, or need help, but not always able to do anything about it, Alisha would periodically call out to her older child, checking in with her. She found herself switching her attention constantly between the two children, making sure to keep both within the circle of her care.

Eating breakfast and putting on jackets, mittens and hats followed much the same pattern. Alisha's attention swung back and forth between the two children: one might spill the cereal, another refuse to eat or just eat slowly, then the first one start whining for another kind of cereal, etc. By the time the children were dropped off, Alisha felt exhausted.

## Exposing the Complex Demands of Motherhood

This is a very demanding morning, requiring work that is challenging, complex and unpredictable. Empathy allows Alisha to be responsive to her children's needs, but it is not always easy. Alisha needs to be attuned to two different children with their differing ways of interacting, their likes and dislikes, and their particular mood that morning. At the same time she must be aware that there is a time constraint, and both the children and she need to be somewhere else. Regardless of what she may or may not be able to do, Alisha is aware that she needs to deal with the pressure inside herself in order to respond to the needs of her children. She is attuned to the press of time as well as the needs of her children, and aware that these can conflict.

Alisha responds to her children's needs, opening herself up to what they need, rather than just what she needs. RCT points to the importance of mutuality in relationships (Jordan, 1986). An individualistic response would be based on the needs of the individual self, rather than the holding of one's own needs as well as the needs of the other during interactions.

Some of the children's needs are visible in the traditional sense. It is apparent that the children will need to be woken up, teeth brushed, clothes changed, beds made, laundry brought downstairs, and so on. But RCT sensitizes us to needs that are not always apparent, and the work of empathy involved in anticipating these needs and responding to them. Alisha is taking account of some "invisible" needs and capabilities of the children. The little one is fussy when she gets up, Alisha says to me. So she, Alisha, is responding to this anticipation by waking Peanut up with remedies for the grouchy mood: the soothing comfort of hugs, the safety net of being picked up and taken to the bathroom, and the holding environment of patience, as this little one launches herself into the developmental task of practicing mastery over daily skills.

On a good day, Alisha balances how much to help Peanut, so that she can support the growth of the child's confidence in her own developing ability. Her focus is on empowering her child. She takes account of the child's need to do things herself. By anticipating the child's limits, and then building in responses that allow her to succeed, Alisha protects her child from feeling shame. When the toothpaste oozes out because the pressure applied by those tiny, hot little hands is too much, Alisha exclaims that the toothpaste is naughty this morning; it is running away.

## Role of the Couples Therapist

A couples therapist can make a powerful intervention by naming and acknowledging the layers of anticipation, thoughtfulness and responsiveness involved in Alisha's seemingly "easy" work of a routine morning. Reframing her work as that of creating a holding environment, a Petri dish so to speak, within which each child is held and nurtured, and her growth fostered, would allow the couple to have a respectful language about Alisha's work.

Alisha shared that Paul was an involved and helpful parent too. He regularly did the grocery shopping, helped with the driving, emptied out the dishwasher each morning, and loaded it up at night. But somehow, his interaction around the children's needs did not work. For example, explained Alisha hesitantly (and with much defending of Paul), he would ask a child to brush her teeth. Upon being told that she wanted to do it herself, he would agree with the child and walk out of the bathroom. When he would return a few minutes later, expecting the job to be done, the child might still be in the bathroom, trying to push the toothpaste back into the tube, after having emptied the entire tube out onto the counter: she was curious to see how much there was inside, she would earnestly explain to Daddy.

This would lead to Paul chastising her, devaluing her judgement that she could "do it on her own," and Peanut bursting into tears or refusing to brush her teeth. Or he might try to help Bunny pull a sweater over her head, and do it in a way that led the child to cry, or the sweater to get stuck. This is where the complexity of empathy needs to be named. An intervention by the couples therapist, giving language to the complexity of empathy, would safely allow Paul to view the children's and his own behavior differently. The dynamics of empathy are not easily available for the learning in the culture at large. Additionally, empathy is often confused with vulnerability, which is equated with weakness in the larger culture. RCT's explication about the role of empathy, as well as its importance for relational zest, can be used effectively to help couples understand how to support each other for mothering as well as parenting work.

## Getting Caught between the Needs of Husband and Children

Without such support, Alisha found herself caught between the expectations of her husband and the needs of the children in her marriage. Pay attention, she would scold the children; children don't just do a task to get it done, she would explain to Paul; it is the *process* of doing it that captures their attention. Hurry up, she would say to the children, feeling constrained to take care of Paul, who was often impatient with the pace of "growth in process." Turning around, she would feel the pressure to also stay true to the children's reality: they are continuously practicing their own capacities, they are discovering a new facet of the world, she would try to explain to Paul. They don't know how to time themselves to suit our adult needs. She tried to be empathic to everyone's needs, but did not know how to ask for empathy for herself (Jordan, 1984). There were days when her head would spin with the non-negotiable needs of each of her loved ones, and she would end up feeling drained.

At other times she had tried sharing that she got frustrated too. There was always so much to do, and not enough time. She tried to explain how motherhood had altered her in response to the needs of her children. She wanted Paul to understand her pressures and to share her mothering experiences, so that she felt less alone. Her stress would reduce if Paul and she could talk about the way she constantly had to juggle her work demands, his expectations, the children's needs, and the necessity to keep the household running. She reported to me that she did try to explain in ways that would help Paul understand her and the children's needs. Children need us to adapt to their capacity to understand the world, she would explain to Paul. Telling a child to lay the table when she was six, and then getting angry because all she did was put out four plates, did not help the child and might even be harmful to her sense of confidence in being able to navigate the world successfully. Teaching such young children how to "stretch" required taking the time to teach skills, in ways that did not shame them or make them feel inadequate. Empathic interactions were the "love" within which they made sense of a sometimes confusing and demanding adult world.

But it did not work. Paul would either refute Alisha or become dismissive of her. He felt that Alisha had her way of doing things, he had his, and that was that. Alisha would get upset, and try to shift the discussion to the children's needs, wanting Paul to understand why she did what she did, and why she often felt overwhelmed, tired or stressed out. Paul would then feel that she was being manipulative and "emotional," or she was controlling. He would blame her for his interactions with the children, or leave it all up to her.

Alisha was left feeling misunderstood, angry, and constantly anxious, with a strange sense of loneliness even though she was surrounded by her family.

She also felt that her work was unseen. There was no space to discuss why she sometimes felt tired, frustrated or anxious around the children's issues, no space to discuss that she needed support too. Over time, the unspoken bottom line between the couple had become that her moods and complaints were because she was unable to manage the children in a way that did not tire her out, or make everything proceed seamlessly. She made too much of the work, she was too sensitive, too caring, too emotional, or too rigid. Alisha had no words with which to defend herself, or to rebut Paul's version of her reality. She resented having to defend herself, and felt that there was something missing in her marriage.

## When Individualism meets Relationality

Something is indeed missing: Paul and Alisha are using different paradigms of relating to the children. Paul is using an individualistic approach in which each person is separate, and is encouraged to be "independent" (Jordan, Kaplan, Stiver, Surrey, & Miller, 1991). He extends this to his parenting style; when Peanut says she wants Daddy to leave the bathroom because she can brush her teeth herself, Paul does so. When he returns to see the job undone, and the bathroom sink a mess, with all the toothpaste out of the tube, he loses his temper because of the pressure of time to get to work, and because the child said she could do something that she could not. He tells her she cannot, she was wrong, and Peanut dissolves into sobs saying, "I can, I can, I can."

Alisha is using a relational approach (Jordan et al., 1991). Upon being asked by Peanut to leave, Alisha assesses the child's desire as well as her lack of ability. She nurtures the desire without shaming the child for her lack of ability. She also tolerates the pressure of time, Bunny's needs in the other room, and her own desire to move the morning along quickly. She balances her own needs with those of the children.

These two markedly different ways of responding to the same situation are very particular ways of organizing self–other interactions. Paul's way, and the dominant way of this society, is the individualistic way. Each individual is a separate unit. There is legitimate permission to place one's own needs as the primary needs to consider in each relational situation. When the "other" is capable of explicitly stating his/her needs, the individualistic person can choose to consider those needs, and then choose to be responsive or not. Mutual responsiveness as a way to be mutually responsible for the wellbeing of a relationship is not a requirement for the individualistic self.

Additionally, there is no responsibility on the individualistic person to hold his/her needs in abeyance for the sake of relational or caring work. There is permission to ignore the needs of the other if these interfere with fulfilling one's own needs. Furthermore, there is also permission to ignore the impact of one's actions on the relational other when fulfilling one's needs. Paul behaves as he does with the children and Alisha not because he does not love them; he does so because in the individualistic model of self–other relationships, he is doing nothing wrong.

Though the above example uses a male/female distribution for individualistic versus relational approaches, this is by no means my intent or the model of RCT. Both men and women are capable of organizing relationships in an individualistic or relational manner. In addition, it is possible and indeed common for men and women to have both relational and individualistic ways of organizing self–other interactions.

Alisha proceeds with her self being "in relationship" to the other. Action taken on her own behalf considers the impact of these actions on the other. She holds herself responsible for ensuring that in the process of fulfilling her own needs, she does not minimize or lose sight of the needs of the relational "other." In addition, her interactions with the children are not about winning or losing the argument or the issue of the moment.

## Communicating Around Difference

Alisha found it very helpful to have a language for the different ways of being in relation with the other, and was able to face the fact that Paul used an individualistic model in which his self needs were above the needs of his family. He did not think this was wrong, and indeed would have been startled to learn that empathy for the other requires holding the needs of the other as equally important. She also found it very helpful to understand that motherhood is a very particular kind of relational contract. With help from the therapist, she slowly found a language and the confidence to begin to challenge Paul's assumptions about a relationship, and about parenting. She learned to say that the "other" in this case is a child. In such a relationship, the child is unable to take care of his/her own needs, and must depend upon an adult for physical as well as psychological sustenance. For a long time, this child will also be unable to articulate her needs in ways that allow for negotiation, compromise, or delayed gratification in the adult sense. It takes sustained effort, cognitive and affective skills, as well as practice to make sense of a child's needs. Her marriage would have been helped by the involvement of a couples therapist who had language for viewing motherhood and the work of empathy through an RCT theoretical framework.

## When Couples Therapy Encounters Difficulties

Priya has been married for 19 years and came to see me because of difficulties in the couple's relationship. They had sought therapy at Priya's initiative, because there had been some significantly disturbing interactions between her husband and the children. He had an authoritarian style with the children, but now they were pushing back. This was making him raise the stakes, by shaming or punishing them.

For example, most recently he had insisted that the children ski down a slope they were not ready for. Both (one 13 and the other 11) refused, whereas earlier they would have felt anxious, cried, but done it. Upon their refusal, he lost his temper, told them they were wimps, and stormed off. Both children became afraid that Dad would not come back, Dad did not love them, and that he was ashamed of them.

Priya told me this had been a pattern, and she had been too intimidated by her husband's authority and self-confidence to look at it. She felt powerless and unable to effect change (Miller, 1982). But her children's repeated meltdowns forced the issue, and the couple decided to go to couples therapy to figure out how to communicate about the children.

During couples therapy, Priya realized that she was fearful of naming her husband's behavior, and let the therapist know this. She was referred to me, with the message from the therapist that she had "issues."

Very quickly, it became clear that Priya felt "less than" her husband. She could not immediately give words to this feeling; it was just a nameless, formless belief. Slowly, however, she was able to realize that she believed his job of earning money was more important than her own. Indeed, she did not quite believe that her work on behalf of her children could be called "important." She was anxious and insecure about finding fault with her husband: she feared his anger, not because he was unusually explosive or abusive, but because if he became angry with her, she felt intensely anxious. She realized that this anxiety made her feel she was somehow not good enough, and this feeling completely disorganized her. She would feel she had to make it all right, get her husband to somehow approve of her again, and get the relationship back to a place where she had his approval. Priya had been a successful career woman before having her children, and did not recall having this intense insecurity and fear around her career issues. She realized that she had had no external validation for anything that she did for 15 years.

Priya has internalized our culture's beliefs about the non-existence of the work of a mother. She dreads the common question "do you work?" When faced with it, she replies, "No, I am a stay-at-home mother." Her "issues" are more than personal shortcomings: they are the result of being in a "low-power" situation. The purpose of her life, to devote herself to caring for her children and making a family, is hardly regarded as a purposeful or high-power life situation in our culture. Priya believes she does nothing of "real" value. She has no reason, evidence or support to believe otherwise.

## The Importance of Contextualizing Feelings

Naming her feelings as the result of her situation, rather than as personal shortcomings, was a very effective intervention with Priya. She quickly understood the impact upon her of the isolation within which she worked, and the low power of her work as a mother. She began to re-view her anxiety as an accumulation of years of feeling minimized and invisible, and feeling powerless to change it. She worked hard in therapy to observe herself, and actively manage these feelings. As a result, she began to respect herself, and expect to be respected for her unfailing love and work for her family. Over time, she found a new balance between mutuality and power in her relationship with her husband (Jordan, 1991). Unfortunately, the couple stopped couples therapy because Priya felt unsupported by the therapist as she grew in her individual work. She felt that there was something missing in the therapist's attempts to name issues, and ended up telling the therapist that she felt that her work as a mother was invisible, devalued or pathologized in the couple sessions.

## Conclusion

This chapter has attempted to give language to the physical and emotional work of motherhood and its impact upon a marriage, using the theoretical framework of RCT. It is suggested that a mother's work on behalf of her family is often an important organizing principle in her life. However, this work can be invisible and devalued. This chapter suggests, through case composites, that a mother's work be a legitimate focus of attention, communication and support during couples therapy.

## References

Coll, C.G., Surrey, J.L., & Weingarten, K. (Eds.). (1998). *Mothering against the odds: Diverse voices of contemporary mothers*. New York: Guilford.

Collins, P.H. (2000). *Black feminist thought* (2nd ed.). New York: Routledge.

Jordan, J. (1984). Empathy and self boundaries. *Works in Progress*, No. 16. Wellesley, MA: Stone Center Working Papers Series.

Jordan, J. (1986). The meaning of mutuality. *Works in Progress*, No. 23. Wellesley, MA: Stone Center Working Paper Series.

Jordan, J. (1991). The movement of mutuality and power. *Works in Progress*, No. 53. Wellesley, MA: Stone Center Working Paper Series.

Jordan, J. (2010). *Relational-Cultural Therapy*. Washington, DC: APA Books.

Jordan, J., Kaplan, A., Stiver, I.P., Surrey, J., & Miller, J.B. (1991). *Women's growth in connection*. New York: Guilford.

Miller, J.B. (1982). Women and power. *Works in Progress*, No. 82-01. Wellesley, MA: Stone Center Working Paper Series.

Miller, J.B. (1976, 1986). *Toward a new psychology of women* (2nd ed.). Boston: Beacon Press.

Miller, J.B. (1988). Connections, disconnections and violations. *Works in Progress*, No. 33. Wellesley, MA: Stone Center Working Paper Series.

Miller, J.B., & Stiver, I. (1997). *The healing connection: How women form relationships in therapy and in life*. Boston: Beacon Press.

Surrey, J., Kaplan, A., & Jordan, J. (1990). Empathy revisited. *Works in Progress*, No. 40. Wellesley MA: Stone Center Working Paper Series.

# 11

# A NEUROBIOLOGICAL-RELATIONAL APPROACH TO COUPLE THERAPY

*Mona DeKoven Fishbane*

## Couple Distress

Couples coming to therapy often feel disconnected, disempowered, and defeated. Not knowing how to reach each other, partners get stuck in polarized positions and reactivity, each setting the other off in repetitive unhappy cycles. These impasses take on a life of their own, as couples are caught in their unhappy dance over and over again (Scheinkman & Fishbane, 2004). The reactivity is driven by the emotional brain, especially the amygdala, which is constantly assessing: Safety or danger? Friend or foe? And for distressed partners, the amygdala frequently determines that the other's behavior signals: Danger! Foe! Then, rather than turning toward each other as allies, partners turn against each other as enemies, or away from each other as strangers (Gottman & Driver, 2005; Wile, 2002). Both may feel like victims, blaming the other and justifying their own behavior. These rationales are often irrational and self-serving. In addition to our amygdala, we have a prefrontal cortex (PFC) that needs to make sense of things. High atop our left PFC is a region that has been called "the Interpreter" (Roser & Gazzaniga, 2004). The Interpreter narrates a story that explains our experience—and unhappy partners often concoct a self-justifying story.

In addition to our neurobiological wiring, other factors support the blame game. Cultural beliefs and practices play a major role in this dynamic. The dominant US culture privileges competition over collaboration, and debate over dialogue. Individualism and independence are core beliefs; autonomy is prized, representing the sanctity of the separate self. Conflict is often perceived as a zero-sum game, with a winner and a loser. When one feels misunderstood or hurt, a narrative with a linear view of self as victim and other as perpetrator is often adopted. These beliefs permeate couples' relationships, as partners interpret slights and injuries through these cultural lenses.

In the relational approach to couple therapy offered here, both the neurobiological and the cultural factors that underlie the couple's impasse are addressed. Other dynamics that contribute to couple distress are identified as well, including family-of-origin issues, past hurts within the couple's relationship, and larger contextual issues such as power, gender, marginalization, and trauma. The therapist holds both partners' pain while challenging problematic behaviors and beliefs that keep the couple polarized. For example, the therapist offers an interactive, circular view of the couple's dance as an alternative to the linear victim–villain narrative. The myth of independence is challenged with a more interdependent view, and autonomy is reframed as including relational accountability (Boszormenyi-Nagy & Krasner, 1986). Constraints based on gender socialization are addressed. And, as we will see, power dynamics are redefined to include a focus on relational empowerment and disempowerment.

## Rethinking Power

Power is commonly understood as Power Over—the power to prevail over others. Power Over dynamics and power differences between partners are real and need to be addressed; risk of violence or intimidation must be assessed. Sometimes there *is* a clear perpetrator and a clear victim. A circular, systemic view does not neglect individual responsibility and accountability. Power differences related to money, class/education, gender, or access to resources affect couples' interactions. Patriarchal cultures typically grant men greater power, as males are socialized to dominate and assume entitlement in relationships, while females are taught to accommodate and caretake.

But for all their ostensibly greater power, men in heterosexual relationships are often at a disadvantage when it comes to navigating the world of emotions. Males tend to be de-skilled in empathy during their development, while many females practice empathy on a daily basis. Patriarchy harms men as well as women, constraining both in ways that contribute to couple polarization. The discourse about power has been enlarged by relational theorists to include a focus on Power To (the ability to self-regulate and live in accordance with one's values) and Power With (the ability to relate with respect, empathy, generosity, and equality) (Fishbane, 2001, 2011; Goodrich, 1991; Surrey, 1991). "Relational empowerment" (Bergman & Surrey, 2004; Fishbane, 2011, 2013; Surrey, 1991) and "relational competence" (Jordan, 2004) encompass these aspects of power, the ability to navigate with skill and generosity in the social–emotional realm. We will explore ways to facilitate relational empowerment in couple therapy. First, let us consider the relational nature of the self, and the neurobiology underlying couples' impasses.

## Wired to Connect

Neuroscience offers support for the interdependent view of the self that has been proposed by relational theory (Fishbane, 2001, 2007; Jordan et el., 1991; Jordan, 2009). We are fundamentally relational creatures, and need others throughout our lives. The field of interpersonal neurobiology explores the neural basis of this interdependence (Siegel, 2010b; Hasson et al., 2012). Human survival has been attributed in part to our highly developed social brain, which adapted to the exigencies of group living (Cozolino, 2006). It is our gregarious nature that allowed us to develop complex coping mechanisms and to build cultures and institutions. Our ability to cooperate and be compassionate is at least as important as our ability to compete (Keltner, 2009). Like other mammals, we know how to "tend and befriend" (Taylor, 2002) as well as contend.

The baby's brain is wired through connection with caregivers, especially right-brain-to-right-brain attunement (Schore, 2003). Secure attachment between child and parents has beneficial consequences throughout life. This parent–child connection is not perfect, however; even in well-attached mother–baby pairs, 70% of the interactions are out of sync (Tronick, 2007). What matters is the repair; in these well-attuned dyads, the mother repairs well and often. Indeed, it has been suggested that these frequent experiences of disconnection and repair build a kind of "quotidian resilience" in the child, who learns that difficult moments can be mastered and turned around (DiCorcia & Tronick, 2011). On the other hand, chronic disconnection, neglect, abuse, and other severe traumas leave a lasting and damaging mark on the brain. Early trauma and chronic stress can negatively affect cognitive function by impacting the hippocampus, an area of the brain key to memory and learning—and loaded with receptors for cortisol, the stress hormone. Experience matters, as it wires the brain by changing connections between neurons (Kandel, 2007) and even affects the expression of genes (Davidson & Begley, 2012).

Our need for others continues throughout life. Social rejection triggers pain centers in the brain (Eisenberger & Lieberman, 2004). Adult love is considered an attachment relationship (Hazan & Shaver, 1987; Johnson, 1996). Loneliness and unhappy relationships in adulthood negatively affect health and longevity (Cacioppo & Patrick, 2008; Kiecolt-Glaser & Newton, 2001). Couples co-regulate each other, for better or worse, each partner's neurophysiology shaping the other's (Solomon & Tatkin, 2011). Women are particularly vulnerable to the ups and downs of their intimate relationships. Whereas men generally experience a health benefit from marriage, for women it depends on the quality of the relationship (Kiecolt-Glaser & Newton, 2001).

We have a deep need to "feel felt" by others (Siegel & Hartzell, 2003). This attunement is particularly important for couple relationships. Empathy is a complex phenomenon, having both automatic and conscious elements (Decety & Jackson, 2004). At the automatic level, we pick up on others' experiences by feeling them in our own bodies. This resonance, or embodied simulation, allows us to feel what the other feels "from the inside out" (Siegel & Hartzell, 2003). Both mirror neurons and the insula have been identified as key to this process (Iacoboni, 2008; Lamm & Singer, 2010). Empathy also requires higher cognitive functions, such as consciously putting oneself in the other's shoes. There are individual differences in empathic accuracy, and motivation can increase empathic accuracy (Ickes, Gesn & Graham, 2000).

## Brain: The Basics

The human brain evolved in such a way that our higher cognitive capacities are built on top of our more primitive brain. The triune brain is composed (in order of evolution) of the reptilian brain (automatic reflexes), the mammalian brain or limbic system (emotional processes), and the neocortex (McLean, 1990). The prefrontal cortex (PFC), at the front of the brain, unique to humans, allows us to think and plan. Thanks to our PFC, we can muse about the past and contemplate the future. This capacity can be distorted into rumination and regret about what we've done, or anxiety about what might happen. The system is not perfect. And our later-evolving higher brain did not supplant the more primitive layers. We carry within us our inner lizard and inner mammal (and they are often running the show!). Evolution does not proceed in a rational, logical fashion; it keeps what works well enough to maximize survival of our DNA into the next generation.

The way our brains evolved can cause us trouble at times, even heartbreak. Couples' kneejerk responses, their dances of reactivity, often reflect the activation of more primitive areas of the brain. The amygdala, at the heart of the limbic system, is dedicated to keeping us safe. It makes snap decisions before we are even aware of what we have seen—or that we are making a decision at all (LeDoux, 1996). When couples escalate quickly—leaving the therapist befuddled as to how things got so heated so fast—it is the couple's amygdalas that are running the show. I call this, with a little poetic license, "the dance of amygdalas" (Fishbane, 2013).

Current neuroscientific research challenges Descartes' separation of thought from emotion, and mind from body (Damasio, 1994; Davidson & Begley, 2012). The neurobiology of emotion has received much attention in recent years; "I feel, therefore I am" balances Descartes' "I think, therefore I am" (Cacioppo & Patrick, 2008). Thought and feeling are inextricably intertwined (Davidson & Begley, 2012). The brain is embodied, with a bidirectional flow of information and influence. Emotion is a body experience. As William James noted long ago, it's not that we cry because we are sad; rather, we are sad because we cry. The physical experience precedes awareness of the emotion. Information from the body travels to the insula in the brain, where we ultimately become aware of what we are feeling. The ability to name one's emotion is an important aspect of emotional intelligence; the inability to do so is called alexithymia. Emotions are not just internal, individual experiences; they are relational processes, communications to others. Emotions can be contagious (Hatfield, Cacioppo & Rapson, 1993). In a couple, one partner's raised eyebrow can send the other partner into a rage—all in an instant. As we will see, emotion regulation is key to mental health, and to couple well-being.

Our higher brain eventually catches up to our limbic system and starts to reason about and reflect upon our emotional experience. As we have seen, the PFC may do this in a self-justifying manner. But the PFC can help us be mindful and thoughtful in our responses, and it can calm down the amygdala. *It is the PFC that allows us to live within our values.* With prefrontal intentionality, the couple can create a healing, relational narrative in lieu of the competitive one that fuels the blame game and the dance of amygdalas.

*Humans are creatures of habit.* The neural basis of habit is conveyed in Hebb's theorem: "Neurons that fire together wire together" (Siegel, 1999). The more we do something, the more likely we will do so in the future. *But humans are also creatures of adaptation and change.* Our ability to adapt to changing circumstances allowed *Homo sapiens* to survive, whereas the more rigid Neanderthals died out. Neuroplasticity, the ability of the brain to change, was, until a decade ago, considered a characteristic of the child's and adolescent's brain, but not available to adults. Recent research has revolutionized our thinking about the adult brain's ability to change. Neuroplasticity, it turns out, can continue in adulthood, especially if we nurture it with healthy living habits. The brain, an "organ of adaptation" (Cozolino, 2006), is constantly being sculpted by experience; learning changes the brain throughout life. *Neuroplasticity allows couples to change and to create relationship plasticity.* Sharing this optimistic view of human adaptability with clients can empower them in their journey of change.

## Working with Couple Reactivity: The Vulnerability Cycle

As partners set each other off, with blame and defensiveness predominating and emotions running high, *both are the victims of and the (inadvertent) co-creators of a circular dance of distress.* In therapy, we work together to understand the dynamics fueling the dance. We map the couple's reactive processes using the Vulnerability Cycle Diagram (Scheinkman & Fishbane, 2004). *As we co-construct the diagram and slow down the dance, amygdala reactivity gives way to prefrontal thoughtfulness and curiosity.* Let us explore how this works with a brief case example.

Steven lost his business in the recent economic recession, and has been unemployed for two years. Early in their marriage, his wife, Carolyn, who works as a nurse, took upon herself the jobs of raising their two children and being the social-emotional expert in the family. The original couple contract—he supported the family financially, she did almost everything else—worked adequately for them, until Steven lost his work and his way. He has become morose and withdrawn. Carolyn has increased her hours at work to keep the family afloat. She is stressed and exhausted, and seeks sympathy from Steven for her plight. But Steven feels ashamed over his failure and does not know how to comfort his wife. Instead, he gets defensive or pulls away, which infuriates Carolyn. She was attracted to Steven because he was strong and protective,

170

unlike her depressed mother. She felt safe with her husband. And while she over-functioned as a wife and mother, the financial security her husband offered gave her peace. When Steven lost his job, she lost that sense of security. And Steven is unable to help more at home as she has increased her work hours. He is limited by his socialization as a man; he has never gotten the hang of empathy, seeing his role only as financial provider. He has been motivated to do better than his father, who never was able to hold onto a job, and who was berated by Steven's mother for his failure to provide. Steven's identity is wholly bound up with his work success. Having lost that, he has nothing to offer his wife or teenage children.

Carolyn's anger grows as she feels that she has to do everything; old feelings from her family of origin are reactivated. Carolyn was a parentified child, over-burdened at a young age, trying to make up for her mother's depressive passivity and withdrawal. With Steven morose since his career collapsed, Carolyn is flooded with old memories of being with her depressed mother. She is not conscious of all this; her amygdala becomes activated when she sees Steven moping around the house. In addition to her realistic concerns about her husband in the present, her amygdala is sending alarm signals from her past.

When his wife angrily criticizes him for being mopey and self-indulgent, Steven is flooded with old memories as well—it feels like his mother berating his father for not being a good provider. Steven vowed at a young age to be a great provider when he grew up, and he dedicated himself to his studies as a child and to his work as an adult. His efforts evoked love and pride from his mother (and from his wife). Now, with his career in shambles, Steven is lost; he is reliving the nightmare of his childhood. His sense of inadequacy and shame, already activated by his unemployment, is heightened further in the face of Carolyn's contempt. He withdraws and shuts Carolyn out, as he did when his mother berated his father. Steven's withdrawal is like salt on a wound for Carolyn, as it reminds her of how her mother would shut herself up in her room for hours at a time. It leaves Carolyn feeling abandoned. And the more abandoned she feels, the more critical she becomes; the more critical she becomes, the more Steven withdraws in self-defense.

Their impasse is informed by cultural beliefs and gender socialization as well as family-of-origin dynamics. Steven has seen his male role as the provider, and has not developed empathic or nurturing skills. He was never a hands-on dad; he was emotionally disconnected from Carolyn and the kids even before he lost his job. As a female, Carolyn was raised to nurture and over-function in the social–emotional realm. Even while she resented their unfair division of labor throughout their marriage, she didn't challenge these traditional gender roles. This imbalanced arrangement collapsed along with Steven's career.

## The Vulnerability Cycle Diagram

Each partner has vulnerabilities; Carolyn feels overburdened and abandoned, Steven feels inadequate. And when their vulnerabilities are triggered, their survival strategies get activated. Carolyn's survival strategies (aside from being very responsible) include anger and criticism. Steven's survival strategies (aside from being a good provider, which he is unable to do at this point) include withdrawal and defensiveness. Each partner's survival strategies trigger the other's vulnerabilities, which activate that partner's survival strategies, which set off the other's vulnerabilities; and the couple become caught up in a vulnerability cycle (Figure 11.1).

*Both Carolyn and Steven have a linear, blaming view of their interaction.* Carolyn claims that she is so angry because Steven withdraws from her and the children, and Steven counters that he only withdraws because she is so critical all the time. I show the couple the blank vulnerability cycle diagram, and have them fill in their own vulnerabilities and survival strategies. They are intrigued, and see how *each one's behavior is creating the other's.* They are able to visualize *the circular nature of their dance.* They see that they are both victimized by this unhappy dance, and that "who started it?" is a pointless question. By drawing the cycle, we have externalized it (Scheinkman & Fishbane, 2004; White, 1989). I encourage the couple to confront their cycle together, as a *team.* I also suggest that if blame shows up, they could invite it to leave. They laugh, understanding that they don't have to be driven by their own automatic, blaming tendencies; they can make conscious choices in keeping with their marital and personal goals.

### Speaking from Vulnerability

I ask them to speak from their vulnerabilities, since this tends to evoke empathy. By contrast, when they lead with their survival strategies of criticize–withdraw,

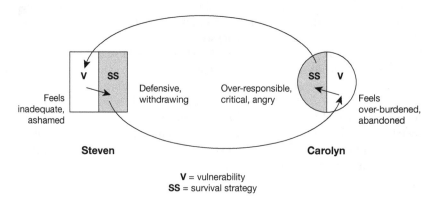

V = vulnerability
SS = survival strategy

*Figure 11.1* A Vulnerability Cycle

they push each other away just when they most need each other. I coach Carolyn to say, "Steven, I am feeling overwhelmed—could you pick up the kids from school and start dinner?" This formulation brings out Steven's protectiveness, and he is glad to oblige. He wants to be helpful (and it helps that Carolyn is specific in her requests rather than complaining globally about his lack of participation at home). When Steven is feeling hurt by Carolyn's tone if she gets critical, I suggest he say, "Honey, I want to hear your concerns, but your anger is pushing me away and making me feel small. Please speak to me more gently so I can listen."

## *"Growing Up" Survival Strategies*

We also work on helping both partners "grow up" their survival strategies. For many couples in distress, their survival strategies are rigid, frozen in the form they were used to in childhood. I encourage clients to *adapt their survival strategies for more flexibility*. Steven learns to negotiate a Time Out break when he is feeling overwhelmed rather than storming off and leaving Carolyn abandoned—and to come back to the conversation when he is calmer (Gottman & Gottman, 2006). Rather than turn away from or against her, he learns to turn toward her, to engage with Carolyn around their differences (Bergman & Surrey, 2004). This is scary for Steven, but when I frame it as empowered and protective behavior, he is willing to try. He also learns to identify his automatic defensiveness and experiments with taking off his defensive shield and listening to Carolyn with an open heart (Fishbane, 2011). *He is enlarging his definition of what it means to be a man.*

I work with Carolyn on her survival strategies of over-functioning, anger and criticism. She sees that Steven wants to help out more at home, but that he withers under her contempt. Hearing that contempt is particularly toxic in marriage (Gottman & Gottman, 2008), Carolyn commits to learning how to put her concerns forth to Steven assertively rather than aggressively. I am not encouraging Carolyn to self-silence, but rather to address the inequity more successfully, in a way that he can hear her. We discuss concrete ways that Steven can contribute to the family's well-being and to greater equality in the marriage.

## *Separating the Present from the Past*

I help the couple identify their amygdala triggers. Steven becomes alarmed and frightened when he hears Carolyn's contemptuous tone. As far as his amygdala is concerned, he is a child again hearing his angry mother berate his father. Carolyn identifies the moments when she feels unprotected, overworked and abandoned with Steven, just as she felt as a child. We work to separate the present from the past (Scheinkman & Fishbane, 2004). Thus, Steven comes to see that he can respond to his wife's concerns more maturely; she is not his mother, and he is not his father. And Carolyn realizes that she is not the parentified, helpless girl of her childhood; she can put forth her needs pro-actively with Steven so the couple can create a more equitable arrangement. In our work, both partners become *less reactive and more reflective*—about their marriage, and about how they express their own needs and manage their own reactivity. In the process, both are becoming more emotionally—and relationally—intelligent.

## Power Dynamics

Men typically have more power than women in our culture. Physical size, earning power, and a sense of entitlement that flows to men in patriarchal societies all stack the deck in favor of males. Prior to his career collapse, Steven certainly fit this picture. While never a bully or violent, he assumed a position of male privilege by refusing to participate in family life with anything approaching equality. Carolyn, accustomed to over-functioning in her family of origin, made her peace with the inequity because she was grateful for the financial stability and the emotional solidity offered to her by her husband. With his unemployment, she lost both, and ended up with a depressed husband. She felt she was carrying the whole family on her back. The couple became mired in a power struggle. Carolyn wanted Steven to seek treatment for his depression and to consult a job coach; and she wanted him to help more at home. Steven was stuck in a narrow view of manhood, and resisted being told what to do by a woman. Their power struggle was laced with gender dynamics.

*Power struggles tend to emerge when couples are stuck in a competitive mindset.* They may struggle over reality, fighting over what really happened in an interaction. I suggest that the couple make room for multiple realities rather than "dueling realities" (Anderson, 1997). Power struggles often reflect *relational disempowerment*; when partners don't know how to get through to each other, they may resort to Power Over behavior. Couples are less likely to engage in Power Over tactics when they are able to self-regulate and communicate their needs respectfully. We turn next to helping partners develop greater emotional and social intelligence, Power To and Power With. *In shifting from power struggle to relational empowerment, both partners work to be their best self rather than "besting" each other* (Fishbane, 2011).

## Power To

### *Emotion Regulation*

Power To is the ability to live intentionally, and to make choices in keeping with one's values. A central aspect of Power To is self-regulation. As the ancient Roman philosopher Seneca said, "Most powerful is he who has himself in his own power." Neuroscientists and psychologists have studied emotion regulation; it entails the PFC calming down the amygdala. In both depression and a propensity to violence, this neural circuit fails to function properly (Davidson, Putnam, & Larson, 2000; Johnstone, van Reekum, Urry, Kalin, & Davidson, 2007). Some people are more prone to temper and stress reactivity than others; neuroscientists are studying these individual differences. Likewise, individuals have an emotional set point, some more upbeat (with a neural profile of greater left prefrontal activation), while others are more negative (right prefrontal profile) (Davidson & Begley, 2012).

Whatever one's natural emotional tendencies, it is possible to learn new techniques for emotion regulation, and even to change one's emotional set point. Mindfulness meditation has been found to be especially effective in this regard (Davidson & Begley, 2012). Learning to identify, name, tolerate, and manage one's own emotions are vital skills for couple relationships. Like many men, Steven doesn't know how to name his emotions, much less manage them. Neuroimaging shows that when we name our feeling, the PFC becomes active and the emotional brain quiets down (Creswell, Way, Eisenberger, & Lieberman, 2007); we "name it to tame it" (Siegel, 2010a). Unable to identify his own feelings or deal with Carolyn's, Steven shuts down and shuts Carolyn out when she gets angry. He becomes highly agitated, his heart racing with anxiety, as he enters diffuse physiological arousal (DPA) (Gottman & Gottman, 2008). He stonewalls with Carolyn in order to calm himself down neurophysiologically; for Steve this is about survival. Learning how to recognize and manage his own emotions—and to be open to Carolyn's—is key for Steven's growth and for relational transformation in the marriage.

### Cultivating Choice: "Tools for your Toolbox"

When offering clients emotion regulation techniques, I call them "tools for your toolbox" (Fishbane, 2007). Men—as well as women—love this "tools" language, as it points to empowerment and focuses on concrete actions. I help both partners cultivate their ability to *choose* their own behavior, so they can live intentionally rather than on automatic pilot. One technique that helps develop choice is The Pause, taking a moment to stop and breathe before responding. Deep breathing activates the parasympathetic nervous system, which counters amygdala reactivity. And stopping to think about one's priorities activates the PFC. These techniques facilitate relational empowerment in both partners, making them less likely to feel like victims or get caught up in mutual blame.

### Making a Relational Claim

Another core relational skill is putting forth one's needs or agenda in a respectful manner. I help partners "make a relational claim" with each other (Fishbane, 2001), holding their own needs, the needs of the partner, and the relationship all at the same time (see also Bergman & Surrey, 2004). This is a complex skill, and many clients find it difficult. In her family growing up, Carolyn learned to defer to others and not make too much noise about her own needs; this family-of-origin training dovetailed with her gender socialization to be a "nice girl" and not make waves. Now, unhappy in the marriage, she resorts to contempt, which is equally problematic. Steven learned in his family to focus single-mindedly on his own achievement so he would not end up a failure like his father. He did not learn how to balance his own agenda with others' needs. His gender training reinforced this self-focus, hampering his ability to develop "relational awareness" (Jordan, 2004). Both partners need to learn how to make a relational claim, and in doing so, to overcome old cultural, gender, and family-of-origin constraints.

### *Healing Intergenerational Wounds*

In our therapy, Steven and Carolyn bump up against unfinished business with their families of origin. Like many clients, Steven and Carolyn carry old wounds and grievances toward their parents. They are "living under the spell of childhood" (Fishbane, 2005), hoping that their parents will one day give them what they need. These adult children feel disempowered and victimized with their parents, a stance that fuels their reactivity in the marriage.

I work to help Steven and Carolyn "wake from the spell of childhood" (Fishbane, 2005), to see their parents with adult eyes rather than through the lenses of a disappointed child. "Think of your mother as your grandmother's daughter, and get to know her that way," advises Michael Kerr (personal communication, 2003). This inspires a more sympathetic and mature perspective on parents, a position of "filial maturity"—which most people don't develop until at least their mid-30s (Fingerman, 2002). Since the PFC isn't fully wired until around age 25, it appears that a mature brain is necessary for a mature intergenerational relationship. Waking from the spell of childhood also involves the ability to take care of oneself. When we can deal with our own upsets and can self-soothe, we are not at the mercy of others' ability or availability to do this for us. "Parenting yourself from the inside out" (Siegel & Hartzell, 2003) gives you the freedom to rely on others when they are available, and to rely on yourself as well. Healthy couple relationships entail a balance between soothing each other and self-soothing (Greenberg & Goldman, 2008).

Some clients choose to update and "grow up" their current relationship with their parents. I call this "the loving update" (Fishbane, 2005). I work with Carolyn and Steven to respectfully invite their parents to a more mutually beneficial way of interacting. Most parents respond positively to such an invitation, especially if it is clear that this discussion will not be a blame-fest, but is geared to improving the parent–child relationship. It is remarkable how positive shifts in the intergenerational realm strengthen the couple relationship. The work is synergistic, as partners become more resilient and competent in both contexts. When Carolyn and Steven are less burdened by fear or resentment toward their parents, they are freer to become more resilient in their marriage.

## Power With

Power With is the ability of partners to care for each other, share power, and co-create a mutually satisfying relationship. Research shows that equality is associated with couple satisfaction (Knudson-Martin & Mahoney, 2009; Walsh, 2006). Gay and lesbian couples are more likely to have equal relationships, since they don't fall into traditional gender roles with each other; they negotiate their roles and division of labor more overtly and more fairly (Gottman et al., 2003; Johnson, 2009). We all assess the balance of fairness in our relationships (Boszormenyi-Nagy & Krasner, 1986); and if, like Carolyn, we feel we are giving a lot more than we are receiving, we can become resentful.

### *Nurturing the Relationship: Proactive Loving*

In a Power With mode, partners work as a team on their relationship to become co-authors of their lives together. I encourage couples to cultivate the "We" (Bergman & Surrey, 2004; Fishbane, 1998, 2011), to think about the impact of their own behavior on the relationship. Thus, when Carolyn feels annoyed with Steven, she learns to think through her comments to him rather than going to contempt. She anticipates his response, and considers how she might bring more relational intelligence into the interaction. Likewise, when Steven feels put upon or insulted by Carolyn's criticism, he tries to see it from her perspective and modulates his response. Both feel more empowered as they bring prefrontal thoughtfulness to their interactions, as they hold the "We" in mind. *They are shifting from reactive to proactive loving.*

I ask the couple to brainstorm about how they would like their relationship to look if they were its co-authors; they create a "relational purpose statement" (Bergman & Surrey, 2004). Both would like more tend-and-befriend and less fight-or-flight in their interactions. Steven wants to be less reactive to Carolyn's suggestions, and indicates a readiness to consult a job coach and to resume his exercise regimen. He prefers not to try medications or psychotherapy at this point, but is willing to revisit this if his depression continues. Both partners want Steven to be more involved with their teenage kids; his (hopefully temporary) free time can be seen as a gift in this regard. Steven agrees to address household chores more equitably—especially when I tell him this is what happy couples do; for many women, the man emptying the dishwasher is an aphrodisiac. Both partners want to rekindle their sexual passion, which has dwindled during their impasse.

Another key issue for this couple is their empathy gap. Carolyn, like many females, has been practicing empathy from an early age; Steven, like many males, was socialized away from the world of feelings. This creates a gender gap in empathy that is troubling to heterosexual couples. Partly based in biology (females have more oxytocin, a hormone/neurotransmitter that affects and is affected by empathy; Uvnas-Moberg, 2003) and largely shaped by socialization, men and women often come differentially capable with regard to empathy. In therapy, I offer to teach empathy skills to the partner who is empathy-challenged, in this case Steven. It turns out that empathic accuracy is a skill that can grow with motivation. Researchers found that men become as empathically accurate as women when motivated to do so either by money or by a message that women find empathic men sexy (Klein & Hodges, 2001; Thomas & Maio, 2008)! Steven is intrigued to learn that empathy releases oxytocin, the same "cuddle chemical" (Taylor, 2002) that is released with orgasm. Thus empathy is framed as a learnable (and valuable) skill rather than an innate or female ability.

Care and connection are not steady states. Connection yields to disconnection, and "we" gives way to me-vs.-you. Happy couples have conflict; but they do not resort to contempt or bullying. And they, like well-attached mother–baby pairs, repair well and often (Gottman & Gottman, 2008). Repair entails processes of guilt, apology, and forgiveness. Many partners are allergic to guilt. The philosopher Martin Buber (1957) contrasted healthy guilt with neurotic guilt. Healthy guilt is an appropriate emotion when we have hurt someone; it leads us to repair. I encourage this healthy guilt, along with repair, in couple therapy. And on the other side of apology is forgiveness. When partners are blocked in their ability to experience healthy guilt, apology, or forgiveness, we work on these issues in therapy.

## The Stories We Tell

Humans are a narrating species, and the stories we tell make a difference. Couples caught up in the individualistic narrative that dominates mainstream US culture view their differences as threat or competition. A relational view of the self creates a more generous and collaborative orientation (Fishbane, 2001). In a relational view of moments of disconnection between partners, "fault" is more about fault lines or gaps of hurt and misunderstanding than about blame. In therapy, couples can be encouraged to "mind the gap" when they feel disconnected or upset with each other.

Gender stories shape us from our earliest days. Outdated stories about sex differences such as "boys are better at math" or "girls are better at empathy" are being challenged by research that points to the power of expectation and socialization in these skills. Research finds that men and women are much more alike than different, in both their brains and their capacities. Small innate differences (male infants are somewhat fussier and more active than females; boys and girls have different play preferences) become enlarged through socialization in the home and most especially with peers (Elliot, 2009; Maccoby, 1999). The games children play have a major impact on their skill development and on their brains. Cultural expectations shape men and women for different relational roles and beliefs, with females over-functioning as caretakers. This leaves many heterosexual couples with an imbalance of responsibilities in the home—and many women angry about the inequity. For both partners to thrive in the relationship, narratives about gender must be enlarged.

Cultures shape brains and behavior. From perception to neurobiological correlates of self- identity, culture impacts brain processes (Ames & Fiske, 2010). The interdependent worldview of many Eastern cultures is evidenced neuro-biologically as Asians perceive more holistically, while Euro-Americans per-ceive figure over ground. Partners from different cultural backgrounds may indeed literally see the world differently. Even when they are from the same cultural background, they have had different life experiences and different family backgrounds that have shaped their brains and beliefs. The narratives that shape us are often not visible to us; yet they affect us profoundly. Conflict between partners often reflects these differing neuro-cultural experiences. The therapist's own personal and cultural assumptions add another layer of complexity. It is vital that the therapist maintains a stance of curiosity and cultural humility with clients, and promotes the same stance between partners.

I help the couple *create a relational narrative that honors multiple perspectives*. I also encourage a *relational ethic* to increase fairness, mutual care and generosity. These values can directly impact couple reactivity. While it is true that our emotional brains often overwhelm our higher brains (bottom-up influence from amygdala to PFC), it is also the case that our goals and expectations shape our reactivity (top-down influence from PFC to amygdala). Automatic, emotional processes are influenced by the stories we tell and the expectations we have. If we hold an individualistic, competitive view of relationships, we will relate to a slight or hurt very differently than if we hold a collaborative perspective. With a relational perspective, caring for the other doesn't detract from one's self, it enhances the self—assuming there is fairness in the give and take in the relationship (Boszormenyi-Nagy & Krasner, 1986).

## Challenges of Change

### *Who's in Charge of Change?*

Change is a complex process. On one hand, habits are self-reinforcing, as neuronal circuits become deeply wired. Change is difficult. Yet we are not doomed to be slaves to our habits; the human brain is constantly adapting to new circumstances. Neuroplasticity allows us to change and grow throughout life. But neuroplasticity is harder for adults, and needs to be nurtured; exercise, paying attention, and openness to learning new things are key to brain plasticity (Doidge, 2007; Ratey, 2008). Our narrative or belief about change is crucial; a "growth mindset" facilitates change, whereas a "fixed mindset" inhibits it (Dweck, 2007). Many couples struggle with this issue, one pushing for change and the other saying, "I am the same person you married! Stop trying to change me!" Indeed, a couple dynamic in which one tries to change the other—with change as a transitive verb with a direct object (as in Carolyn trying to change

Steven)—is likely to fail. Most people do not want to "be changed" by another; they want to author their own change.

Clients are similarly wary of the therapist trying to change them. Old survival strategies may be getting in the way in the current relationship, but people hold onto their survival strategies for dear life. Indeed, in many cases these very strategies literally allowed survival during a traumatic or troubled childhood. Giving up familiar coping mechanisms is terrifying. If a client feels pressured to change by the therapist or partner, "resistance" is likely to result. When I encounter "resistance" in therapy, I assume I am stepping on a survival strategy and am pushing too hard for change. The delicate balance of accepting clients while challenging them to choose change is at the heart of the work. It is not my job to change the couple, but rather to provide them with a safe space for relational transformation. I work collaboratively and transparently, without hidden agendas or secret techniques. Rather than pathologizing their dynamics, I partner with couples' strengths and resilience. I ask what works well in their relationship and in other areas of their lives. We borrow from these positive skills already in their repertoire, and see if they can be applied to their distressed interactions.

## Safety

Clients must feel safe and respected in order to risk change. It is crucial to attend to the alliance with both partners. This can be challenging when sympathy with one feels like a betrayal to the other. Indeed, couples often look to the therapist to be the judge of who is right or wrong in the relationship. I sidestep the judge role, and work to hold the pain and concerns of both partners, adopting a position of "multilateral partiality" (Boszormenyi-Nagy & Spark, 1973), siding with both at the same time. Both must feel the therapist is on their side, even as unproductive behavior is challenged. The partiality shown to each of them is emotional as well as cognitive; clients need to feel felt as the therapist allows herself to be emotionally engaged and moved by the work (Jordan, 2009).

## Neuroeducation

Change is more easily embraced when framed as relational empowerment. The goal is for both partners to become more aware and thoughtful about their own reactions, so they can choose to live within their values. A bit of "neuro-education" can be helpful in this regard (Fishbane, 2008). I might explain, for example, that when they become reactive and go to fight or flight, it is their amygdala that is running the show. The PFC can calm down the amygdala, bringing back their ability to think and choose their own behavior. I suggest imagery work in which clients imagine their PFC coming in to soothe their rowdy amygdala (Fishbane, 2008). In addition, I might offer a brief training in mindfulness meditation, helping partners slow down their breathing and pay attention to their experience in the present moment (Davidson et al., 2003). If we are working on empathy skills, I encourage them to attune to their body experience to understand their own emotion, and to attend to their partner's emotional experience as well.

### Rewriting Scripts: The Fork in the Road

I invite partners to review a fight they had during the week, asking how each would rewrite their own script in the interaction. This Monday morning quarterbacking or "retrospective reviewing" (Atkinson, 2005)—done in a moment of calm reflection rather than in the emotional intensity of the fight—allows partners to consider their relational and personal goals. It allows them *to choose to live within their values*, a prefrontal capacity. Eventually, clients are able to catch themselves *during* an interaction and make a better choice. I call this "the fork in the road" (Scheinkman & Fishbane, 2004); rather than go down the old, automatic, unproductive path, partners consciously choose a better way. In this moment they are living in a more empowered—and more generous—way.

### Maintaining Change

For couples to change old habits and rewire neural circuits, much repetition of new habits is necessary. At first new behaviors may feel awkward; but with time and "massed practice" (Doidge, 2007), they become the "new normal." Maintaining change is a concern in all therapies; clients can easily revert to old behaviors in times of stress, illness, or fatigue. Predicting this and working with the couple on relapse prevention is important. I make it clear that I am available should the couple want to return for some "refresher" sessions down the road. When couples end therapy, our relationship doesn't necessarily end. Holding our work and their goals and new strategies in mind helps the couple stabilize their changes over the long haul.

### Journeys

When a couple comes to me for therapy, I am aware that they have been on a journey, sometimes for decades, that predates their current crisis and request for treatment. They may have had many good years together, weathered painful losses in their relationship, and seen other therapists along the way. I hold in mind their couple journey, aware that our paths will intersect for a while, and that they will continue without me, either together or separately. During our time together, I hope to help each partner become more empowered and generous, so they can navigate their ongoing journey proactively rather than reactively. Understanding the multilayered complexity of intimate relationships—from the macro level of social-contextual issues to the micro level of neurobiology to the reciprocal interactions between two partners—can facilitate the couple's relational empowerment and transformation.

# References

Ames, D.L. & Fiske, S.T. (2010). Cultural neuroscience. *Asian Journal of Social Psychology*, *13*, 72–82.

Anderson, H. (1997). *Conversation, language and possibilities: A postmodern approach to therapy*. New York: Basic Books.

Atkinson, B. (2005). *Emotional intelligence in couples therapy: Advances in neurobiology and the science of intimate relationships*. New York: WW Norton.

Bergman, S.J. & Surrey, J.L. (2004). Couple therapy: A relational approach. In J.V. Jordan, M. Walker, & L.M. Hartling (Eds.), *The complexity of connection: Writings from the Stone Center's Jean Baker Miller Training Institute*, pp. 167–193. New York: Guilford.

Boszormenyi-Nagy, I. & Krasner, B.R. (1986). *Between give and take: A clinical guide to contextual therapy*. New York: Brunner/Mazel.

Boszormenyi-Nagy, I. & Spark, G.M. (1973). *Invisible loyalties: Reciprocity in intergenerational family therapy*. New York: Harper & Row.

Buber, M. (1957). Guilt and guilt feelings. *Psychiatry, 20*, 114–129.

Cacioppo, J.T. & Patrick, W. (2008). *Loneliness: Human nature and the need for social connection*. New York: WW Norton.

Cozolino, L. (2006). *The neuroscience of relationships: Building and rebuilding the human brain*. New York: WW Norton.

Creswell, J.D., Way, B.M., Eisenberger, N.I., & Lieberman, M.D. (2007). Neural correlates of dispositional mindfulness during affect labeling. *Psychosomatic Medicine, 69*, 560–565.

Damasio, A. (1994). *Descartes' error: Emotion, reason, and the human brain*. New York: Penguin.

Davidson, R.J. & Begley, S. (2012). *The emotional life of your brain*. New York: Penguin.

Davidson R.J., Kabat-Zinn J., Schumacher J., Rosenkranz M., Muller, D., Santorelli S.F., et al. (2003). Alterations in brain and immune function produced by mindfulness meditation. *Psychosomatic Medicine, 65*, 564–570.

Davidson, R.J., Putnam, K.M., & Larson, C.L. (2000). Dysfunction in the neural circuitry of emotion regulation—A possible prelude to violence. *Science, 289*, 591–594.

Decety, J. & Jackson, P.L. (2004). The functional architecture of human empathy. *Behavioral and Cognitive Neuroscience Reviews, 3*, 71–100.

DiCorcia, J.A. & Tronick, E. (2011). Quotidian resilience: Exploring mechanisms that drive resilience from a perspective of everyday stress and coping. *Neuroscience and Biobehavioral Reviews, 35*, 1593–1602.

Doidge, N. (2007). *The brain that changes itself*. New York: Viking.

Dweck, C. (2007). *Mindset: The new psychology of success*. New York: Ballantine.

Eisenberger, N.I. & Lieberman, M.D. (2004). Why rejection hurts: A common neural alarm system for physical and social pain. *Trends in Cognitive Neurosciences, 8*, 294–299.

Elliot, L. (2009). *Pink brain, blue brain: How small differences grow into troublesome gaps; and what we can do about it*. New York: Houghton Mifflin Harcourt.

Fingerman, K. (2002). *Mothers and their adult daughters*. Amherst, NY: Prometheus Books.

Fishbane, M.D. (1998). I, thou, and we: A dialogical approach to couple therapy. *Journal of Marital and Family Therapy, 24*, 41–58.

Fishbane, M.D. (2001). Relational narratives of the self. *Family Process, 40*, 273–291.

Fishbane, M.D. (2005). Differentiation and dialogue in couple therapy. In J. Lebow (Ed.), *Handbook of clinical family therapy*. Hoboken, NJ: Wiley.

Fishbane, M.D. (2007). Wired to connect: Neuroscience, relationships, and therapy. *Family Process, 46*, 395–412.

Fishbane, M.D. (2008). "News from neuroscience": Applications to couple therapy. In M.E. Edwards (Ed.), *Neuroscience and family therapy: Integrations and applications* (pp. 20–28). Washington, DC: American Family Therapy Academy Monograph.

Fishbane, M.D. (2011). Facilitating relational empowerment in couple therapy. *Family Process, 50*, 337–352.

Fishbane, M.D. (2013). *Loving with the brain in mind: Neurobiology and couple therapy*. New York: WW Norton.

Goodrich, T.J. (1991). Women, power and family therapy: What's wrong with this picture? In T.J. Goodrich (Ed.), *Women and power: Perspectives for family therapy* (pp. 3–35). New York: WW Norton.

Gottman, J.M. & Driver, J.L. (2005). Dysfunctional marital conflict and everyday marital interaction. *Journal of Divorce & Remarriage, 43*, 63–77.

Gottman, J.M. & Gottman, J.S. (2006). *Ten lessons to transform your marriage*. New York: Crown.

Gottman, J.M. & Gottman, J.S. (2008). Gottman method couple therapy. In A.S. Gurman (Ed.), *Clinical handbook of couple therapy* (4th ed., pp. 138–164). New York: Guilford.

Gottman, J.M., Levenson, R.W., Gross, J., Frederickson, B.L., McCoy, K., Rosenthal, L., et al. (2003). Correlates of gay and lesbian couples' relationship satisfaction and relationship dissolution. *Journal of Homosexuality, 45*, 23–43.

Greenberg, L.S. & Goldman, R. (2008). *Emotion-focused couples therapy: The dynamics of emotion, love, and power*. Washington, DC: American Psychological Association.

Hasson, U., Ghazanfar, A.A., Galantucci, B., Garrod, S., & Keysers, C. 2012). Brain-to-brain coupling: A mechanism for creating and sharing a social world. *Trends in Cognitive Sciences, 16*, 114–121.

Hatfield, E., Cacioppo, J.T., & Rapson, R.L. (1993). Emotional contagion. *Current Directions in Psychological Science, 2*, 96–99.

Hazan, C. & Shaver, P. (1987). Adult love conceptualized as an attachment process. *Interpersonal relations and group processes, 52*, 511–524.

Iacoboni, M. (2008). *Mirroring people: The science of how we connect with others*. New York: Farrar, Straus & Giroux.

Ickes, W., Gesn, P.R., & Graham, T. (2000). Gender differences in empathic accuracy: Differential ability or differential motivation? *Personal Relationships, 7*, 95–109.

Johnson, N. (2009). Carrying equal weight: Relational responsibility and attunement among same-sex couples. In C. Knudson-Martin & A.R. Mahoney (Eds.), *Couples, gender and power: Creating change in intimate relationships* (pp. 79–103). New York: Springer.

Johnson, S. (1996). *The practice of emotionally focused marital therapy: Creating connection*. New York: Brunner/Mazel.

Johnstone, T., van Reekum, C.H., Urry, H.L., Kalin, N.H. & Davidson, R.J. (2007). Failure to regulate: Counterproductive recruitment of top-down prefrontal–subcortical circuitry in major depression. *Journal of Neuroscience, 27*, 8877–8884.

Jordan, J.V. (2004). Toward competence and connection. In J.V. Jordan, M. Walker, & L.M. Hartling (Eds.), *The complexity of connection: Writings from the Stone Center's Jean Baker Miller Training Institute*, pp. 11–27. New York: Guilford.

Jordan, J.V. (2009). *Relational-Cultural Therapy*. Washington, DC: American Psychological Association.

Jordan, J.V., Kaplan, A.G., Miller, J.B., Stiver, I.P., & Surrey, J.L. (1991). *Women's growth in connection: Writings from the Stone Center*. New York: Guilford.

Kandel, E. (2007). *In search of memory: The emergence of a new science of mind*. New York: WW Norton.

Keltner, D. (2009). *Born to be good: The science of a meaningful life*. New York: WW Norton.

Kiecolt-Glaser, J.K. & Newton, T.L. (2001). Marriage and health: His and hers. *Psychological Bulletin, 127*, 472—503.

Klein, K.J.K. & Hodges, S.D. (2001). Gender differences, motivation, and empathic accuracy: When it pays to understand. *Personality and Social Psychology Bulletin, 27*, 720–730.

Knudson-Martin, C. & Mahoney, A.R. (2009). The myth of equality. In C. Knudson-Martin & A.R. Mahoney (Eds.), *Couples, gender and power: Creating change in intimate relationships* (pp. 43–61). New York: Springer.

Lamm, C. & Singer, T. (2010). The role of anterior insular cortex in social emotions. *Brain Structure & Function, 214*, 579–591.

LeDoux, J. (1996). *The emotional brain: The mysterious underpinnings of emotional life*. New York: Simon & Schuster.

Maccoby, E. (1999). *The two sexes: Growing up apart, coming together*. Cambridge, MA: Harvard University Press.

MacLean, P.D. (1990). *The triune brain in evolution*. New York: Plenum.

Ratey, J.J. (2008). *Spark: The revolutionary new science of exercise and the brain*. New York: Little, Brown.

Roser, M. & Gazzaniga, M.S. (2004). Automatic brains—Interpretive minds. *Current Directions in Psychological Science, 13*, 56–59.

Scheinkman, M. & Fishbane, M.D. (2004). The vulnerability cycle: Working with impasses in couple therapy. *Family Process, 43*, 279–299.

Schore, A. (2003). *Affect regulation and the repair of the self*. New York: WW Norton.

Siegel, D.J. (1999). *The developing mind: How relationships and the brain interact to shape who we are*. New York: Guilford.

Siegel, D.J. (2010a). *Mindsight: The new science of personal transformation*. New York: Bantam/Random House.

Siegel, D.J. (2010b). *The mindful therapist*. New York: WW Norton.

Siegel, D.J. & Hartzell, M. (2003). *Parenting from the inside out*. New York: Penguin.

Solomon, M. & Tatkin, S. (2011). *Love and war in intimate relationships: Connection, disconnection, and mutual regulation in couple therapy*. New York: WW Norton.

Surrey, J. (1991). Relationship and empowerment. In J.V. Jordan, A.G. Kaplan, J.B. Miller, I.P. Stiver, & J.L. Surrey (Eds.), *Women's growth in connection: Writings from the Stone Center* (pp. 162–180). New York: Guilford.

Taylor, S.E. (2002). *The tending instinct: Women, men, and the biology of our relationships*. New York: Henry Holt.

Thomas, G. & Maio, G.R. (2008). Man, I feel like a woman: When and how gender-role motivation helps mind-reading. *Journal of Personality and Social Psychology, 95*, 1165–1179.

Tronick, E. (2007). *The neurobehavioral and social-emotional development of infants and children.* New York: WW Norton.

Uvnas-Moberg, K. (2003). *The oxytocin factor: Tapping the hormone of calm, love, and healing.* Cambridge, MA: DaCapo Press.

Walsh, F. (2006). *Strengthening family resilience* (2nd ed.). New York: Guilford.

White, M. (1989). The externalizing of the problem and the reauthoring of lives and relationships. In M. White, *Selected papers.* Adelaide, Australia: Dulwich Centre Publications.

Wile, D. (2002). Collaborative couple therapy. In A.S. Gurman & N.S. Jacobson (Eds.), *Clinical handbook of couple therapy* (3rd ed. pp. 91–120). New York: Guilford.

# 12

# HEALTHY RELATIONSHIPS DURING UNHEALTHY TIMES

## Relational-Cultural Theory Group for Partners Facing Cancer

*Constance A. Johannessen*

> It is only when we truly know and understand that we have limited time on earth and that we have no way of knowing when our time is up, that we will begin to live each day to the fullest, as if it was the only one we had.
>
> (Elisabeth Kübler-Ross)

Millions of individuals face the diagnosis of cancer every year. An almost equal number of people are impacted simply through their marriage or commitment to the newly diagnosed patient. Over many years of practice, this author has witnessed the devastating effect the illness can have on relationships. The stress couples experience often creates intolerable situations, leading to physical and/or emotional abandonment. These outcomes only make the cancer journey more difficult and painful and can have significant impact on the patient's healing.

This chapter is a guide for professionals who work with couples to find ways to strengthen and maintain the health of the relationship while enduring the strains of cancer treatment. With their backs against time, cancer patients consistently identify their relationships as meaning the most to them. Often they wish they could feel closer to the person they love, or at least more fully share their innermost thoughts during this difficult course. This is the very moment when professionals can assist couples to strengthen their relational resilience.

Groups have long been a helpful setting for cancer patients to grasp the treatment culture and provide support. This chapter describes the development of cancer groups for couples that is embedded in Relational-Cultural Theory. The basic premise of these groups is that an emotionally connected couple will better cope with and manage the relational storm that can occur.

What follows is the introduction of a couples group, the unique struggles of each partner and my experiences and perspectives as co-leader.

## Introduction to Group

I stood at the door waiting for the new members to arrive. The parking lot was still near empty as I anxiously stared out. Upstairs, my co-leader continued to welcome the first couple into the group. They were friendly and animated, with the wife revealing that she was overcoming Stage III breast cancer.

Five couples had signed up for the group. Three out of the five people with cancer were still undergoing chemotherapy. In a moment of self-doubt, I wondered, "Would they physically be up for this meeting?" As I looked out at the still vacant parking lot, I longed for everyone to arrive and the session to begin.

Then two pick up trucks pulled in, followed by another vehicle. I breathed a sigh of relief; the members were finally here. I relaxed and invited everyone to the meeting area. That evening each couple shared their story, the personal weight of cancer and the changes it made in their lives. Throughout, their narratives were punctuated by the struggles of having cancer and the occasional inability to find the words to communicate their emotion.

Although physically with their partners, each individual appeared uniquely lonely when discussing the impact cancer had on their lives. While each couple had different ways of relating to each other, they all said they wanted to connect, or reconnect, more fully with their partner. At times, it seemed as if they were estranged from each other.

Each person described why they entered the group. One husband could not sleep because he was burdened by anxiety and fear that his wife's cancer would return. One woman perceived her husband as silently and valiantly attending to her needs, yet they never spoke about her cancer. Another wife was angry. Life had dealt her a "raw deal." She was furious that her young husband would not fight harder to secure their finances, their daily routines, and, most of all, his life. To her, his lack of fight implied an impending defeat.

One man retired from his work early to be with his wife. She was his "miracle gal." She had been told she would not survive her first round of lung cancer treatment. Experiencing remission for a brief time period, she again suffered the same diagnosis. In light of the cancer, he wanted to be with her each and every day.

As a therapist, I heard some emerging themes:

- the loneliness and isolation associated with cancer
- a desire to connect more fully with each other
- common challenges and struggles couples encounter when striving to relate more closely with one another
- the continued influence of old, unresolved issues/patterns that interfered with couples' attempts at dealing with cancer

- differences both people never envisioned, yet acquired from their new roles as the one with cancer or caregiver
- the rapid unpredictable shifts in emotions each person experienced from their partner.

Members expressed wishes to feel closer to the person that they love, or at least more fully share their innermost thoughts during this difficult life chapter. It seemed couples lacked the communication skills necessary to navigate their cancer crises and they longed to connect more completely.

Miller (1986) stated that all emotional growth occurs in connection with another. She described "connection" as being at the core of all relationships and when it is not, it is strongly desired. A healthy connection is mutually empathic and empowering (Miller & Stiver, 1997, p. 26).

The power in connecting becomes the catalyst for hope and healing. Miller and Stiver (1997) identified five growth-enhancing qualities that emerge in healthy connection. They are: increased energy, empowerment, empathy, authenticity, and positive experiences that result in the desire for more similar interactions. As a consequence of fully connecting, couples are likely to feel what Miller and Stiver describe as "zest."

## The Diagnosis of Cancer: Beginning the Journey

No one is ready for the diagnosis of cancer. This was certainly true for Kate as she drove to the hospital with her husband for a routine colonoscopy. Kate, a 40-year-old woman, underwent the unpleasant preparations and entered the hospital expecting the procedure to involve minor discomfort. The doctor and nurses were friendly. However, during the screening four polyps were identified, and immediately removed. The doctor and nurses' faces shifted from light-hearted to a bit more serious.

Due to fasting and anesthesia, Kate needed transportation home. Her husband Jake stayed and listened to the report. They were met with unexpected news. One of the polyps was especially large and had to be biopsied. In a kind manner, the doctor suggested that this was common and staff would contact her with the results.

When leaving the hospital, Kate tried to express her fears. Jake's response was, "Don't worry, everything will be fine." Although Jake's reassurance was well-meaning, Kate needed to communicate more. She interpreted his message to mean "stop talking." Like many people, Jake believed that by not communicating, their worries and conditions didn't exist. However, it is the complete opposite. Couples need to be aware of their emotions and how to communicate them.

Upon hearing the diagnosis of cancer, most people experience shock. As one 50-year-old woman whose breast cancer was in remission said, "Being diagnosed with cancer is such a lonely experience, even when loved ones are around. It was reminiscent of my first husband's funeral. I had a crowd of people around me, wanting to console me, yet I felt so alone. Everyone wanted to be helpful, but no one knew what it was like."

It is natural to feel emotionally disconnected from others when receiving a cancer diagnosis. It causes a rupture (the shock due to illness) within the relationship. This initial rupture feels overwhelming and dangerous and threatens the normal routine and predictability of life (Banks, 2000). In this overwhelmed state, it is natural that the person with cancer may feel isolated from loved ones.

## The Neurobiological Connection

Although their lives have been interrupted by the demands and treatments for cancer, couples can still sustain emotional growth. Research demonstrates that positive interpersonal connection not only decreases the physical pain (Eisenberger & Lieberman, 2005; Zaza & Baine, 2002), but can also improve quality of life. Couples experience a gamut of emotions throughout their course with cancer. These include: initially experiencing shock, withdrawing into survival mode, anxiety, grieving losses, depression, questioning recovery, confronting the prospect of dying, and dealing with the surge of emotions following treatment. Anderson (2006) emphasizes the importance of giving quality attention to each emotional phase and preventing isolation when addressing these agonizing emotions.

Eisenberger and Lieberman's (2005) research shows an important correlation between pain and social contact. They argue that without social connections, people will experience an increase in physical pain. They suggest that social and physical pain share the same brain pathways. Other research has shown that individuals with an increase of social support experience less pain (Eisenberger & Lieberman, 2005; Zaza & Baine, 2002).

Neurobiological studies have also shown that healthy relationships improve the immune system (Picardi, 2007). Further studies suggest that experiencing or enhancing sensitivity to one type of pain is shown to reduce the other type of pain, thus social and emotional support appears to regulate physical pain (Eisenberger & Lieberman, 2005). Eisenberger and Lieberman conclude that social connection is imperative for both happiness and survival.

This is exemplified by one woman in the group who worried that her husband would feel abandoned if she did anything for herself. She believed her presence was the key to her husband's survival. He apparently could tolerate the pain when she was there, yet felt severe emotional and physical pain when she went out.

Studies by Gallese (2003) and Iacoboni et al. (2001) have identified mirror neurons, and have shown that one individual's brain has the ability to create representations of the other's mind (Iacoboni et al., 1999; Rizzolatti & Craighero, 2004; Rizzolatti et al., 2001; Siegel, 2007). The combined studies reinforce the significant effect a couple's relationship has on each of them, especially when one is experiencing pain.

## Relational-Cultural Theory and Couples Cancer Groups

A common goal for most Relational-Cultural Theory (RCT) groups is to decrease isolation (Fedele, 1994). The majority of cancer support groups are focused on coping skills, education and acquisition of needed resources. All of these areas are certainly important, yet they differ from RCT cancer groups. By building and strengthening communication, combined with recognizing the culture brought on by cancer, RCT interventions differ from other supportive treatments by focusing, holding and strengthening relational connections.

RCT can be helpful for a couple dealing with cancer because it pays particular attention to the process and development of healthy interpersonal connections. The strength of the interpersonal connection is in the quality of power, authenticity, empathy, mutuality, and zest (Jordan et al., 1991).

The core theoretical underpinning in RCT groups is mutuality. As noted in Kayser and Scott's (2008) research, mutuality is the most significant factor in coping with cancer because "couples who are mutually responsive in their coping tend to appraise the cancer as a stressor that affects them both" (p. 39). The RCT group focus is on mutuality, as well as awareness, authenticity, mutual empathy, mutual empowerment and strengthening courage (Shem & Surrey, 1998).

However, in seeking mutuality, couples often feel stuck or unable to move forward in their communications. This inability to progress is defined as an impasse. As Stiver (1992) described, "In an impasse, both people feel increasingly less connected, more alone and isolated, and less able to act effectively in the relationship" (p. 3). Bergman and Surrey (1992) discussed the importance of couples moving beyond emotional impasses, as impasses create a disconnection in the relationship (Miller, 1998; Surrey, 1992).

One way of moving beyond an impasse is to include others outside of the partnership. Anne, an oncology social worker, spoke to this when discussing her work with couples. She described the first appointment as couples joining her and then requesting to be seen alone for a subsequent session. During their individual meetings, people would report both how strong their partners were and how frightened they themselves felt. They stated an inability to disclose their fears because this could ultimately erode their partner's strength. In her role, Anne recognized the impasse and helped these individuals return to their relationship and reconnect.

This relational paradox was initially formulated by Miller (1988) in her paper "Connections, Disconnections and Violations." Miller describes a process where an individual emotionally pulls away and holds back from the relationship. The person stops disclosing and chooses to limit communications for fear they will damage the relationship. The relational paradox is that the person believes the emotional distancing is the solution to maintaining a close connection. In this situation, couples hold back their fears from each other in order to maintain the bond of courage and sustain the strength to engage in treatment.

The importance of a third person, or group connection, is that it allows the opportunity to share fears without deflating a partner's positive energy. This process can be considered a protective triangle which facilitates strength and decreases feelings of isolation. Without a third person or group available, the fears can become extreme, potentially leading to severe anxiety or depression.

## Group Setting and Process

A preferred setting for a cancer group is a healing environment. A healing environment is a warm atmosphere that feels comforting, non-judgmental, and reflects a nurturing tone. Strasburg and Teraoka (2003) initiated "healing environments" in California and define them as settings "that offer sustenance to the soul and give meaning to experience" (p. 5). Research pertaining to the impact of healing environments for cancer patients was conducted at the Barbara Karmanos Cancer Clinic in Michigan (Rich, 2002; Strasburg & Teraoka, 2003). Rich's (2002) results showed a 45% decrease in patients' need for pain medications as compared to patients hospitalized in traditional sterile institutions. Healing environments can be created by simply adding serene pictures, flowers, a small buffet of food, or other gestures that enhance the setting.

### Week 1: The Initial Session

The group is co-led and short-term, eight weeks in duration. The first meeting is intended for couples to introduce their journey with cancer (Spira & Reed, 2003) and then shift their focus from the illness to how it has impacted their relationship. Each individual is asked to share their story, describe how they have coped thus far, define transformations in their relationship since being diagnosed with cancer, and express what they hope to gain from the group.

Their stories begin by their entry into the medical culture. They will need to depend on and trust this culture during their course with cancer. Couples describe their immersion in western medicine culture as outwardly marked by familiar medical language, roles, medications, surgeries, numerous appointments, and constant interactions with nurses and doctors. Often professionals are portrayed as cold and clinical and emotionally vacant, with a heavy focus on symptoms and treatment protocols. This medical culture is so ingrained that most couples have internalized it without realization or examination, and expect very little from this system in the way of emotional support.

In contrast to the traditional medical model, beginning in the first session the goal is to assist couples in embracing their illness and treatment for cancer from

191

the Relational-Cultural Theory perspective. A major belief of this theory is that all relationships play a major role in healing, including the relationship with the medical staff.

Within our culture physicians have historically been elevated to such high levels that the average person often fears openly communicating with them. Dunham (2008) reported research administered from the Veterans Affairs hospital in Houston and the Rochester Medical Center in New York that showed people with lung cancer found their physicians express little emotional support. "When patients made comments on topics such as personal impact of cancer, their diagnosis and treatment, and their struggles with the healthcare system, doctors responded with words of empathy only 10 percent of the time."

In every RCT group meeting, leaders help couples determine how they can best interact with the institutions and staff they are engaged with. The group offers camaraderie with others who have similarly entered the medical culture and encountered major losses. Couples are immersed in letting go of life as they once knew it. Changes often include personal loss, such as loss of hair, and loss of control of one's body. Couples also face unemployment, financial stressors and insurance complications. Some lose important relationships or the quality of their relationships significantly changes. For example, one woman whose husband suffered from cancer described friends as pulling away when they learned of his illness. She pointed out that many friends simply did not know how to respond and communicated less. In markedly worse scenarios, partners were unable to tolerate their partners' illness and engaged in affairs or completely abandoned the relationship.

Cancer is undoubtedly hard on any relationship. Changes can feel overwhelming as former routines are interrupted and days become unpredictable, especially when compared to everybody else's life that appears to proceed as usual.

The first session shifts from each couple sharing their personal journey to identifying relational strengths and positive characteristics, defining their complementary relational style, discussing the transformations the couple's relationship has endured since the diagnosis of cancer, and sharing how, as partners, they have coped with cancer. It is essential that everyone participates. Although couples share the same events, their individual experience of the event may differ. This initial meeting determines the foundation and establishes the tone. The goal is to create a non-judgmental, positive, and accepting environment.

### Weeks 2 through 7

Meetings begin with check-ins that last for approximately 15 minutes. These serve as a time to discuss hospital visits, medications, financial challenges, insurance issues, jobs, the week's progress and daily activities. In general, the check-in offers an opportunity to gain insight into how each person is doing physically and emotionally.

One common issue reported during check-ins is the countless hours couples spend sitting and waiting for appointments. Seigel (1993) was concerned with the atmosphere in waiting rooms and the significant amounts of time couples wait with their heads down in silence. He initiated a cultural shift by stressing the importance of communicating with others while waiting and gaining a more positive experience.

Following a group discussion on this subject, one member chose to initiate conversation in a waiting room and realized he looked forward to seeing the same people at each appointment. He learned from the other patients and when his treatment ended, he really missed his friends from the waiting room.

## Small Groups

People with cancer and caregivers break into groups defined by their role. The purposes of the two groups are:

- to identify areas each has hesitated to discuss with their partner
- to discuss fears openly
- to explore feelings and thoughts with others in similar roles
- to provide a forum where each can express difficult feelings regarding the impact cancer has on their life
- to allow empathic responses from others who can identify with their challenges.

## Large Group Participation

Following the small group work, individuals rejoin their partners in the larger group setting. This enables discussions from the small groups and the opportunity to embrace core RCT principles applicable to fostering couples' communication.

## Group Exercises

At the end of each meeting, using group exercises can be a meaningful, positive, and fun way to wrap up and create closure. One example of an exercise originates from Bergman and Surrey's (1992) work with couples groups. They asked each couple, "What animal is your relationship like?" (p. 12). For RCT cancer groups, the questions could be: "What animal would you choose to describe your relationship prior to the diagnosis of cancer? What animal best describes your relationship since being diagnosed with cancer?"

## Week 2: Small Group

The question proposed for discussion in Week 2 is: "Since dealing with cancer, what are some things you would like to speak more effectively about with your partner?"

As previously depicted in the example of Kate and her husband Jake, couples often reach an impasse, preventing further emotional interactions. The following are common impasse scenarios:

- *Scenario 1*. One man experienced pervasive anxiety because he feared his wife's cancer would return. He acknowledged reading extensively to find relief and possibly gain control. His thoughts about the cancer were obsessive in nature. His life of being "Mr Fix It" wasn't happening this time. The lack of control fueled his anxiety. Caregivers identified with this man and helped him live with uncertainties more effectively and to realize, define, understand and accept what he could/could not control.
- *Scenario 2*. One woman, also in the caregiver group, described difficulty discussing the depth of her depression with her husband. She was so angry that he was not fighting harder to survive. This woman benefited from a nonjudgmental member who listened to her anger, responded kindly and asked her the question "Is this how you want your husband to remember you? Do you want your husband to think of you as an angry woman?" The third person was able to suggest ways that she could cope more effectively with her husband's illness.

## Week 2: Large Group

In Week 2 the emphasis is on the couple's connection. "Being in the connection means being emotionally accessible" (Miller & Stiver, 1997, p. 3). A healthy, growth-fostering connection is "an interaction between two or more people that is mutually empathic and mutually empowering" (Miller & Stiver, 1997, p. 26).

Leaders can guide the discussion with the following questions. What does empathy mean to you? Why is it important to be empathic at this time? What role does empathy play in healing? What do you most want to understand about your partner? What do you most want your partner to understand about you? Also: Describe recent moments you experienced your partner as empathic.

Empathy is at the core of a healthy connection and is the heart of relating. By striving to understand and express empathy, the couple is engaged in a sensitive journey of growth. Empathy is defined as the "fundamental mode of human relatedness. It is the accepting, confirming and understanding human echo . . . A psychological nutrient without which human life as we know and cherish it could not be sustained" (Kohut, 1978, pp. 704–705). Empathy for another person decreases a sense of isolation (Jordan, 1987; Jordan, Kaplan, & Surrey, 1983; Surrey, Kaplan, & Jordan, 1990).

The following two scenarios are illustrations of partners being empathic and moving their relationship forward:

• *Scenario 1.* Tim, a 50-year-old man, experienced the debilitating process of working hard his whole life and becoming financially strapped as a consequence of kidney cancer. His wife Terri was also devastated. She dealt with the financial losses by being angry. Her anger devastated him more. Tim felt shame. He needed his wife to listen to his experience. He wasn't intentionally trying to make her world more difficult. He too was angry that all he had striven for was incrementally being taken away. He needed her to understand how physically sick he was and that he was doing the best he could. He needed compassion and understanding from her. Terri was not so much angry at Tim as she was at how drastically their financial situation had changed. She was working two jobs while being Tim's caretaker. She too was doing the best she could and needed compassion for her struggles.

How does a couple maintain empathy in the face of loss? Like Tim and Terri, they need to acknowledge and grieve their losses. They can listen closely to how their partner has been affected. They can also express their experience of the setbacks in a non-blaming manner. Sadly, their lives changed in a brief moment and it is important they acknowledge what they are dealing with consequently.

Throughout this discussion, the leaders and members have to be sensitive to the couple's connection. They protect each individual as they share or vent in order to prevent emotional damage. The group guides each partner toward listening, understanding, and finding compassion for their partner.

• *Scenario 2.* Couples experience many humiliating moments as a result of cancer. One unexpected embarrassing situation is bedwetting. Bedwetting often is a challenging conversation to have with a loved one. One woman who was physically modest resisted wearing adult Depends to bed and, as a result, frequently wet the bed. Her husband "happened" to fall asleep on the couch each evening. He obviously struggled to communicate how much he desired to return to their bed. When he initially requested that she use the support wear, she responded with shame and anger. She thought the "diaper" was too regressive. In hearing other members, she gradually realized he was not wishing to humiliate her but, instead, wanted to be physically close to her.

In summary, what these few examples show is that only through finding the courage to discuss hardships together can couples express and experience empathy. To be empathic requires listening closely, trying to understand the other's experience and exhibiting compassion. The group goal is to help the couple to have mutual empathy, recognizing this as a truly difficult chapter for both.

### Week 3: Small Group

In both the small groups the leaders pose the following questions: What is mutuality when partners are in different roles? Why is it essential?

### Week 3: Large Group

In the larger group, the leaders encourage the members to experience empathy for their partner's undertakings. They ask, "How can you empathize with some of the differences in your partner's role? How can you empathize with the unique challenges in your role?"

Cancer research by Kayser and Scott (2008) has credited mutuality as the most significant factor in coping with cancer. According to Jordan (1986), "Mutuality involves an appreciation of the wholeness of the person's experience and respect for the other person's differences and uniqueness. Mutuality values enhancement of the other's growth and most importantly, leaves all participants open to change" (p. 7). With mutuality comes an interpersonal balance of power.

Mutual responsiveness includes genuine listening and validation from each person (Jordan, 1986; Kayser & Scott, 2008, p. 40). Research shows that partners "who are satisfied with the support they give and receive are skilled in communicating their support needs to each other. They mutually shape the nature of their support process in a way that positively enhances both partners' adjustment to cancer" (Kayser & Scott, 2008, p. 37).

Immediately upon diagnosis, roles shift with one becoming the patient and the other the caregiver. Many couples struggle to accept the inherent differences in these roles and by discussing these differences they can help establish mutuality. Both have challenging roles. Even though both are dealing with the same critical event, the experience may feel dissimilar. Unique to the role of the cancer sufferer is the constant attention to the physical self and the invasive experience in one's body. The caregiver, on the other hand, is consumed by the welfare of their partner. This new identity as cancer sufferer is a highly vulnerable role. The caregiver, or the "healthy" one, carries the strength, yet is similarly vulnerable.

Jordan (1990) recognizes the difficulties people experience when allowing themselves to be vulnerable and that shame is often associated with being vulnerable in a competitive patriarchal system. This competitive system rewards winning/success and devalues losing or being in a vulnerable state.

In her work, Jordan (1990) sees acknowledging one's vulnerability as an opportunity for growth. She stresses the importance of compassion from another when the vulnerable person emotionally opens up. She states, "Compassion aims at finding the shared passion or suffering with the other. It brings us into deep joining in vulnerability, where strength is fostered" (p. 7).

Emotionally sharing during vulnerable times often requires internal courage. Jordan (1990) defines courage as the "capacity to act meaningfully and with integrity in the face of acknowledged vulnerability" (p. 7). For each couple, it is this balance of shared courage and empathy that is important to sustain while feeling vulnerable and coping with cancer.

The two members share lifestyle changes, hefty sacrifices, and financial stressors. According to Kayser and Scott (2008), "Successful coping behaviors result from this process of emotional response and validation" (p. 121).

Kate and Jake experienced an impasse right from the beginning. As Kate noted, "We haven't talked about cancer at all." Jake feared if he discussed cancer, it would become real and he might have to face fears of losing Kate. He lost his mother to cancer only six months prior to Kate's diagnosis. Jake could discuss issues pertaining to treatment, just not his emotions. She fully appreciated his practical help, yet yearned to connect emotionally with him.

### Week 4: Small Group

Leaders ask, "Based on dealing with cancer, what do you most want to understand about your partner and his or her coping process?"

### Week 4: Large Group

Leaders pose the questions: How do you, as a couple, address your fears? What are some healthy ways to address fears? How can you maintain empathy when confronting fears?

Fears and anxiety associated with cancer can become overwhelming. Anderson's (2006) work with cancer patients suggests that people experience varying degrees of anxiety. Some people encounter generalized anxiety which affects every aspect of one's life, and can negatively impact concentration and daily functioning. There is also cancer-specific anxiety which is characterized by disturbing recurring images, avoidance, and suppressed feelings associated with the cancer (Anderson, 2006).

Many couples have no idea how to emotionally manage this new occurrence of anxiety. An initial question might be, "What in this emerging difficulty can I control?" The following is a short vignette of how one couple proceeded, took control, and navigated their journey with cancer.

Kendall, a 60-year-old man, addressed his fears and with his wife Tonya's help, mobilized his interpersonal power. Kendall was diagnosed with pancreatic cancer. His first physician from his western hometown told him that he had only a few months to live and no treatment was available. He refused to accept this prognosis. Through researching treatments, they learned of the Whipple operation performed in a few hospitals throughout the country. Both he and

Tonya thought this was the best way to proceed. They chose a surgeon on the East Coast near their son's family, uprooted their lives and relocated.

When they met the East Coast surgeon for the first time, Kendall was concerned. The physician seemed brilliant; however, he lacked any positive bedside manner.

Then he gave his new surgeon a hug. This disarmed him. When Kendall next threatened to kiss him if he didn't warm up, the surgeon laughed and they established a warm working bond. Kendall faced his fears by asserting control when he could. In this example, Kendall directed his relational course with his doctor.

According to Kayser and Scott (2008), the "Strongest predictor of long term adjustment to cancer is not medical variables, but rather coping abilities" (p. 121). Fears are often the thin ice on which couples do not want to venture. It is in facing fears together, drawing from each other's strengths, and feeling empowered that the impact of the fears will lessen and coping will unfold. Birds instinctively do this by facing into the wind. They land and take off that way because facing windward helps keep their feathers unruffled.

### Week 5: Small Group

In the small groups, leaders ask, "Are there ways you could feel more empowered in the relationship so it could grow?"

### Week 5: Large Group

Leaders pose the questions: What can you control as a couple? How can you make peace with cancer and find ways to become empowered as a couple? Are there ways you could both feel more empowered in your relationship, allowing growth and enhancing your connection? Could you give an example or share a story?

People with cancer often feel so disempowered that they become depressed. For example, Eileen was diagnosed with lung cancer for a second time following a few years in remission. Initially, she was embarrassed and was angry at herself for smoking. Following chemotherapy, Eileen sank into a deep depression.

Family and friends worried and encouraged Eileen to leave her couch and try something different by joining a group. Surprisingly, during the first session, Eileen immediately connected with other survivors. Instead of having difficulty leaving her home each week, she looked forward to being with others who were also trying to survive cancer. Hearing how hard they tried each day to engage in life empowered and spurred her to work harder. She felt understood and believed they realized the courage she needed for each challenging day. She felt encouraged and empowered, which resulted in her depression lifting.

Depression impacts the healing process for most forms of cancer. A study (Monahan et al., 2007) in Europe shows that people dealing with prostate or GI cancers are most positively impacted by the lifting of their depression. The quality of their lives significantly improves when depressive symptoms are successfully treated, which helps the healing process.

Because the diagnosis of cancer has such a major emotional impact, and the focus on treatment is intensive, couples may miss seeing the relationship as a source of power. Surrey (1987) defined psychological empowerment as: "The motivation, freedom and capacity to act purposefully, with the mobilization of the energies, resources, strengths, or powers of each person through a mutual, relational process" (p. 7).

A compelling example is Tim's journey with Stage IV renal cancer. Tim felt totally stripped of his power by cancer. His illness and his losses overwhelmed him. He sobbed when he shared his struggle to see ways he could regain power. He looked to others to listen to his pain and help him define what was in his reach and what he could control. In experiencing comfort for his grief, he was able to shift his attention to what was possible. He identified a desire to go up north to his camp with his wife, Terri. This simple opportunity was extremely important to him. The next possible weekend, just the two of them spent time at the camp. They talked, played cards, read, and took short walks. Tim was able to be in nature and celebrate his interests and passions. Terri experienced the prior normalcy of heading off to the camp, which was their "get away place." Both felt nurtured and revitalized.

Empowerment includes realistically making what is possible happen and accepting the "capacity to move or produce change" (Miller, 1982, p. 3). With cancer, it is important to be patient, especially since unexpected setbacks may temporarily derail goals. For example, Tim and Terri were not able to head up to the camp immediately. Tim became dehydrated following chemotherapy and was temporarily hospitalized. When he was considered stable, they were able to venture to their camp.

### Week 6: Small Group

Leaders suggest the following questions: How do you encourage your partner to live each day fully? What could you do to make this happen?

### Week 6: Large Group

In the larger group the discussion pertains to hope. The leader asks, "What does having hope mean to each of you?" If possible, invite a couple who have survived cancer or whose cancer is in long-term remission in to speak.

How does hope, or lack of hope, impact couples? Studies by Siegel (2007) pertaining to the brain illustrate the power of relationships. Researchers from Italy (Gallese, Fadiga, Fogassi & Rizzolatti, 1996) have discovered the "social nature of our brains" (Siegel, 1996), which suggests that in a relationship, hope may be experienced by one individual and mirrored neurologically by another.

Whether genuine hope is a feeling in hearts, souls, or minds, it encompasses positive energy that helps couples persevere and have positive outcomes. In summary, genuine hope often includes empathy during challenging moments. It is empowering and suggests a future optimistic outcome.

## *Week 7: Small Group*

Leaders ask, "Are you able to attend to personal needs, as well as your relationship needs?"

## *Week 7: Large Group*

Leaders bring the group to focus on, "What opportunities can be created to experience empowerment together? And alone?"

During this session couples also reflect on life after cancer. It is clear that a couple's life never will be what it was prior to cancer. How could it be? In facing and escaping mortality, they are profoundly affected. Returning to normal life requires reclaiming physical and emotional strength that had been dedicated to the cancer battle.

Physically, the partner who has cancer is likely dealing with changes to their body. The radiation, chemotherapy or surgery has assuredly left its mark. The survivor has to adjust and accommodate to this new sense of self and body awareness. For example, Jenny had a mastectomy as a consequence of breast cancer. While healing and awaiting reconstructive surgery, she grieved her old body. Initially, Jenny felt embarrassed and shied away from having her husband see her naked breast. She needed constant reassurance from him. His understanding and kindness fostered their reconnection. Jenny and her husband talked openly as they both emotionally healed and accepted the changes.

For cancer survivors, shifting roles from patient to non-patient can feel alien and overwhelming. Couples describe the importance in re-entering at their own pace, setting realistic expectations while regaining stamina. In conjunction, they often experience lingering fears about the cancer returning. This is a natural concern given their recent experience of facing the constant, pervasive plausibility of death.

Couples change as a consequence of this journey. For some, the changes may be so great that it is unlikely they will transition back to all of their former activities. After assessing their life and identifying missed opportunities, they may choose a different, more preferred lifestyle. For example, Graham chose to retire significantly earlier from his full-time position to spend more time with Eileen. This allowed them new adventures and opportunity to simply enjoy each other.

### *Closing Meeting*

The last meeting is a time to reflect on the group in its entirety and effectively say goodbye to each group member. The following is what Kate, the 40-year-old woman diagnosed with colon cancer, shared as her reflections.

Kate and her husband entered the group following her last radiation treatment and chemotherapy. Prior to the group, Kate believed she could not think of the "C word," never mind express it. She cried while warmly describing details of her ordeal and expressed appreciation for what Jake must have experienced. On a day-in and day-out basis he worked full time and came home to nurse his sick wife. As she gratefully cried about his remarkable care for her, he looked on, internalizing her words.

Jake is a burly, Harley-Davidson-type guy. He was tender to Kate. He did everything he could to keep Kate alive. Kate felt empathy for him, his losses and stressors. In turn, Kate's expression of empathy towards him helped him open up and express his feelings about his part of the experience, his earlier losses and his desire to get back to a normal life. Prior to entering the group, Kate felt emotionally isolated. While in the group, Kate and her husband gained the tools they needed to communicate and cope more effectively.

In summary, as part of the reflective process, couples are asked to discuss what they learned about their partner, the strengths and positive changes noticeable in their partner, and what role hope plays in their relationship at this time and in the future.

Inevitably the topic of dying surfaces in this last group session. Research from the Dana Farber Cancer Institute speaks to the importance of communicating openly during the final life stage (Wright et al., 2008). Wright and associates (2008) showed that cancer patients who talked about death with loved ones in their last days experienced greater comfort and less stress. In their study of 322 people with terminal cancer, they found that people who did not have end-of-life conversations got significantly more aggressive care in their final week in life which was linked to lower quality of life near death (Wright et al., 2008). The loved ones who discussed impending death said they felt less regret, and better quality of life, during their bereavement than their counterparts who not only suffered from regret, but were more prone to depression (Wright et al., 2008).

Couples address what they perceive as important decisions. Couples need to continue to experience empowerment through their daily decisions. They can define visitations by family and friends and work on closure tasks, such as the obituary, the funeral service or the closing memorial tribute.

## What Overall Impact Can an RCT Cancer Group Have on Couples?

Graham sent a letter expressing his experience and the impact the groups had on his relationship with Eileen. The following are excerpts:

For well over ten years Eileen has been plagued with a mild form of depression. When we got the original diagnosis of small cell lung cancer and then as the months passed the physical effects of the treatments it wasn't surprising that her depression symptoms returned. I was really desperate to find some additional help for her at this time. Fortunately the oncology group at the Hospital suggested that we contact you for possibly getting involved in a cancer support group. At first Eileen didn't want to go so I simply insisted.

As time passed I noticed a marked improvement in her overall attitude. You, your co-leader and the group really made a difference during a very difficult time. Much to my surprise I also found our weekly visits to your facility helped me too. Being a caregiver to a person you love is a very draining experience. To watch your wife of over forty years go from a strong, warm, loving intelligent person of a very young sixty three years of age to a frail person who needs near constant support and assistance in just a few months is, to say the very least, a near impossible cross to bear.

I found the sessions where we went into two groups, the cancer patients and the caregivers particularly helpful. I was having a hard time but others seemed completely overwhelmed to the point of being angry with their sick partners. The group didn't judge, but rather added to what the other person was saying which seemed to help the person. It helped me to try and help them ... It was also a real pleasure to meet with so many truly brave and determined people. You're good at what you do and I hope you can continue to help in desperate situations. Respectfully, Graham.

In summary, whether it is a chapter in a couple's history or their last days together, engaging in more connecting interactions will make their time together significantly more meaningful. RCT gives couples the much needed support and tools to have a healthy relationship in unhealthy times.

## References

Anderson, B. (2006). *We can do more: Capturing meaning and improving health for cancer patients with psychological intervention.* Presentation at the 3rd Annual Conference of the American Oncology Society.

Banks, A. (2000). PTSD: Post-traumatic stress disorder: Relationships and brain chemistry. *Project Report No. 8.* Wellesley, MA: Stone Center Working Paper Series.

Bergman, S. & Surrey, J. (1992). The woman–man relationship: Impasses and possibilities. *Work in Progress*, No. 55. Wellesley, MA: Stone Center Working Paper Series.

Dunham, W. (2008, September 23). Amid deadly illness, doctors offer little empathy, study finds. *The Boston Globe.*

Eisenberger, N. & Lieberman, M. (2005). Why it hurts to be left out: The neurocognitive overlap between physical and social pain. In Williams, K., Forbes, J., & von Hippel, B. (Eds.) *The social outcast: Ostracism, social exclusion, and bullying.* New York: Cambridge Universal Press, pp. 109–127.

Fedele, N. (1994). Relationships in groups: Connection, resonance and paradox. *Works in Progress*, No. 69. Wellesley, MA: Stone Center Working Paper Series.

Gallese, V. (2003). The roots of empathy: The shared manifold hypothesis and the neural basis of intersubjectivity. *Psychopathology*, 36: 171–180.

Gallese, V., Fadiga, L., Fogassi, L., & Rizzolatti, G. (1996). Action recognition in the premotor cortex. *Brain*, 119: 593–609.

Iacoboni, M., Koski, L., Brass, M., Woods, R., Dubeau, M., Mozzietta, J., et al. (2001). Reaffirm copies of imitated actions in the right superior temporal cortex. *Proceedings of the National Academiy of Sciences of the United States of America*, 98: 13995–13999.

Iacoboni, M., Woods, R.P., Bekkering, M., & Rizzolatti, G. (1999). Cortical mechanisms of human imitation, Science, 286: 2526–2528.

Jordan, J. (1986). The meaning of mutuality. *Work in Progress*, No. 23. Wellesley, MA: Stone Center Working Paper Series.

Jordan, J. (1987). Clarity in connection: Empathic knowing, desire and sexuality. *Work in Progress*, No. 29. Wellesley, MA: Stone Center Working Paper Series.

Jordan, J. (1990). Courage in connection: Conflict, compassion, creativity. *Work in Progress*, No. 45. Wellesley, MA: Stone Center Working Paper Series.

Jordan, J., Kaplan, A., Miller, J., Stiver I., & Surrey, J. (1991). *Women's growth in connection.* New York: Guilford Press.

Jordan, J., Kaplan, A., & Surrey, J. (1983). Women and empathy – Implications for psychological development and psychotherapy. *Work in Progress*, 82-02. Wellesley, MA: Stone Center Working Paper Series.

Kayser, K. & Scott, J. (2008). *Helping couples cope with women's cancers: An evidence-based approach for practitioners.* New York: Springer.

Kohut, H. (1978). The psychoanalyst in the community of scholars. In P. Ornstein (Ed.). *The search for the self: Selected writings of Heinz Kohut*, Vol. 2 (pp. 685–724). New York: International Universities Press.

Manne, S. & Ostroff, J. (2008). *Coping with breast cancer: A couples-focused group intervention.* New York: Oxford University Press.

Miller, J.B. (1982). Women and power: Some psychology dimensions. *Work in Progress*, No. 1. Wellesley, MA: Stone Center Working Paper Series.

Miller, J.B. (1986). What do we mean by relationships? *Work in Progress*, No. 22. Wellesley, MA: Stone Center Working Paper Series.

Miller, J.B. (1988). Connections, disconnections and violations. *Work in Progress*, No. 33. Wellesley, MA: Stone Center Working Paper Series.

Miller, J.B. & Stiver, I. (1997). *The healing connection: How women form relationships in therapy and in life.* Boston: Beacon Press.

Monahan, P., Champion, V., Rowl, S., Giesier, R., Given, B., Burns, D., et al. (2007). What contributes more strongly to predicting QOL during 1-year recovery from treatment for clinically localized prostate cancer: 4-weeks-post-treatment depressive symptoms or type of treatment? *Quality of Life Research*, 3: 399–411.

Picardi, A. (2007). Insecure relationships may drain immune system. *Psychosomatic Medicine*, I, 69: 40–46.

Rich, M. (2002, November 27). Healing hospital design. *Wall Street Journal.*

Rizzolatti, G. & Craighero, L. (2004). The mirror neuron system, *Annual Review of Neuroscience*, 27: 169–192.

Rizzolatti, G., Fogassi, L., & Gallese, V. (2001). Neurophysiological mechanisms underlying the understanding and imitation of action. *National Review of Neuroscience*, 2: 662–670.

Seigel, B. (1993). *How to live between office visits: A guide to life, love, and healing*. New York: Harper Collins.

Shem, S. & Surrey, J. (1998). *We have to talk: Healing dialogues between women and men*. New York: Basic Books.

Siegel, D. (1996). Attachment, emotions, memory and narrative: Cognitive neuroscience encounters psychotherapy. *Psychiatric Times*, XIII(3).

Siegel, D. (2007). *The mindful brain, reflection and attunement on the cultivation of well-being*. New York: W.W. Norton.

Spira, J. & Reed, G. (2003). *Group psychotherapy for women with breast cancer*. Washington, DC: American Psychological Association.

Stiver, I. (1992). A relational approach to therapeutic impasses. *Work In Progress*, No. 58. Wellesley, MA: Stone Center Working Paper Series.

Strasburg, K. & Teraoka, F. (2003). Healing elements of design. *Healing Environments Publications*, Vol. 10, No. 2.

Surrey, J. (1987). Relationship and empowerment. *Work In Progress*, No. 30, Wellesley, MA: Stone Center Working Paper Series.

Surrey, J., Kaplan, A., & Jordan, J. (1990). Empathy revisited. *Work In Progress*, No. 40. Wellesley, MA: Stone Center Working Paper Series.

Wright, A., Zhang, B., Ray, A., Mack, J.W. Trice, E., Balboni, T., et al. (2008). Associations between end-of-life discussions, patient mental health, medical care near death, and caregiver bereavement adjustment. *Journal of the American Medical Association*, 300(14), 1665–1673.

Zaza, C. & Baine, N. (2002). Cancer pain and psychosocial stressors: A critical review of the literature. *Journal of Pain and Symptom Management*, 24(5): 526–542.

# 13

# A RELATIONAL-CULTURAL PERSPECTIVE OF DIVORCE

*Dana L. Comstock-Benzick*

Marriage failure plus grief, minus social approval multiplied by emotional distress and divided by low self-esteem, equals depression, anxiety, perhaps panic, and the behavior these emotions elicit.

(Roman and Haddad, 1978)

At the time of this writing, nearly three years had passed since my divorce was finalized. For the record, this is the first piece I have written since the divorce, and in all honesty it began as some of the most difficult research and writing I had ever done. Two days of crying marked my initial immersion into this project. From that point, I had trouble pulling my thoughts together and had difficulty expressing myself. I had a hard time getting into a productive rhythm, and never felt quite satisfied that things were coming together in "just the right way." I suspected that my initial trouble resulted from revisiting my own experiences while reviewing literature on divorce in preparation for this project. In the midst of my early discouragement, I feared I simply might not be able to get through it. I then came across a quote that read, "To recount experiences of shame or humiliation, we risk revisiting painful images of being devalued, disempowered, or disgraced, perhaps triggering or reinforcing further feelings of shame" (Hartling, Rosen, Walker, & Jordan, 2000, p. 1).

While that quote summed up my writing struggles in a nutshell, it was also relevant to much of what is experienced in the divorce process. From that perspective, I began to feel that there may not be any "reward" in writing about disconnection, dissolution, or divorce. Divorce is final. Given that the kind of relational movement that leads to divorce represents surrendering to a series of disappointments, relational ruptures, interpersonal violations or even abuse, I found it hard to accept that there was even a place for divorce in the Relational-Cultural Theory (RCT) scholarship. While that might sound extreme, I will own that it reflects the position I held in relation to the dissolution of my own marriage. Simply put, I never anticipated a divorce, nor did I want to divorce, at least not at *that* time.

While I was aware there were some struggles in my former marriage, I also knew that our lives weren't greatly out of sync with those of other white, same race, middle-class families working to balance careers with the demands of raising two small able-bodied children and caring for aging parents. In fairness (after all, *I'm* the one writing this chapter), I'm not perfect. From my perspective, we had a lifetime of change to look forward to, which I also believed would undoubtedly come with more challenges *and* rewards. I felt empathic about the intensity that seemed perfectly normal for where we were in our family life development. Sadly, and again like other married couples, spouses have variable levels of tolerance for difficult periods for any number of reasons.

In spite of the outcome, I value marriage now as much as I did then and it turns out I share this sentiment with the majority of people living in this country (Cherlin, 2010). While I have come full circle and am set to remarry in a few weeks, lurking through divorce literature, endless statistics and risk factors was depressing and frightening. With respect to statistics, last year in North America, one million marriages ended in divorce, and three fourths of them involved children. Conservative estimates suggest that ten million people were personally impacted by the one million divorces (Irving, 2011).

Over time, it became clear to me that I wouldn't be able to pull together a thorough Relational-Cultural perspective of divorce without looking at the historical and contemporary trends of divorce *and* marriage. That was when the fun started, and perhaps some long overdue healing. Let me preface this transition by clarifying that I had a multitude of sources on the history of marriage and divorce from which to choose, and found very few of them to be exhaustively inclusive. I'm not even sure that is a reasonable expectation of any one source. Because marriage holds such a sentimental place in our culture, the rights to marry have been, and continue to be, a hotbed of political debate. For this reason, I was hard pressed to find sources that were written without a political agenda. There were more books, articles, essays, statistics, political commentaries and opinions on the topics of marriage and divorce than I had *ever* imagined.

In the end, I was left feeling that this chapter may be the first of many needed explorations of divorce from the RCT perspective. The United States is an immigrant country. And those of us who were born here tend to be quite "migratory," a fact that some suggest is very hard on relationships (Cherlin, 2010). The big picture of our country's history and the current economic, global and political climate do not afford us a single marriage or divorce context which we can view through the RCT lens. Racial, cultural, economic, religious and other variations in family life and lifestyle are stratified and divisive in this country. As I studied marital and divorce trends and practices from around the globe, I imagined them making their way into, and finding a place in, this country. A wide array of experiences make up the "American" divorce experience, and many of these narratives are absent from the mainstream literature and research.

The purpose of this chapter was twofold. Efforts were made to (a) explore the historical route through which we arrived at the predominant mainstream ideals about marriage and divorce in the United States, and (b) present an RCT perspective of divorce that considers current trends within a historical context. It is essential to understand that divorce narratives represent *only those who have both the option and the resources to divorce.*

For some married couples in this country, culture and/or religious mandates prohibit divorce, as does a lack of financial resources. Just as there are a variety of more or less acceptable coupling options, separation does not always involve divorce. Therefore, many of the trends and experiences presented in this chapter may apply to those who are currently wrestling with the effects of a dysfunctional marriage or relationship, as well as to those who have not married but have experienced the permanent rupture of a romantic relationship.

## A *Very* Brief History of Marriage and Divorce

One of the more frequently cited and politically balanced historical accounts of marriage and divorce is presented in Stephanie Coontz's (2005) book, *Marriage, A History: From Obedience to Intimacy, or How Love Conquered Marriage.* Coontz details historical trends in marriage and "the marriage crisis" from around the world, and proposes an alternative to commonly accepted myths about the original purpose of marriage. She also gives some much-needed perspectives on the modern marriage in the hope that we can learn from our mistakes and work towards managing the destructive effects of divorce.

Coontz (2005) asserts that "when it comes to the overall place of marriage in society and the relationship between husbands and wives, nothing in the past is anything like what we have today, even if it may look similar at first glance" (p. 2). For thousands of years, marriage *and* divorce had been nothing short of an economic, social and political negotiation which was transacted in such a way as to benefit the "collective" or greater good, whatever that meant in a given context. This negotiation was in no way left up to the two individuals marrying, and whether or not they were in love did not figure in the equation. Coontz (2005) suggests that these arrangements were so important to a social fabric that divorce rates, however small, have resulted in some form of a marriage crisis or concern about the decline of family life for as long as people have been marrying!

In other words, such concerns are not unique to contemporary Western cultures including the United States. Coontz (2005, p. 1) makes the point that:

> The ancient Greeks complained bitterly about the declining morals of wives. The Romans bemoaned their high divorce rates, which they contrasted with an earlier era of family stability. The European settlers

in America began lamenting the decline of the family and the dis-
obedience of women and children almost as soon as they stepped off
the boats.

Kaler (2001, as cited in Coontz, 2005) states that the "invention of a past filled
with good marriages" is likely a common way that people throughout history
and across cultures have expressed their dissatisfaction with the respective
hardships of their time. I would assert that the same holds true today in the US.

Inevitably, the fallout of such difficulties, be they economic, political, etc.,
impacts the ways in which women and men relate. Coontz (2005) argues that
the "relations between men and women have changed more in the past thirty
years than they did in the previous three thousand" as has the "role of
marriage" in relation to the broader culture (p. 4). She also suggests that any
kind of coupling arrangement or family lifestyle we might think of as odd or
even deviant in our day and age has very likely been practiced somewhere
around the globe. In other words, it's *all* been done before.

Anthropologists and archaeologists have proposed many theories as to why
marriage was invented by our Stone Age ancestors. Of the two predominant
theories, the first asserts that marriage was created for men to protect women
(and their offspring) and the second suggests it was created so men could exploit
the talents of women and children for their own survival. Coontz (2005) suggests
that marriage was created in an effort to expand familial ties, and is most
certainly the *only* way to acquire in-laws. She writes that "marriage turned
strangers into relatives and enemies into allies" (p. 44). Divorce in this day and
age turns relatives into strangers, and allies into enemies.

Marriage as a way to obtain in-laws is the theory best suited to RCT in that
it is consistent with the developmental goal of expanding relational networks
rather than growing increasingly autonomous or independent over our life
span. Any efforts for individual survival by our Stone Age ancestors would have
likely been suicidal! However, marriage, as a way of building family ties and
group alliances, moved from being beneficial to the well-being of both family
groups to a means by which families with wealth could merge, or alternatively
hoard, wealth (Coontz, 2005). Families with claim to extensive territories could
expand their boundaries, obtain political allies, and produce legitimate heirs,
who, in turn could be married off, and produce more legitimate heirs.

Family expansion served to further social, material, territorial and political
gains while simultaneously increasing class divides. Men and women entering
into marriage during this era were primarily loyal to their own side of the
family, or perhaps the more powerful side of the family, and *not* to their
respective spouse. For millennia,

> Elites jockeyed to acquire powerful in-laws. If, after they agreed to seal
> a match, a better one presented itself, they maneuvered (and some-
> times murdered) to get out of the old one . . . Formal rules detailed

what kinds of marriage could and could not produce legitimate heirs
... From the Middle Eastern kingdoms that arose three thousand
years before the birth of Christ to the European ones fifteen hundred
years later, factions of the ruling circles fought over who had the right
to legitimize marriages or authorize divorces. These battles often
changed the course of history.

(Coontz, 2005, p. 48)

The age of Enlightenment, accompanied by the emerging market economy,
prompted the decline of arranged marriages. While this was not the case in all
parts of the world, the idea of freely choosing one's partner based on love and
companionship took hold in Western Europe and eventually spread all the way
into Russia (Coontz, 2005).

### The Emergence of the Love-Based Companionship Marriage

The idea of freely choosing one's spouse based on love and companionship was
not designed to promote egalitarian relationships based on the Relational-
Cultural theoretical concept of mutuality as we know it, or at least strive to,
today. The trend, however, did begin to prompt questions and objections
related to women's lack of legal rights. The idea of a love-based companionship
marriage spread to various parts of Europe and eventually made its way into
colonial America. The proponents of this new idea about marriage simply
aimed "to make marriage more secure by getting rid of the cynicism that
accompanied mercenary marriage and encouraging couples to place each other
first in their affections and loyalties" (Coontz, 2005, p. 149). Critics of this new
type of marriage were concerned that breaking with a tradition that had been
practiced for thousands of years would "produce rampant individualism" and
likely increase divorce (p. 149). Coontz writes:

Conservatives warned that 'the pursuit of happiness,' claimed as a
right in the American Declaration of Independence, would undermine
the social and moral order. Preachers declared that parishioners who
placed their husbands or wives before God in their hierarchy of loyalty
and emotion were running the risk of becoming 'idolaters.' In 1774 a
writer in England's *Lady Magazine* commented tartly that 'the idea of
matrimony' was not 'for men and women to be always taken up with
each other' or to seek personal self-fulfillment in their love. The
purpose of marriage was to get people to 'discharge the duties of civil
society, to govern their families with prudence and to educate their
children with discretion.'

(2005, p. 150)

Old traditions die hard. It took a while for the love-based companionship marriage to catch on during the Victorian era. My take on the initial resistance to the love-based marriage stems from the idea that this kind of relationship was quite frightening and awkward in that day and age. Emotional expression, in a time of reason, along with new courtship rituals based on this kind of marriage, was very out of line with the rules for social interactions between men and women in the Victorian era. Generally speaking, men and women socialized in segregated spheres (Coontz, 2005). While marriages may not have remained "arranged" in the way or at the same rate as they had in the past, a system of "referrals" emerged. Matches were made based on social standing and other commonalities, and the approval of the prospective mate by one's parents or potential in-laws was still very much desired, if not needed.

Transitioning from arranged marriages to those based on love, companionship, and individual choice ultimately resulted in a slight decline in marriage in the late 18th century. Women's continued financial dependence on men often left them with no other choice but to marry, with or without love. Paradoxically, some women in the US today choose to have children without marrying because they don't want to risk taking on a husband who may prove to be a financial burden (Clarke-Stewart & Brentano, 2006)!

The mutuality that might accompany our expectations of a love-based companionship marriage was elusive to Victorian-era wives. In addition to being financially dependent (with some exceptions where a woman would enter marriage with an inheritance, some land, or perhaps even slaves she could rent for income), they were legally controlled by their husbands (even *after* marriage to some degree). Bleser and Heath (1991) noted that women of moderate social standing eagerly accepted their lot and "believed that marriage would provide them with social rank, material benefits, freedom, and companionship and, thus, was far more desirable than remaining single".

Coontz (2005) indicated that in the absence of equality and mutuality, some "nineteenth-century women felt that their own marriages were based on mutual consideration, despite their husbands' legal authority over them" (p. 181). Whether a marriage was based on love, companionship, or mutual respect, scholars have documented that men were the heads of households and that patriarchy was alive and well in the families of the earliest European settlers of colonial America (Bleser, 1991). A continuum of successes with respect to the new love-based marriage continued to unfold as increasing opposition to slavery began to create the national divide that led to the civil war.

### *Slavery and Marriage in the Antebellum South*

With respect to marriage in the context of slavery, enslaved individuals had no legal rights and were allowed to marry, or not, based on the position of their owner. Ultimately, allowing (and sometimes forcing) slaves to marry, albeit informally, was possible but only in the interest of the white slave owner as a means to increase forced, free labor and to reduce the likelihood that members of a nuclear family would run away. In spite of marriage, enslaved couples and families were routinely separated. In these circumstances, "kin" were very important and extended families would assist mothers with the care of their children, who were often sold by the age of six. Many enslaved women, married or not, were raped by their white owners and had no legal recourse (Clinton, 1991).

Clinton (1991) noted that "colonial America witnessed a legislative frenzy" in an attempt to deal with the "thorny question of interracial sex". The solution, at least in the courtrooms of Virginia in 1662, was to defy centuries of English tradition by declaring that children born to slaves would follow the status of the mother, regardless of who the father was (Clinton, 1991). This prevented any legal claim these children might assert with respect to their white father's wealth. The sexual exploitation of slaves resulted in the "disruption of the slave family and the creation of destructive elements which affected the lives of African-Americans" (Clinton, 1991). Over time, states began creating elaborate laws intended to discourage any kind of interracial relations not only between whites and free blacks, but between whites and *any* person of color.

Interracial sexual encounters or cohabitation were especially taboo between white women and men of color. Upon discovery, black men suffered severe punishments, even death. On the other hand:

> A white woman discovered in an interracial sexual relationship would have to deny consent or suffer drastic consequences; this topic would not be one for polite society, and polite society would not tolerate any gossip about such matters. Gossip failed to stain males involved in interracial liaisons unless they flaunted or publicly acknowledged such conduct.
>
> (Clinton, 1991)

In spite of clearly delineated social rules, Southerners, particularly white men, are documented to have lived by double standards. Clinton (1991) writes that "sexual contact[s] with slaves . . . were 'pardonable' offenses which protected white female purity." When these relationships became exclusive, or even long-term, white wives were potentially objectionable. It is unclear how often these conflicts led to divorce, but there are documented cases of white men who had exclusive long-term affectionate relationships with black women. Clinton (1991) cites the case of Thomas Foster, Jr., who "abandoned his Mississippi home in 1826 in the company of his beloved Susy, a slave his wife had tried to sell away. Foster gave up his land, his status, and his legitimate white wife and children when he exiled himself for love"—only to sell her in his later years.

Marriage and divorce narratives, such as those presented by Bleser (1991), demonstrate that white supremacy produced a system of marginalized, taboo, and socially stratified marriages, cohabitations and love relationships in the earliest days of this nation. Up to the time of this writing, I have been unable to reconcile the sexually repressed nature of those living during the Victorian era with the blatant sexual exploitation and abuse perpetrated by slave owners. It has been suggested that rural life in the Victorian era, free of the watchful eyes of neighbors, close kin, etc., loosened the grip of social norms, resulting in relational and familial violations (Cherlin, 2010). Rural life, such as that in the antebellum south and in the undeveloped west, coupled with "the new emphasis placed on the cultivation of affection and sentiment among family members combined with great concern about the need to control sexuality produced profound strains in the household" (Bardaglio, 1991).

Such strains included infidelity, abandonment, alcohol abuse and even incest (Bleser, 1991). State courts scrambled to create regulations intended to protect marriage and families, which were seen as the "foundation of social order" (Bardaglio, 1991) in much the same way that family is viewed today. Paradoxically, demands for more liberal divorce laws ensued. Over the past 200 years, divorce laws have expanded from narrow criteria to what we now know as the "no fault divorce" (Cherlin, 2010; Coontz, 2005).

Coontz (2005) notes that between 1880 and 1890 there was a 70% increase in divorce. My integration of the literature leads me to believe that individuals, in pursuit of personal happiness, may have chosen to leave loveless marriages wrought with abuse and betrayal, while others left love-based marriages that had failed to live up to their romantic expectations. It is also likely that emancipation followed by subsequent gains in the woman's suffrage movement destabilized gender relations and gender roles.

Since the 1890s, rates of both marriage *and* divorce have continued to rise in the US, although at varying rates at different points in history for a number of reasons (Cherlin, 2010; Coontz, 2005). To date, the "United States has one of the highest levels of both marriage and divorce of any Western nation" due, in large part, to the contradictory cultural ideals of both marriage and individualism (Cherlin, 2010).

## Marriage and Expressive Individualism

Anthony Cherlin, in *The Marriage-Go-Round: The State of Marriage and the Family in America Today* (2010) writes that:

> In the space of half a century . . . we have seen the widest pendulum swing in family life in American history. We have gone from a lockstep pattern of getting married young, then having children, and for the most part staying married, to a bewildering set of alternatives that includes bearing children as a lone parent and perhaps marrying at some later point; living with someone and having children together without marrying; or following the conventional marriage-then-children script, perhaps later divorcing, then probably living with a

212

new partner and maybe remarrying. We have gone from concerns over the costs of conformity—think *The Organization Man*—to troubles over the tyranny of too many choices.

Consequently, we choose and choose again, starting and ending cohabitating relationships and marriages . . . this distinctive pattern of multiple partnerships is related to the central place in American culture of both marriage and a kind of individualism that emphasizes self-expression and personal growth.

Cherlin (2010) is careful to delineate that the cultural values of marriage and expressive individualism are not binary constructs over which opposing groups favor one more than the other. He asserts that we carry *both* cultural models and flip from one to the other without even recognizing what we're doing. As both relate to how we conduct our personal lives, it evokes a very real sense of urgency with respect to the RCT concept of relational awareness!

In some respects, marriage and individualism are interrelated in that people tend to "view the success of their partnerships in individualistic terms. And it suggests that commitments to spouses and partners are personal choices that can be, and perhaps should be ended if they become unsatisfying" (Cherlin, 2010). Cherlin integrates the two and proposes an unflattering individualistic cultural model of family life that essentially reads like a justification for divorce. His model includes the following tenets:

• One's primary obligation is to oneself rather than to one's partner and children.
• Individuals must make choices over the life course about the kinds of intimate lives they wish to lead.
• A variety of living arrangements are acceptable.
• People who are personally dissatisfied with marriages and other intimate partnerships are justified in ending them.

The emergence of the love-based marriage, coupled with the cultural value of individualism, resulted in increasingly high expectations of personal rewards within marriage. Whitehead and Popenoe (as cited in Cherlin, 2010) suggested that marriage as a means through which one can achieve personal happiness "is gaining popularity as a SuperRelationship, an intensely private spiritualized union, combining sexual fidelity, romantic love, emotional intimacy, and togetherness". With such high expectations, disappointments and divorce seem inevitable.

At first glance, these expectations of marriage seem quite naïve and qualify as fodder for romantic novels. This seems more than paradoxical, as those who marry are choosing to do so later in life after achieving educational and financial goals. In other words, the expectation that "love conquers all" seems uncharacteristic of a mature demographic (Demo & Fine, 2010, p. 52). With regard to maturity and preparedness, Demo and Fine (2010, p. 53) state that many individuals entering into marriage:

> may not have a very realistic and clear sense of what marriage entails and how difficult it is to forge a strong bond, which might lead some individuals to enter into marriage prematurely before they understand the challenges that lie ahead as they forge a life together.

From the RCT perspective, individual maturity and understanding the challenges of married life do not equate to relational competence.

Cherlin (2010) actually goes so far as to suggest that some individuals marry without giving much thought to what lies ahead after the actual wedding! He writes that, "the focus on the wedding is so complete that they sometimes seem unprepared for how to live their married lives after the celebration is over." As such, the wedding, in and of itself, is a form of expressive individualism. This is especially the case when the couple, rather than their parents, pay for the wedding.

Given the elaborate expense of a wedding along with increasingly diverse and acceptable lifestyles from which to choose (not to mention divorce rates), Cherlin (2010) offers that marriage is desirable over cohabitation in that it gives couples what he refers to as "enforceable trust." He explains that:

> Getting married requires a public commitment to a long-term, possibly lifelong, relationship. This commitment is usually expressed in front of relatives, friends, and religious congregants . . . As a result, marriage lowers the risk that your partner will renege on promises to act in ways that would benefit you and your children. It allows you to put time, effort, and money into family life with less fear of abandonment by your partner.

In spite of enforceable trust, the success of a marriage in the United States depends largely on whether or not both spouses maintain the cultural value of marriage.

## Individualism and the Nuclear Family

The cultural values of marriage and expressive individualism are inextricably linked to the idealized image of the nuclear family. In the US, the nuclear family is thought of as "the basic unit of society," which serves as the "connective tissue" of communities (Sarkisian & Gerstel, 2012, p. 36). Individualism permeates the ideology of nuclear families in the belief that they "should be self-sufficient and not rely on others for help" (Sarkisian & Gerstel, 2012, p. 43). Expectations of self-sufficiency are reflected in social policy, including Medicaid and welfare reform, which tend to encourage marriage as the solution to poverty and to devalue, invisibilize and neglect the role extended family members play in supporting one another (Sarkisian & Gerstel, 2012). Such support is reciprocal between married and unmarried family members and is described by Sarkisian and Gerstel (2012) as "kinkeeping" or "carework," which includes emotional, physical and financial support (p. 3). This trend mirrors much of the foundation on which Relational-Cultural Theory was built: Relational practice is necessary for human survival, but is devalued in favor of individualism and autonomy as markers of healthy psychological development.

It is important to note that the structural aspects and expectations of contemporary married life (two people going off to make it on their own) produce what is referred to as "isolationist effects" (Sarkisian & Gerstel, 2012, p. 41). Isolationist effects result in a transitional redistribution or rearrangement of the way support flows from married and unmarried family members to their extended family. These changes are based on the expectation that a married individual will be (and should be) preoccupied with their spouse, and thus less available to tend to the needs of their extended family in the same ways they may have prior to marriage.

While it is beyond the scope of this chapter to provide an exhaustive discussion of how these dynamics play out in families, Sarkisian and Gerstel (2012) note, for example, that unmarried family members are more often expected to care for aging relatives than are their married counterparts. In short, individualistic cultural ideals related to marriage and "nuclear family life" undermine the relational resources on which all members of the extended family depend for survival! Scholars speculate that this dynamic has contributed to the fragility of marriage in the US (Cherlin, 2010; Sarkisian & Gerstel, 2012). In other words, married couples fare better with the love and support of their extended families, but paradoxically, and under the cultural ideal of expressive individualism, marriage potentially evokes a mutual sense of ambivalence between married individuals and extended family members and in-laws.

Just as marriage can evoke relational ambivalence, divorce becomes a family affair. Divorce is undoubtedly a family crisis, and, in some ways, operates to reverse the isolating effects of marriage (Sarkisian & Gerstel, 2012). Extended family direct care to the individual going through a divorce by providing financial assistance, emotional support, help with young children and even housing. Just as family members are often present to witness the enforceable trust at the couple's wedding, so do they witness the disintegration of the marriage (with some exceptions when difficulties are kept secret until the marriage implodes), and ultimately the divorce.

Any number of circumstances can lead a couple to divorce. Because marriage is a contract, and for some a covenant, the effects are devastating, and potentially traumatic (Birrell & Freyd, 2006). The pain of divorce extends to couples' children, extended family and throughout their communities of support. While not all divorces are highly adversarial, many are, especially when young children are involved. At their extreme, high-conflict divorces unfold as a public spectacle with the estranged spouses working in opposition to re-establish separate identities, obtain or retain financial assets and defend their relational value as a parent and a partner (Demo & Fine, 2010). At their worst, marriages come to an end in what Barbara Whitehead (as cited in Cherlin, 2010) refers to as the "expressive divorce."

## Developing Relational Competencies

Under the cultural ideal of expressive individualism, marriage is a means by which one can achieve and attain "self-development and personal satisfaction" (Cherlin, 2010). In the context of the well-established cultural ideal of expressive individualism, divorce is an acceptable option (although not ideal) if one's personal happiness needs are not being met, or if the marriage has been determined to be detrimental to one's personal growth. From the relational-cultural perspective, the hyper-focus on expressive individualism leaves little room for an emphasis, much less an "ideal," on the relational competencies that help us create and maintain growth-fostering relationships, particularly those outside of the immediate or nuclear family. Instead of working towards relational competence, the capstone of adulthood seems to be the "achievement of marriage." Culturally, and psychologically, we are locked in a binary relational system in which we either win or lose.

Traditional research, or at least research from the individualistic perspective, indicates that when we lose at one relationship, the majority of us will set out to achieve some degree of personal fulfillment in another one (Cherlin, 2010; Clarke-Stewart & Brentano, 2006). Relational-Cultural Theory offers an alternative to this pattern, namely the idea that over the life span, and in the context of all relationships, efforts are made to move towards better connection. RCT also posits that creating and maintaining growth-fostering relationships, in an ever-expanding number of relational networks, are essential to our *collective* emotional development and well-being. Relational networks would include those of the immediate family, extended family (to include in-laws), and social and professional networks. RCT further asserts that the ability to foster the growth of those in our care, and to be affected or moved by their experiences, is indicative of individuals' healthy psychological and family-life development. This perspective is in stark contrast to the broader culture's hyper-focus on the nuclear family, and to the idea that marriage serves to provide personal growth and fulfillment to each spouse, respectively.

The distinctive feature (and the focus of this chapter) of Cherlin's (2010) cycle of relationship "creation, destruction, and recreation," is that of destruction. For those that are married, destruction means divorce. In RCT language, divorce equates to the permanent rupture of a relationship and is referred to as a "disconnection" (Jordan, 1995, p. 2). In RCT language, all relationships go through periods of connections, disconnections and reconnections. In short, the

216

connections we experience in relationships are characterized by what Jean Baker Miller (1986) describes as the "five good things" (p. 3). In connection:

> each person feels a greater sense of 'zest' (vitality, energy); each person feels more able to act and does; each person has a more accurate picture of her/himself and of the other person(s); each person feels a greater sense of worth; and each person feels more connected to the other person(s) and feels a greater motivation for connections with other people beyond those in the specific relationship.

These qualities and/or experiences of connections are characteristic of *mutual* growth (rather than personal growth) and typify what RCT scholars refer to as *growth-fostering relationships* (Jordan & Dooley, 2000). Over time, and in spite of our best efforts, relationships move into periods of disconnection. Jordan and Dooley (as cited in Comstock, 2005) describe disconnections as the opposite of the five good things in that each person experiences "decreased energy; inability to act; a lack of clarity or confusion regarding self and other; decreased self worth; and we turn away from relationship" (p. 33).

All relationships have their ups and downs, and spouses often have mixed feelings about the other, and the relationship. The very essence of the RCT scholarship, unlike that on divorce, is an elaboration of the ways by which individuals, couples, families, groups, institutions, the mental health professions and even the broader culture can transform disconnections (Comstock et al., 2008). Jordan (1992) states that transforming disconnections "involves awareness of the forces creating the disconnection, discovery of a means for reconnecting, and building a more differentiated and solid connection" (p. 8). Key to transforming disconnections is what Jordan (1995) refers to as "relational awareness" (p. 5). Jordan emphasizes that developing relational awareness is a complex process that involves more than "personal awareness" (p. 5). Specifically, Jordan states that relational awareness involves "awareness of the other, awareness of the impact of oneself on the other, the effect of other on oneself, and the quality of energy and flow in the relationship itself" (p. 5).

While RCT posits that relationships are fluid and cyclic, many people enter into marriage under the assumption that the nature of their relationship is essentially static (e.g. "It is strong now, and will remain strong"), as is the fundamental character of their spouse. Mouradian (2004) captures this belief by stating that "early in a relationship, many of us attribute our partner's positive traits as inherent to their natures and their bad behavior to passing aberrations based on circumstances or outside influences" (p. 8). Early in marriage, couples may attempt to "self-correct," but not without a degree of conflict. Conflict is tricky as it is often expressed via some degree of anger. Miller and Surrey (1990) suggest that "anger is an emotion which arises when something is wrong or something hurts and needs fixing" (p. 2). Some couples have little if any tolerance for conflict, and so begins a slow breakdown of any hope for reparation. If change does happen as a result of conflict, more often than not, one of two things happens: (a) there is a redistribution of power (e.g. increased financial transparency, a more egalitarian approach to the accessibility of resources, a redistribution of household labor and/or childcare), or (b) a systematic effort to maintain power-over ensues in the form of emotional, physical and/or sexual abuse.

It is fair to say that most people enter into marriage with the expectation they will remain married, and that they will be challenged to work through a host of hurts and disappointments. Mouradian (2004, p. 4) describes this expectation by stating that:

> Even in a well-functioning relationship that is mutually supportive, loving, safe, and satisfying, we must overlook, forgive, and learn to accept the imperfections of our mates. A relationship cannot be maintained if we fail to do this, and we are socialized to do it in preparation for marriage.

Couples enter into marriage with some degree of confidence that they can and do have at least some capacity to forgive and move forward. These capacities, however, vary in degree from one spouse to another. Jordan (1995) reminds us that we all have varying degrees of tolerance for hurt, disappointment, forgiveness, and that "we all have particular ways we disconnect" (p. 2). She goes on to state that there are "particular situations that render us most vulnerable to disconnections" (1995, p. 2).

Bergman and Surrey (1994) state that "in all relationships, minor disconnections are inevitable" and add that they are "a sign of life and change" (p. 5). At best, they see these as opportunities "to move out of past and into new connection." When couples can do this successfully, they grow "through and toward connection, or relational development . . . when disconnections cannot move in this way there is an experience of impasse" (p. 5). As indicated above, couples' attempts to resolve minor disconnections or impasses often involve identifying and changing the behavior of the offending party, and/or removing negative outside influences. From the RCT perspective, neither of these efforts represents any kind of *mutual* effort to examine the ways each person may have contributed to the disconnection.

What results is a pattern of blame. Once a pattern of blame is established, so too is a pattern of withdrawal, defensiveness, isolation and fear (Jordan, 1995). Bergman and Surrey (1994) warn that "'when one person meets fear and protection in the other, each becomes more locked into the past, more into protection, and less capable of opening or expanding" (p. 5). They go on to describe "a feeling of being trapped or taken over by this habitual, stereotypical movement, less sense of freedom or range of motion, less space and energy for any creative insight or action, a feeling of being locked into a power struggle" (p. 5).

Some couples grow tired of the chronic, gnawing disconnections indicative of power struggles characterized by unrelenting efforts to assert and attain individual (versus relational) needs, and mutually initiate divorce. This is not always mutual. Reaching a decision to divorce is often a long process that unfolds over a period of time and only after spouses engage in "dyadic processes" (Demo & Fine, 2010, p. 90). Demo and Fine (2010, p. 90) state that:

> Dyadic processes involve 'relational talks' that focus on the current status and future of the relationships. Members may discuss reasons for staying in the relationship as well as reasons for ending the relationship. These talks may end in reconciliation or dissolution, or they may end ambiguously when individuals do not know what will happen with the relationships. Dyadic processes may occur over and over in a circular fashion until one or both people determine that the relationship cannot be salvaged and that termination is either inevitable or the best outcome.

Demo and Fine (2010) also suggest that relational talks eventually move outside of the marriage and into "social networks" (p. 91). At this phase, "individuals may seek advice, develop accounts of relational problems, seek support and provide updates on the status of the relationship" (Demo & Fine, 2010, p. 91). Efforts at this phase involve creating relational narratives that are consistent with "cultural scripts" and allow the individual to "present a self that is still relationally desirable" (2010, p. 91).

RCT therapists describe couples at this stage as having "developed a story about their relationship that is so problematic that it no longer allows them to be empathic toward each other" (Mirkin & Geib, 1995, p. 3). Without empathy, or recognition of the complexities or context of their marriage, these couples have reduced the story of their relationship into "tiny, redundant or defending statements" that leave them "feeling incompetent and disempowered" (p. 3). Mirkin and Geib (1995) suggest that without intervention, these kinds of blaming, confining, and stationary stories are typically those in which couples find themselves entrenched, leaving them with no option but divorce. It is these kinds of stories that encroach on the litigation process.

## Relational Violations during Divorce Litigation

When marriage comes to an unfortunate end, it potentially unfolds as a public spectacle wrought with fear, shame, humiliation and terror. The latter is a far cry from the initial bliss that serves as the impetus for marriage. The paradoxical nature of marriage and divorce is best captured by Jordan (2005), who asserts that, "because connection is so basic to our well-being . . . the fear of isolation is probably the most profound fear that human beings experience"

(p. 4). In short, the overriding emotion as marriage heads towards divorce is fear. Irving (2011) writes that divorce is the

> 'perfect storm,' in which all the 'right' conditions for creating maximum marital and family suffering come together. These conditions include the couple's hurt, or perhaps even shock, that their marriage is coming apart. This in most cases sparks strong feelings of anger, resentment, and regret. The fact that society accepts divorce as a solution to personal problems, rather than seeing it more accurately as a different and much worse problem, is also a factor. Finally, all of the above conditions are channeled into a legal system that feeds on parents' fear that if they don't fight for their rights they could lose everything, including their children.

Before any litigation process can begin, someone has to initiate the process. The way in which this is done can set the tone for the entire divorce process. In short, the initiator will take their narrowed, defining statements about the relationships and turn them into the marriage story. The isolating nature of the disconnection experienced during the litigation process stems from the initiator's deep investment in rewriting all aspects of the history of the relationship (emotional, financial, social, etc.) and the character of the estranged partner. For the spouse unaware that divorce was inevitable, it can feel like a large chunk of time in the relationship, or perhaps the relationship as a whole, was just an illusion. All the time, love and energy that had maintained the relationship are "disappeared."

For the initiator (who legally becomes the "petitioner"), strategies of survival and disconnection involve a constant focus on those factors that led to the end of the marriage. The other spouse (the defendant), however, may not have those factors at the core of their relationship narrative and sometimes will resist the divorce process altogether by refusing to cooperate, or by simply giving in to the initiator's requests in the hopes of a reconciliation. The latter can be very risky, as often the individual (defendant) is left without their marriage and/or any assets. At this phase, formal legal processes begin through either mediation or litigation. Typically, the initiator/petitioner will present their relationship narrative to an attorney who will begin the litigation process. Litigation exacerbated by a jury trial is the worst case scenario, especially when young children are involved. While it is beyond the scope of this chapter to explore all the complications and relational violations that can happen in families with young children, it is worth noting that Judge Paula J. Hepner (as cited in Irving, 2011) warns:

> What little civility is left between two parents before walking into court is almost always destroyed by their posturing in the litigation. However, the only information parents will present is a list of their

injustices portraying each other in the worst possible light: the most inconsiderate, the most immoral, the most inadequate, the most controlling, the most . . . the most. Indeed the majority of parents view the case as their chance to get their day in court when, in actuality, it is their children's day in court.

Clarke-Stewart and Brentano (2006) warn that lawyers trained in family law are "programmed to argue for their client's position, right or wrong. It is not their job to be conciliatory, to negotiate, or to decide what is right or best. Their role is to win the case" (p. 64). Relational violations in the litigative process result when attorneys for both the petitioner and the defendant objectify the opposing spouse by focusing on the most horrific aspects of the respective dueling narratives. To "win" a case, the attorneys will intimidate and instill fear during depositions and cross-examinations. Humiliation is used to disempower, shame, devalue and silence the opposing spouses into being unable to authentically represent themselves and/or their narrative. Given that not all individuals have defensive natures, representing oneself becomes even more complicated when the respective attorney has to speak for their client and when cross-examinations control and limit responses.

Relational violations related to litigation, coupled with those resulting from the ending of the relationship, are nothing short of traumatic. In the process, friends of the former couple are often forced to take sides. Relationships that were initially built on connection and mutual respect are aligned against the "other" spouse and are constructed in an adversarial nature. Family and in-law connections are ruptured and, as mentioned earlier in the chapter, allies become enemies and family members become strangers. Recovering from the aftermath of the relational devastation post-divorce takes time. Research indicates that it is possible to survive divorce, and that most individuals report a "new normal" within three to four years (Clarke-Stewart & Brentano, 2006).

## Conclusions, Recommendations, and Lessons Learned

This writing and relational journey, while tedious and overwhelming, has been healing. I have been forced to reflect on some of the obstacles to my own healing and on some of the regrets and lessons I learned along the way that I hope will be helpful to therapists and/or their clients who are dealing with divorce. I want to first emphasize that I agree with Jordan (1995), who states that "one of the most important skills a person can develop is to be able to discern which are the relationships in which one is safe being open or vulnerable and where one should be appropriately self-protective" (p. 5). She goes on to assert that "there are clearly situations when people must move out of non-mutual, hurtful relationships . . . At such times, disconnecting is healthy" (p. 5).

When my former spouse requested a divorce, I was taken by surprise. While there were times I had struggled, it turned out much better for me to be the "defendant" in our litigation process. While this might not be the case in all divorces, I would recommend a close examination of the potential for high levels of conflict before filing for a divorce. If one is facing the potential for a highly conflicted divorce, I recommend attempting collaborative law first (if available in your state) and/or mediation. I tried both, and they failed. Looking back, I would have regretted not having made those efforts.

I also recommend having a support network in place and expecting the emergence of a host of new vulnerabilities along the way. I attended a support group for individuals going through a divorce at a local church, and spent many hours wondering how anyone survived this process without a support system. The support group in which I participated was faith-based. From that experience I took with me a fitting metaphor for the experience of divorce: Divorce is painful in that it involves the tearing of flesh. When times felt to be unbearable, I reflected on that metaphor, which helped to normalize my pain.

The support group helped me to understand how my vulnerabilities affected my ability to parent, how my depression impacted my children, and how I was at risk for internalizing the negative relational images that emerged from the litigation process. It is very important to recognize, and resist, internalizing negative relational images because they can put one at risk for making poor relationship choices in the future.

Divorce litigation can take months, even years and can bring financial ruin. It is my opinion that some family law attorneys base the length of the process and the expense of the litigation on the income and/or financial value of their client. It is also my opinion that some "opposing attorneys" (representing the petitioner and the defendant) collude in dragging out divorce proceedings until they have earned a predetermined amount of money. The risk of being financially exploited adds yet another relational vulnerability. With the exception of Irving (2011), most of the divorce literature I reviewed was silent on this subject, and most often made general references to the fact that most couples who divorce through a litigation process come away feeling dissatisfied about the outcome of their settlement (Clarke-Stewart & Brentano, 2006; Demo & Fine, 2010).

While I was fine with the outcome of my divorce litigation, it was an expensive process from which I continue to recover. During my divorce, I often found myself wondering how anyone without financial means could ensure a fair process and often felt that divorce assistance should be a public service. Irving (2011) presents a compelling case for mediation and spells out how lengthy, highly conflicted divorce proceedings impact children, and their parents' ability to work cooperatively as co-parents. Irving also reports that mediation is a fairly new process in our country. I am happy to be able to report that at least one state is making serious efforts to reform its legal system. During the course of this project I learned that the Supreme Court in Anchorage, Alaska has introduced a pro bono program to resolve potentially high-conflict divorces quickly. So far, the program has been 80% effective, and other states are considering creating similar programs (National Public Radio, 2012).

For therapists working with couples, it is important to identify and deconstruct any conflict related to expressive individualism and to create and/or identify a foundation to the marriage or relationship that is built on mutuality. To this end, Bergman and Surrey (1994) recommend helping couples identify and resist obstacles to mutuality and build "on the qualities that support creativity in relationship: curiosity, flexibility, persistence, playfulness, paradoxical thinking, risk-taking, openness to the new, patience, and capacities for sustained attention and imagination" (p. 5). It is also important to help couples recognize that there are seasons to their marriage, that their relationship is fluid and that enduring tough times involves relational awareness. "Introducing new positive imaginal ways of describing and naming the 'we' makes more available in the moment the whole history, energies, and resources of the relationship" (Bergman & Surrey, 1994, pp. 5–6).

As this project came to an end, I had been remarried for nearly a month. I had been adjusting to being a new wife, to parenting two additional sons, and had been assisting my two children adjust to a new kind of family life with the support of my former spouse. My former spouse, who recently took up surfing, and I have been on good terms. As fate would have it, my divorce attorney also surfs and just as this project was wrapping up, I'd gotten word that he and my former spouse "bumped into each other" at the beach and ended up spending the whole day surfing together. My recommendation is that in the face of overwhelming, and traumatic disconnections, one should remain open to unexpected, healing relational possibilities. Life and relationships have a way of taking us full circle.

# References

Bardaglio, P. (1991). An outrage upon nature: Incest and the law in the nineteenth-century south. In C. Bleser (Ed.), *In joy and in sorrow: Women, family, and marriage in the Victorian South, 1830–1900*. New York: Oxford University Press.

Bergman, S. J., & Surrey, J. L. (1994). Couples therapy: A relational approach. *Work in Progress*, No. 66. Wellesley, MA: Stone Center Working Paper Series.

Birrell, P. J., & Freyd, J. J. (2006). Betrayal trauma: Relational models of harm and healing. *Journal of Trauma Practice*, 5(1), 49–63

Bleser, C. (Ed.). (1991). *In joy and in sorrow: Women, family, and marriage in the Victorian South, 1830–1900*. New York: Oxford University Press.

Bleser, C., & Heath, F. (1991). The Clays of Alabama: The impact of the Civil War on a Southern marriage. In C. Bleser (Ed.), *In joy and in sorrow: Women, family, and marriage in the Victorian South, 1830–1900*. New York: Oxford University Press.

Cherlin, A. J. (2010). *The marriage-go-round: The state of marriage and the family in America today*. New York: Vintage.

Clarke-Stewart, A., & Brentano, C. (2006). *Divorce: Causes and consequences*. New Haven, CT: Yale University Press.

Clinton, C. (1991). Southern dishonor: Flesh, blood, rage, and bondage. In C. Bleser (Ed.), *In joy and in sorrow: Women, family, and marriage in the Victorian South, 1830–1900*. New York: Oxford University Press.

Comstock, D. L. (Ed.). (2005). *Diversity and development: Critical contexts that shape our lives and relationships.* Belmont, CA: Brooks/Cole, Cengage Learning.

Comstock, D. L., Hammer, T. R., Strentzsch, J., Cannon, K., Parsons, J., & Salazar II, G. (2008). Relational-cultural theory: A framework for bridging relational, multicultural, and social justice competencies [Special Issue: Multicultural Counseling]. *Journal of Counseling & Development, 86*(3), 279–287.

Coontz, S. (2005). *Marriage, a history: From obedience to intimacy or how love conquered marriage.* New York: Penguin.

Demo, D. H., & Fine, M. A. (2010). *Beyond the average divorce.* Thousand Oaks, CA: Sage.

Hartling, L. M., Rosen, W., Walker, M., & Jordan, J. V. (2000). Shame and humiliation: From isolation to relational transformation. *Work in Progress,* No. 88. Wellesley, MA: Stone Center Working Paper Series.

Irving, H. H. (2011). *Children come first: Mediation, not litigation when marriage ends.* Toronto: Dundurn.

Jordan, J. V. (1992). Relational resilience. *Work in Progress,* No. 57. Wellesley, MA: Stone Center Working Paper Series.

Jordan, J. V. (1995). Relational awareness: Transforming disconnection. *Work in Progress,* No. 76. Wellesley, MA: Stone Center Working Paper Series.

Jordan, J. V. (2005). Commitment to connection in a culture of fear. *Work in Progress,* No. 104. Wellesley, MA: Stone Center Working Paper Series.

Jordan, J. V., & Dooley, C. (2000). *Relational practice in action: A group manual.* Wellesley, MA: Stone Center Publications.

Kaler, A. (2001). Many divorces and many spinsters: Marriage as an invented tradition in southern Malawi 1946–1999. *Journal of Family History, 26,* 547–548.

Miller, J. B. (1986). What do we mean by relationships? *Work in Progress,* No. 22. Wellesley, MA: Stone Center Working Paper Series.

Miller, J. B., & Surrey, J. (1990). Revisioning women's anger: The personal and the global. *Work in Progress,* No. 43. Wellesley, MA: Stone Center Working Paper Series.

Mirkin, M. P., & Geib, P. (1995). Consciousness of context in relational couples therapy. *Work in Progress,* No. 73. Wellesley, MA: Stone Center Working Paper Series.

Mouradian, V. E. (2004). Women's stay-leave decisions in relationships involving intimate partner violence. *Wellesley Centers for Women Working Paper Series,* No. 415. Wellesley, MA: Wellesley: Stone Center Working Paper Series.

National Public Radio (2012, April 4). *Alaska Program Resolves Divorces Quickly, Amicably.* Retrieved from www.npr.org

Roman, M., & Haddad, W. (1978). *The disposable parent: The case for joint custody.* New York: Holt, Rinehart & Winston.

Sarkisian, N., & Gerstel, N. (2012). *Nuclear family values, extended family lives: The power of race, class, and gender.* New York: Routledge.

# 14

# HELPING REMARRIED COUPLES SURVIVE STEPKIDS

*Harriet Lerner*

When a marriage involves rearing children from a previous relationship, it challenges everyone in the system. Stepfamilies are complex on every front: historically, emotionally, logistically, structurally, financially, and practically. The potential for competition, jealousy, loyalty conflicts and enemies within and between households is built into the system. It's no surprise that the couple relationship quickly becomes overloaded, even when both partners are doing their very best to make the new marriage work.

Adding to the stress is the fact that much of the advice and couples counseling out there assumes that marriage in a stepfamily can operate like marriage in an original nuclear family. It can't—or at least, not well. When therapists attempt to help couples using the same theoretical perspective that guides us with an original nuclear family, we may unwittingly make things worse. Different family forms require a different understanding of family functioning to guide us.

At least half of marriages that occur every year are remarriages, and about one out of three children will live with a stepparent at some point. I thank family therapy pioneers, Betty Carter and Monica McGoldrick for teaching me about the particular challenges that face couples in remarried families with stepkids. All that follows in this chapter reflects their work and what I've learned from them.

## Forget about Blending

Some of my colleagues like the term, "blended family" ("just add kids and stir"). But here's the problem: families don't blend. Obviously, life is simpler when stepkids are already launched at the time of a remarriage, or are so young that there's lots of time to develop a new history with them. But stepfamily life is rarely simple with kids in the house. It usually takes three to five years for all family members to make some kind of adjustment, and often much longer. Rather than blending, the couple may be more likely to feel that they have been put through the blender.

Therapists can help couples embrace, or, more realistically, appreciate the complexity. When two people marry or couple up for the first time, they bring to their relationship the usual emotional baggage from their family of origin. When they form a stepfamily, one or both also carry the emotional baggage from a first marriage and from the painful termination of that marriage through divorce or death. When the woman becomes a stepmother, the whole world will expect her to take care of his children along with any she might have, because this is "what women do." The natural father is likely to feel tied in knots from the negativity between his new wife and his child—or between his wife and his ex—without a clue how to make things better. The stepfather, for his part, may try to step into an authority role with his wife's children, only to find that his well-intentioned efforts are rebuffed.

When couples expect that all the children and adults will quickly feel "at home" in their new stepfamily, the therapist can help them drop the dream of blending everyone into a family "smoothie." Forging a new family takes time, and couples need to move against the natural wish to push closeness. In RCT terms this would involve honoring the disconnection (Miller, 1986; Miller & Stiver, 1997; Shem & Surrey, 1998; Jordan, 2010). Slowly the conditions for building a solid and growth-fostering relationship may develop, but in the early phases of stepfamily life, both stepmoms and stepdads need to be sensitive to the importance of hanging out on the periphery. For example, if the mother enjoyed a special birthday ritual with her son before her marriage, the therapist can help the stepdad support them continuing the ritual as usual—just the two of them—rather than insisting that he come along. With time, we can help the family to create new rituals of their own.

If there is a teen in the house, hanging out on the periphery is essential. I tell couples to forget their well-intentioned plans to form one big happy family, family dinners and all. Betty Carter (Carter & Peters, 1996) notes that teens are especially confused by demands that they deal with new family members, because they're trying to separate from the family they already have. Eldest daughters are protective of their mothers and may have enjoyed a special position of caretaker with their divorced dads; anyone stepping into a family that includes his teenage daughter should reduce her expectations for closeness to near zero. As Carter notes, elder daughters are their mother's loyal torch-bearers and thus become the stepmother's greatest provocateur.

Monica McGoldrick (1996) puts it this way: If your stepkids are young, or if you're very lucky, you may develop a parent-like relationship over time. If this happens that's wonderful, but it's an extra—not a given and not something to be expected. All that should be expected is that stepmothers and stepchildren treat each other with courtesy, decency and respect. *It's the parent (not the stepparent) that has the primary responsibility to see that this particular expectation is enforced.*

## Challenge Those Traditional Gender Roles!

The old gender expectations lurk at the heart of most stepfamily problems. Even in the most modern and egalitarian of couples, these expectations can be quietly sleeping in the bushes only to leap out five minutes after the remarried couple settles under one roof. To help couples strengthen their marriage, therapists need to challenge them.

When a typical heterosexual couple is about to re-tie the knot, family therapist, Betty Carter (personal communication) reminds us that they are both likely to be thinking along the following lines.

"He says to himself, *'Great! I'm getting married again!* My kids will have a mother now, and we'll be a real family again!' (Translation: I'll go to work, she'll raise my kids and we'll look like a traditional nuclear family again.) Or, worse, he says to himself, 'Great! My kids will have a good mother now, who will do a much better job raising them than that selfish, neglectful bitch I'm divorced from.'

"She says to herself, *'Great, I'm getting married again!* Now I'll have someone to support me and the kids, since we can hardly make it on the child support I get from their father. I'll raise his girls since his work keeps him so busy and my schedule is flexible. Plus, he obviously doesn't have a clue about disciplining them. And the poor little darlings never had a mother who put them first, so if I just try hard enough I can give them what they really need.'"

Therapists can help couples push against these grizzled old gender expectations, which can be a disaster for remarriage. We can help Dad to discipline his own kids, and assume the daily, hands-on job of parenting even when it seems simpler for his on-the-scene wife to do so. Men should know that turning parenting responsibilities over to a new wife will place her in the "wicked stepmother" role and cause his kids to act up. There are plenty of activities that stepmothers and stepchildren can do together (they need alone time) that don't involve putting the primary parenting responsibilities in her lap.

Even seasoned therapists can slip into taking the traditional path of thinking the man can't be expected to do the primary parenting if his wife is the one on the scene. I recall seeing a couple that was having family problems partly because the husband's business took him out of town on weekdays. His wife of about a year was left to take charge of his three boys (her stepchildren), who always acted up around bedtime.

When the husband insisted that he couldn't possibly take charge of bedtime because he was away so much, I found myself reflexively nodding in agreement. Suddenly I recalled a comment I heard Betty Carter make to a father in a similar situation nearly a decade earlier. In her disarming way, she asked: "Have you ever heard of the telephone?"

Jarred awake by this memory, I put the dad in charge of calling his boys every night he was on the road. His job was to find out how their day at school went, to let them know his expectations about bedtime, and to insist that they treat their stepmother with respect and good manners when she reminded them it was time to go to bed. All family relationships and especially their marriage improved remarkably when he rose to the occasion.

### What Stepmothers Are Stepping into

I think we should light a little candle for stepmothers, because the difficulty of their position can't be overestimated. It's much harder than anyone could possibly anticipate at the time she decides to marry a guy who just happens to have children in a package deal. Even the term *stepmother* is loaded with false assumptions. The word *step* is derived from a word for *orphan*, so right away the label *stepmother* implies something less than optimal, as our time-honored fairy tales illustrate so well. But the real problem with the word *stepmother* is the "mother" part. Women marry because they've fallen in love with a guy, and not because they're necessarily looking to be anybody's mother. Most importantly, nobody can walk into a family that has a history of its own and become an instant mother. The role of mother—any kind of mother—cannot be automatically conferred on a woman when she marries a man with children.

It's useful to help our clients recognize the absurdity of such an expectation, and the problems it creates. The harder the new wife tries to become some kind of mother, the more resistance she'll get from her stepchildren and their actual mother. The man's natural tendency to fade into the woodwork will be amplified, especially if he's working harder to support two families. The ground is fertile for mother and stepmother to blame each other.

Meanwhile, the child is caught between two women who are parenting with a hostile edge, and the stepmother provides an on-site target for a distressed child who is acting up. Dad, for his part, may feel like he's caught in the crossfire and is helpless to make things better. The marriage is suffering, which no one anticipated because everyone got along splendidly together before a girlfriend became a new wife and thus a stepmom.

I explain to couples that children rarely voice a wish for another parent. They aren't looking for another mother or father. When Carter and McGoldrick (McGoldrick, Carter & Garcia-Preto, 2011) asked children at the end of family therapy to describe what kind of relationship they'd like with their parent's new husband or wife, kids expressed a wish for a friendly relationship of some sort— say, like an aunt or uncle, basketball coach or special pal. No one ever replaces a parent, not even a dead or absent parent, or one who is in jail on charges of grand larceny.

Stepmothers labor under impossible expectations that they may fail to question. A therapy client told me that she said the following to her two stepdaughters one week after marrying their widowed father: "I know I'm not your mother and I'll never replace her. But I want you to know that I'll love you every bit as much as I love my own kids." This woman had nine and twelve years of history with her own children, respectively. She has been with them since their conception. In contrast, she has five minutes of history with her stepchildren. What moves her to make a promise like this? How can she expect something so unrealistic from herself? Does she see it as her job magically to heal their grief through her love? Does she expect her stepchildren to believe such an unrealistic promise? It's amazing what women learn to expect from themselves on the nurturing front.

### Helping Stepdads Become a Behind-the-Scenes Coach

Generally speaking it's stepmothers and natural mothers who get stuck in the most tension and negativity. Fathers and stepfathers tend to have far less conflict because they're socialized to lay low and hang out on the periphery of family emotional life. That said, being a stepdad is no walk in the park.

If men want to be a positive force in their marriage, we can encourage them to be kind and responsible with their stepchildren and show interest in their activities and projects. If a kid wants to spend one-on-one time with their stepdad, he should go for it. But it's important to help a stepdad understand that he can't step into an authority role with his wife's children, no matter how loving he is to them, and no matter how stellar his leadership skills. Parental authority is something to be earned slowly, over time.

Therapists can help a stepdad to be a supportive husband and behind-the-scenes coach around parenting problems—if and when his wife wants coaching. It's an important role and key to making a marriage last. My advice (Lerner, 2012) to stepdads in *Marriage Rules* reflects what I say in the consulting room:

> Believe in your wife's capacity to raise her children in a way that works for her. Of course, she may be struggling to find her way with discipline for little Jonny, but bite your tongue and stay on the sidelines. If, for example, your wife asks Jonny to set the table and he stays glued to the television, it's not helpful to jump in with, "Jonny, did you hear what your mother said? She said come here and set the table!" If you have a positive suggestion, tell your wife later in a respectful way. Likewise, don't be a critic. Avoid saying things to your wife like, "I can't stand watching how your daughter treats you!" or saying to your stepdaughter "I can't stand listening to you smart-mouth your mother!" Such comments (even if your wife makes them herself, which she may) can undermine your partner's confidence and competence as a mother, and will ultimately strain the marriage.

Here's my advice to moms who may well have absorbed the myth that being female precludes them from raising boys into good men (Lerner, 2012):

> Trust yourself to raise your own children, even if you've married a wonderful man who has always wanted to be a father, and you're convinced that your children will benefit by his assuming some of the

discipline because he's better at it than you are. Don't surrender your authority, even if you've had nothing but Bad Mother Days since your re-marriage. If you're in the middle of a screaming battle with your twelve-year-old son, it may be tempting to throw up your hands and yell to your partner "I can't deal with this anymore! Get in here and take over!" Resist this impulse and handle the situation yourself, even if you're at a total loss, as parents often are.

Encourage your husband to leave the room if he can't stand witnessing the interaction between you and your child. Let him know that you value his feedback, if it's out of earshot from the kids, and if it's presented respectfully. In sum, be open to your husband's feelings and good ideas, while holding tight to your ultimate authority as the parent. Support his important role as behind-the scenes coach. Doing so will help your kids and can literally save your marriage.

While traditional gender roles are at the heart of the problem in many stepfamilies, same sex couples are not immune to the same difficulties. Consider this abbreviated stepfamily story as a model for how stepfamilies typically get in—and out—of trouble, irrespective of whether they are straight or gay (Lerner, 1998).

## Case Example: A Stepfamily in Action

Amy was thirty-three years old when she and her husband Joe, divorced. They worked out a flexible co-parenting arrangement for their eight-year-old son, Jake, who divided his time pretty evenly between them. Amy was a warm, energetic parent who had a deep appreciation of the importance of family connections in her son's life. She deserved a gold medal for fostering every thread of connection between Jake and Joe's family, even though she felt provoked and put down by her ex-in-laws, who blamed her for the divorce.

Amy (the youngest in her family of origin) was a free-spirited mother who acted spontaneously, rarely planning ahead. For example, she'd be driving Jake home at dinnertime and suddenly remember there was no food in the house. They'd pick up pizza or hamburgers and coke at the drive-through and eat dinner in front of the television having a contest over who could belch more loudly. Like many youngests, Amy sometimes acted more like a peer than a parent. But Amy and Jake adored each other, and although Amy sometimes expressed insecurity about her parenting, she and Jake were doing just fine.

Two years post-divorce, Amy surprised herself by falling in love with Victoria. Her relationship with Victoria was the most intimate she had ever known, and both women felt that they had found in each other their true life partner. When Jake was twelve, Amy and Victoria had a commitment ceremony, and they considered themselves married. With the help of therapy, Amy was able to deal calmly and non-defensively with Joe and his family when they hit the ceiling about Jake living with two lesbians. The earlier work Amy had done maintaining communication and connection between the two households paid off during this difficult transition period.

## The Honeymoon is Over

When Amy was dating Victoria, everything bubbled along beautifully. They each had their separate living arrangements, and Victoria got along fine with Jake, then ten, who was affectionate and warm toward her. But when Victoria moved into Amy's house, the trouble began. Victoria discovered that she couldn't tolerate Amy's "looseness" when it came to parenting and household organization. She met only token resistance from Amy when she began to impose her own rules on the household. Fast food was out, as was eating in front of the television. Jake was to make his bed every morning and was allowed to watch a maximum of seven hours of television a week.

Victoria was five years Amy's senior. She had just launched her college-age daughter, Alice, and she had strong opinions about how a family should function. By her own report she was something of a control freak. As I worked with the couple in therapy, I learned that Amy accommodated Victoria for three reasons.

First, there had been so much fighting in Amy's first marriage to Joe that she preferred walking on eggshells with her new mate to risking open conflict. Amy was so desperate for this relationship to work, that she swept her feelings under the rug, even knowing that this "solution" only created more problems in the long run. She kept more and more of her authentic experience out of the relationship in order to remain connected, but the connection suffered (Lerner, 2005; Jordan, 2010).

Second, Amy wasn't confident in her own mothering, despite the fact that she had raised Jake for almost four years following the divorce and he was doing fine by any standard. "I'm not good at the 'take charge' aspect of parenting," Amy explained. "Victoria is better than I am at setting rules and consequences." It didn't occur to Amy

231

that she could learn to do these things, to the extent that she now saw them as important. Instead of considering Victoria's good ideas and putting some of them into practice while staying central in the decision-making process, Amy totally deferred to her.

Third, society didn't affirm Amy's new family, including her deep love for Victoria. Amy wanted to battle homophobia in all its manifestations, starting on the home front. In her zeal to support Victoria's status as a bona fide stepmother, Amy would say things to Jake like, "We are a family and you should listen to your stepmother's rules. You should feel lucky to have two mothers."

Of course, Jake didn't feel especially lucky. The divorce had been a temporary crisis in his life, as divorce always is. It had taken him and his mom time to settle into a new routine, and it took him time to figure out how to be part of a two-household family. Nineteen months after the divorce, his dad had gotten remarried to a woman with two children of her own, causing more change and disruption in Jake's life, at least in the short run. Now another new adult had entered the scene, dramatically altering his relationship with his mom, whom he no longer had to himself. Worst of all, this new person was acting like she was a better mother than his real one, and his real mother was abdicating her job, which Jake experienced as an abandonment. On top of this his classmates made hateful jokes about homosexuals. Feeling lucky was not exactly Jake's experience.

### *"You're Not My Mother!"*

The more Victoria moved toward the emotional center of family life, the more Jake rejected her. "I don't want you to come to the school picnic!" he'd insist. "You're not my mother!" Amy and Victoria saw this as rude behavior to be punished or they heard it as Jake's homophobia, which they would try to talk to him about, while educating him on the subject of discrimination against lesbians and gays. But homophobia, although undeniably a big problem in the world we live in, wasn't *the* problem for Jake. The biggest problem was that Amy had relinquished the daily responsibility of parenting him and that Victoria was attempting to enforce new rules and discipline. It was a blueprint for failure, and Jake and Victoria were increasingly at odds.

When I first saw this couple in therapy, Jake's grades had dropped from mostly As to mostly Cs. Amy, caught in the middle of angry struggles between Jake and Victoria, was depressed, tied up in knots, and terrified that Victoria would end up leaving. Victoria was trying hard to make things work. She had moved in with Amy with such different expectations. Now she felt stressed out, overwhelmed and unappreciated, and she didn't know what had gone wrong.

There were other problems as well. Victoria's daughter announced that she wouldn't be coming home from college during spring break because she didn't have a room in her mother's new home with Amy, and she didn't want to sleep on the couch. Victoria understood that losing her room had contributed to Alice's feeling like an outsider in the new family, but she saw no immediate solution to the problem. Jake complained to his dad that Victoria bossed him around, and Joe's wife began criticizing Victoria to anyone who would listen, making reference to "that lesbian lifestyle." Amy and Victoria then forbade Jake to criticize Victoria in his dad's house, which made Jake feel muzzled and constrained to "watch himself" in his other home.

Victoria also felt increasingly resentful that she had so little time alone with Amy that didn't revolve around Jake or some family problem. "Who do you love more, Jake or me?" she'd demand of Amy. Her own mothering years with a child at home were behind her, and she was frustrated that Amy wasn't more available. It's not unusual for a stepparent to feel jealous of the bond between parent and child because it pre-dates the couple bond and is usually stronger. Also, it's difficult for the new couple to get the time they need to be together given the needs of kids and the relationship challenges everyone is facing.

Victoria realized the question "Who do you love more?" was unfair, since the love and responsibility a parent feels toward a child can never be compared to what one feels for a partner. But chronic stress doesn't bring out the maturity in any of us. Welcome to a typical first year of stepfamily life.

### *Making Changes*

It was crucial that Victoria get out of the "wicked stepmother" role and that Amy support her in the process. To this end, Amy needed to be in charge of her own son, which meant making the primary decisions along with Jake's dad about how he would be raised, being in charge of enforcing rules, and ensuring that Jake treat Victoria with courtesy and respect. When the threesome first became a stepfamily, Amy did a great job of telling Jake "Victoria will never replace your dad." The part she left out was that "Victoria will never replace *me*."

*Kids need to hear both messages loud and clear if they are ever going to truly accept a new adult on the scene.*

Victoria and Amy were also trying too hard to create a cohesive new family. As McGoldrick and Carter (McGoldrick et al., 2011) explain, it takes a long time before a stepmother can graduate from being a total stranger, to a parent's new partner, to the child's friend and then (with some luck) to the position of a loved or respected adult or parent-like figure. If the new partner comes along with a teenager (Jake was almost thirteen when Victoria moved in), a strong emotional bond may never develop, which is totally normal.

Because Amy, Victoria and Jake were all in so much distress, both women were ready to change their part of the problem. Amy once again took charge of raising her son, and she got better at setting rules and enforcing them. Victoria had the more difficult job of taking a back seat and lightening up about how different Amy's parenting style was from her own. It was extremely hard for her to move to the periphery as she watched Amy struggle to get a little more order and structure in Jake's life. It was also hard for Amy to assert her authority as Jake's mother when Victoria became controlling. With therapy, Amy learned to say something like this: "Victoria, you have wonderful ideas about parenting and I want to hear them. But it's not helpful when you criticize me or tell me what to do. And there are some things we simply see differently. I need to raise Jake in a way that makes sense to me, even if I make mistakes."

Both women were ultimately empowered by the changes they made. They were motivated by knowing that they couldn't continue in the old way and still stay ambulatory and breathing. In our final therapy session, Victoria said, "If things hadn't improved, I was going to write a book called, *Steptales from the Crypt.* I assured her it certainly would have been a bestseller.

I also encouraged Victoria to reach out more to her daughter, Alice, who was distancing with a vengeance in response to feeling shut out of her mother's new life just at the time that she herself had left home. Working to stay connected to Alice helped Victoria to focus less on Jake. At the termination of therapy, Victoria and Amy had purchased a house together a few blocks down from their old one that had an extra room that Victoria decorated with Alice's things, so that her daughter knew she had a place in the family. Buying a new house also put Victoria and Amy on a more solid and equal footing as their new family continued to evolve.

## *A PostScript on Gender Roles*

One advantage Amy and Victoria had going for them in becoming a stepfamily was being a lesbian couple. This may sound absurd, given the fact that homosexuals are still being denied the right to marry, are discouraged from loving openly and face endless discrimination and enforced invisibility. But Amy, being a woman, knew what I was talking about when I challenged her to get back in charge of her own kid.

A father, in contrast, might have given me fifty-two reasons why it wasn't possible for him to assume the hands-on job of parenting and his new wife might agree that it was only practical for her to take over. Or, if Victoria had been a man, Amy might have felt that it was important that Jake have a strong male role model who would take over the challenge of discipline, especially since it wasn't her strong point. Olga Silverstein, in *The Courage to Raise Good Men* (Silverstein & Rashbaum, 1994), notes how thoroughly mothers have been brainwashed into worrying about turning their sons into "mama's boys" and believing that only a father can help a boy become a proper man. This myth is problematic in the original nuclear family, but is a disaster in stepfamilies where a stepdad, with the best of intentions, tries to assume the role of disciplinarian with a child with whom he has not built a long, shared positive history.

# The Larger Relational Network: Helping Couples Take the High Road

Whether therapists work with one or more people in the consulting room, we'll be of limited help if we aren't paying attention to the larger relational context in which the couple is embedded (Bergman & Surrey, 1994; Lerner, 2012). A couple relationship can't flourish when triangles and cutoffs rigidify as they do in the face of painful tensions between stepparents, natural parents and other family members. Children, of course, are the most vulnerable members of the system and most at risk of losing family connections when one or both parents remarry.

Plain old education is invaluable in helping our clients calm down, be their best selves and take the high road with other difficult adults in the system. In *Marriage Rules* (Lerner, 2012) I explain how supporting kids' connections in both households can be seen as a spiritual practice:

> If you want your marriage and stepfamily to grow stronger support the children's relationships with everyone in the other household. If you

can't imagine feeling positively toward some other adult in the system, pretend kindness and respect. Consider it your spiritual practice.

This means that if your fifteen-year-old stepdaughter, Anna, comes home and reports that her mother says you're a control freak, you need to under-react. Don't criticize back. If you add fuel on the fire, family relationships will intensify and your marriage will ultimately suffer.

Sure it may be tempting to say, "Well, Anna, your mother thinks I'm controlling because she's a loose cannon." Or, "Your mother just doesn't like me and never will." Or, "I think your mother is threatened and wants to turn you against me." Maybe you say nothing but your stepdaughter can see that you're seething. Or you act sad and wounded, and withdrawn from the conversation. Maybe you confront your husband with how pissed off you are. You may insist he call his wife that very evening and tell her to stop poisoning your relationship with Anna with her crazy lies.

Try mightily to avoid all of the above. Instead, let it go. Take some deep breaths and remind yourself that it is totally normal for your stepdaughter's mother to be anxious and threatened by your position in the family. Under-reacting means you don't take the bait and you don't intensify the triangle further.

Instead you might laugh and say, "Well, I may be a bit of a control freak. I'm probably not as spontaneous and free as your mom is." Or, "Well your mom and I are two different people, and it makes sense that we have pretty different styles." Or (if Anna quotes her mother as saying you're some kind of dangerous weirdo), "You know, I see that differently from your mom. I really don't recognize myself in that picture."

It makes an enormous difference if you can say these things in a low-key way, with no edge in your voice. Nothing is more important than learning to pass on less intensity than you receive. Lightness and humor tend to loosen up triangles, while intensity only makes them more rigid.

Keep in mind that the primary concern of children is how their actual parents are treating them and how the grownups on both sides are treating each other. They don't want you to circle the wagons around your stepfamily, or do anything to threaten their ties with family members on the "other side." More than anything, they don't want a negative or critical focus among any of the adults involved in their care.

Keep trying to support your stepkids' relationships with all family members. Ditto for supporting your own child's relationship with your ex and his family. This is a position of integrity that over time will strengthen your marriage. Try to view the obnoxious behaviors of adults on the "other side" as nothing more than a barometer of their anxiety level and their immature way of managing it. Take the high road. It's hard. And it's worth it.

(Lerner, 2012)

## Conclusion

Making a marriage work with stepchildren at home requires courage, fortitude, and grace under pressure for all involved, including the therapist. Whether you work with couples or with individuals who are part of a couple, the challenge is this: Stepmothers and stepfathers should do only what's realistic and no more, while mothers and fathers must step up to the plate and take charge of their own kids. It goes without saying that things will go more smoothly if the therapist can help one or both members of the couple truly resolve the pain and anger from the dissolution of a previous marriage through death or divorce, and help both partners treat *all* of the adults involved in a child's life with courtesy and respect, even when those other adults are behaving badly. Like most things that are worthwhile, this is easier said than done.

To acknowledge the complexities of stepfamily life is certainly not to suggest that this family form is second-best to the original nuclear family, or that kids can't thrive. Half of the marriages that occur each year are remarriages, and stepfamilies are fast becoming the predominant family form, soon to outnumber nuclear families in the United States, if they haven't already (McGoldrick et al., 2011). A well-functioning stepfamily can enrich everyone involved. Despite the unique challenges for the couple, there are countless well-functioning, happy, and thriving marriages in stepfamilies. Marriages with stepchildren have the very best chance to thrive when the therapist vigorously challenges the many myths and half-truths that surround them, and when the therapist understands that "good couples therapy" with an original nuclear family doesn't fit the territory when stepchildren enter the picture.

## Note

1. Parts of this chapter appeared in Harriet Lerner's *The Mother Dance* (Harper Collins, 1998) and *Marriage Rules* (Gotham, 2012). Parts from *Marriage Rules: A Manual for the Married and the Coupled Up* by Harriet Lerner, PhD, copyright (c) 2012 by Harriet Lerner. Used by permission of Gotham Books, an imprint of Penguin Group (USA) Inc.

## References

Bergman, S. and Surrey, J. (1994). Couple therapy: a relational approach. *Work in Progress*, No. 66. Wellesley, MA: Stone Centre Working Paper Series.

Carter, B. & Peters, J. (1996). *Love, Honor, and Negotiate*. New York: Pocket Books.

Jordan, J. (2010). *Relational-Cultural Therapy*. Washington, DC: American Psychological Association.

Lerner, H. (2012). *Marriage Rules: A Manual for the Married and the Coupled Up*. New York: Gotham Books.

Lerner, H. (2005). *The Dance of Anger*. New York: Harper Collins.

Lerner, H. (1998). *The Mother Dance*. New York: Harper Collins.

McGoldrick, M. (1996). *Making Stepfamilies Work* (audiotape), recorded at the Annual Family Therapy Networker Symposium, Washington, DC.

McGoldrick, M. Carter, B., & Garcia-Preto, N. (Eds.) (2011). *The Expanded Family Life Cycle*, fourth edition. Boston: Allyn & Bacon.

Miller, J. B. (1986). *Toward a New Psychology of Women*. Boston, MA: Beacon Press.

Miller, J. B. & Stiver, I. (1997). *The healing connection: How women form relationships in therapy and in life*. Boston: Beacon Press.

Shem, S. & Surrey, J. (1998). *We Have to Talk: Healing Dialogues between Women and Men*. New York: Basic Books.

Silverstein, O., & Rashbaum, B. (1994). *The Courage to Raise Good Men*. New York: Penguin Books.

# 15

# CONCLUSION

## The Pain of Disconnection, the Power of Connection

*Judith V. Jordan and Jon Carlson*

Disconnections are ubiquitous in relationships. Even with the best of intentions and substantial relational skills we all fail each other empathically, misunderstand one another, hurt one another. It is intrinsic to human experience. Acute disconnections can be reworked into stronger connection. For instance, if you hurt me and I am able to register my pain and be listened to by you . . . if, better yet, you let me know that you are troubled that you hurt me, that you are sorry . . . the relationship benefits. We build trust, a sense of being responsive to one another. This contributes to a stronger "We." If, on the other hand, a more powerful person misunderstands or hurts a less powerful person and the less powerful person tries to register their pain but is dismissed, criticized, humiliated or treated abusively, the less powerful person learns that these aspects of her experience cannot be expressed in the relationship. She learns to keep aspects of herself out of relationship in order to maintain the illusion of relationship. That is, the relationship becomes less authentic, less full. This contributes to chronic disconnection or isolation in which the hurt person begins to feel disconnected and as if she doesn't matter, her feelings don't matter. There is a diminishment of mutual empathy.

When couples come into treatment they are often either ensconced in chronic disconnection or struggling at the edge of feeling deeply disappointed, and acutely disconnected. Often their efforts to retrieve meaning and connection with their partner drive the partner further into disconnection. Sometimes the members of the couple begin to exclude one another from their most vulnerable places, or build walls of blame; acute disconnections harden into chronic disconnection. Without intervention that could help the couple reconnect, many well-meaning and potentially fulfilling relationships end in stagnation or permanent separation. With its emphasis on relational resilience and repair, RCT searches for ways to reconnect that will contribute to the wellbeing of both partners. It also acknowledges that all couples deserve support and assistance and that the culture offers little help and encouragement to people coming together to build satisfying lives with one another.

RCT endorses intervention for couples who are in pain and moving toward chronic disconnection, but it also encourages action to change the cultural conditions that contribute to these problems: unequal, sometimes abusive, power arrangements; marginalization of groups; an over-emphasis on "stand on your own two feet" which deprives individuals of the help we all need to cope and flourish in life; rigid gender, race, and sexual identity expectations that limit human potential; failure to act strongly enough to protect vulnerable populations; and lack of intervention to prevent physical and sexual abuse of these populations. Wellbeing in and out of couples depends on working to: minimize economic and power disparities; encourage the growth of mutual empathy between people; develop socialization ideals that align with our neurobiological predispositions toward connection and empathy.

At the heart of RCT is mutual empathy (Jordan, 2010; Jordan et al., 1991). Mutual empathy fuels understanding between people—a sense of mattering—and provides the glue for community; it allows us to extricate ourselves from the polarities of you versus me. It is always us. It supports our expansion of the sense of WE. It is what supports growth in connection. Jean Baker Miller once noted that, "In a relationship if both people aren't growing, neither person is growing" (Miller & Stiver, 1997). Growth happens in relationship and it is not a one-way street. We do not have to engage in endless debate about selfish versus selfless. Mutual empathy places the emphasis on the "and also" rather than the "either or". And we now have hard data that supports the RCT core concepts of empathic responsiveness, growth in connection, the need to be a part of meaningful connection (Cozolino, 2006; Eisenberger & Lieberman, 2004). We are hardwired to connect and we are biologically constructed to flourish in relationship and suffer in isolation (Cacioppo & Patrick, 2008; Cozolino, 2010; Love & Carlson, 2011; Siegel, 2007, 2012; Banks, 2005). It is sad that our socialization puts us in direct conflict with our neurobiology: We are taught to stand alone, to excel in separation, to compete and achieve at the cost of our fellow beings. This opposition of our core human nature with the narrative of success, which we are taught to live out, creates enormous stress for us; it creates anxiety, feelings of inadequacy, a never quenched thirst for more and more success, comparative achievement. It hurts our bodies and brains (Banks, 2006). And it makes couple relationships unsatisfying.

Mutual empathy is not just a concept that would allow couples to have more satisfying and productive relationships (not a bad goal in itself). It is a recognition of the positive outcome that can happen when we realign our expectations for human development. When we move from a model of separate self to mutual empathy, we are suggesting that: safety is found in connection, not in exercising power over others; we are hardwired to connect and to contribute to the wellbeing of others; human nature is not innately and solely selfish and self-interested; it behooves all of us to transition away from the understanding that at our core we are greedy, selfish and out for ourselves (or our individual genes). Our best chance at survival, personally and collectively, is through building on our capacity for empathy and mutuality, with our fellow beings and with the earth. Our greatest achievement will not be the stockpiling of money or status or weapons; it will be in attending to people's needs for connection and helping them develop the skills with which to support mutual empathy in one another. Instead of creating societies that put us at odds with our more generous and kind inclinations, we need to focus on supporting and expanding the repertoire of relational longings and skills that our brains are ready to bring forward.

We are not suggesting that people are only good and kind and compassionate. We can be petty and selfish and aggressive. We hurt each other, intentionally and inadvertently. But this is all the more reason to develop programs to help people reconnect and repair wounded relationships and rebalance destructive power imbalances. This is the work of couples therapists, social workers, psychologists, mental health counselors and psychotherapists. It is also the pledge of those engaged in social justice (Kottler, Englar-Carlson, & Carlson, 2013). A just society is one that honors and respects the needs of all its citizens. It is a place where "power over" dynamics are replaced with "power with" and "power for". Where our need for connection throughout the lifespan is respected and honored rather than pathologized as "too dependent" or "too needy". We should not be shamed for our most human capacities: the ability to feel the suffering and the joy of our fellow beings and our desire to contribute to other individuals and to the collective wellbeing. WE are social beings. WE are empathic beings.

In this book we have explored differing applications of RCT, providing a range of practices and interpretations. There are vast areas we have not covered. For those interested in delving deeper into the philosophy and practice of RCT, we refer you to a rich literature, including several core books and over 110 works in progress (see jbmti.org). From its inception, RCT has been concerned with social justice as well as providing an accurate understanding of the psychologies of (and interventions with) marginalized groups, starting with women. Jean Baker Miller once said (and it since became the title of Chris Robb's book on the relational revolution in psychology): "This changes everything." By that she meant that when we move from an emphasis on separation, on the separate self, the individual to an understanding of the primacy of relationship rather than self, we move into a world of new possibility.

"Power over" relationships increase chronic disconnection and disempowerment in couples, in families and in the world. In order to honor our deepest human yearnings for connection and love, couples therapists must pay attention to the distorting forces of "power over" (exercising dominance) and stratification. No one can achieve the standards of independence, self-sufficiency and "power over" others that the dominant culture espouses. Rather than emotional resilience, in such a system we see emotional rigidity and increased stress. Community is eroded as hyper-individualism is celebrated. We are cut off from the natural system of support and growth. Human beings have a need to contribute to the growth and wellbeing of others; in our couple relationships and with our children we have an opportunity to practice that generosity. Chris Robb (2006) commented, "It changes everything to see and hear relationships. Not selves" (p. xvi) while Jean Baker Miller noted that to embrace the power of relationships will revolutionize society as well as psychology (Robb, 2006). This book, dedicated to helping couples find greater zest, worth, clarity, creativity and engagement in the community at large (the five good things) will hopefully also contribute to greater social justice, an expansion of our sense of human possibility, and an increasing appreciation of the power of connection to heal us.

Some of the authors in this book have been at the core of RCT theory-building from the beginning. Several are primarily guided by other conceptual systems but appreciate the power of connection in their work, and we felt that their contribution to RCT is important. This model is a "work in progress". If we are not open to being changed by other theory-builders and thinkers, we are failing our own precepts. When we work with couples, it is quickly clear that we are not just working with individuals who have selfish agendas for happiness. We are working with systems, with relationships, with complex tapestries of joy and pain. But what is also abundantly clear in couples work is how important love and connection are in people's lives, despite all our conditioning to the contrary. Some therapists have noted that couples therapy is their most challenging work. Witnessing two people trying to come to a place of union and love, struggling with their internal narratives of separation and fear in a culture that mostly leaves them on their own to figure it all out, can be daunting.

It is important that therapists doing couples work find communities of support for their wellbeing as they provide this to their clients. We personally believe it is important for therapists, who after all are primarily change agents, to put their work in a larger frame. We are importantly dedicated to healing the suffering of individuals, couples, and families. But we have an obligation (sorry if this seems preachy) to change the larger social patterns, the destructive power arrangements, the unachievable demands (for both men and women) to be singular, separate, competitively successful, independent, and invulnerable (Kottler et al., 2013). We are simply not meant to live out those stories. And our efforts to do so are only destructive for us as individuals, for our communities and for our planet. We have an enormous capacity for love and compassion. In our primary couplings we have the opportunity to nourish and expand those capabilities with one another. The Editors and chapter authors believe that the RCT approach offers a deeply effective way to do just that.

# References

Banks, A. (2005) The developmental impact of trauma. In D. Comstock (Ed.), *Diversity and development: Critical contexts that shape our lives and relationships* (pp. 185–213). Belmont, CA: Brooks/Cole.

Banks, A. (2006) *The neurobiology of connection.* Presentation at Summer Training Institute, Jean Baker Miller Training Institute, Wellesley, MA.

Cacioppo, J.T. & Patrick, W. (2008) *Loneliness: Human nature and the need for social connection.* New York: W.W. Norton.

Cozolino, L. (2006) *The neuroscience of human relationships: Attachment and the developing social brain.* New York: W.W. Norton.

Cozolino, L.C. (2010) *The neuroscience of psychotherapy: Healing the social brain* (second edition). New York: W.W. Norton.

Eisenberger, N. & Lieberman, M. (2004) Why rejection hurts: A common neural alarm system for physical and social pain. *Trends in Cognitive Sciences*, 8, 294–300.

Jordan, J. (2010) *Relational-Cultural Therapy.* Washington, DC: APA Books.

Jordan, J., Kaplan, A., Miller, J., Stiver, I., & Surrey, J. (1991) *Women's growth in connection.* New York: Guilford Press.

Kottler, J., Englar-Carlson, M., & Carlson, J. (2013) *Helping beyond the fifty minute hour: Therapists involved in meaningful social action.* New York: Routledge.

Love, P. & Carlson, J. (2011) *Never be lonely again: The way out of loneliness, isolation and a life unfulfilled.* New York: HCI Books.

Miller, J.B. & Stiver, I. (1997) *The healing connection.* Boston, MA: Beacon Press.

Robb, C. (2006) *This changes everything: The relational revolution in psychology.* New York: Farrar Strauss.

Siegel, D.J. (2007) *The mindful brain: Reflection and attunement in the cultivation of well-being.* New York: W.W. Norton.

Siegel, D.J. (2012) *Pocket guide to interpersonal neurobiology: An integrative handbook of the mind.* New York: W.W. Norton.

# INDEX

access to therapy 33
action 1–2, 26, 155, 199, 240
adolescents: sexuality in 124, 125; in
  stepfamilies 226
Alger, Horatio 27
amygdala 72, 166, 169, 171, 180
Anderson, B. 189, 197
anger 25, 49, 50, 112, 217; of women 14,
  39, 81–2, 171
anticipatory empathy 5, 71
anxiety 86; of cancer sufferers 197–8
assumptions 134, 142, 151; cultural 24,
  27, 179
attachment 122, 168
authenticity 2, 5, 6, 40, 71, 190; empathy
  and 14–15; gay men and 95–6, 102,
  106, 111; and good conflict 72, 77
autonomy 166, 167, 215
awareness 190

Bardaglio, P. 212
Bergman, S. 8, 93, 132, 190, 218, 223
blame 32, 131, 146, 172, 218; moving
  away from 50; narratives of 28;
  neurobiology and 166
Bleser, C. 210, 211
blind spots, privilege and 29, 41–2, 110
boundaries 124; in sexuality work 124–5
Boyd-Franklin, N. 36
brain 50, 72, 168, 169–70; social nature
  of 199–200
Brentano, C. 221
Buber, M. 178

cancer: diagnosis of 188–9; coping
  behaviours 196–7; effect on
  relationships 186, 187–8, 192;
  support groups 186, 187, 190–201
care-receiving learning 107–8

caring: devalued work of 154–6; in
  extended family 215; naming 152–4,
  156–8
Carlson, J. 8
Carter, Betty 1, 225, 226, 227, 229, 234
central relational paradox 38–40, 77–8,
  190–1; gay men and 95–7, 101, 104,
  112
change 122, 179–81, 241–2; challenges
  of 179–82; maintaining 181
check-in/check-out 18
Cherlin, A. 212–13, 214
children: caring for 152–4, 155; gender
  differences 3–4, 92–3, 178; gender
  power imbalance 126–7; sexual
  development of 123
circle of connection 143–7
Clarke-Stewart, A. 221
Clinton, C. 211
"coming out" 83–4, 99
communication 131, 135; during illness
  187, 188, 190–1, 201; of emotions
  188, 201
community 242
compassion 3, 25, 49, 98, 168, 195,
  196–7
Comstock-Benzick, D. 9
conflict 62, 133, 143–4, 166, 217;
  cultural assumptions and 179; healthy
  4, 6, 72, 76–7, 112, 178; marital
  135–6, 217–18
Connor, J. 53
contempt 132, 171, 173, 176, 177
context 14, 24, 147; consciousness of
  23–8; cultural 136–7, 147, 240;
  expansion of 26–36; for gay male
  couples 92; for lesbian couples 83–5
contextual awareness 26–7, 33
continuity of connection 21

244